Also by Frederick Exley

A Fan's Notes

PAGES FROM A COLD ISLAND

Frederick Exley

PAGES
FROM
A COLD
ISLAND

RANDOM HOUSE · NEW YORK

Acknowledgments to Attorney Jack Scordo and to Captain Floyd "Big Daddy" Majors, without whose kindness this book would not have been written.

Under the title "Saint Gloria and the Troll," Chapters 6 and 7 first appeared in somewhat different form in *Playboy*; under the title "Goodbye, Edmund Wilson," Chapters 8 and 9, also in different form, appeared originally in the *Atlantic*.

Library of Congress Cataloging in Publication Data

Exley, Frederick.
    Pages from a cold island.

    Autobiography.
    I. Title.

PZ4.E964Pag   [PS3555.X58]   813'.5'4   74–28321
ISBN 0–394–49440–7

Manufactured in the United States of America
First Edition

For David I. Segal (1928–1970)
And for Col. William R. Exley (1926–1973)

But this is preposterous? A character is either "real" or "imaginary"? If you think that, *hypocrite lecteur*, I can only smile. You do not even think of your own past as quite real; you dress it up, you gild it or blacken it, censor it, tinker with it . . . fictionalize it, in a word, and put it away on a shelf—your book, your romanced autobiography. We are all in flight from real reality. That is the basic definition of *Homo sapiens*.

—John Fowles, *The French Lieutenant's Woman*

I did not tell them what bound me closest to you. I did not say . . . how your willful resolution to wrest the secret of life gave me heart, and how in your absolute indifference to public canons of art, friends and shibboleths you walked in the light of your inward heroism.

—A nineteen-year-old Joyce to Ibsen

NOTE TO THE READER

Although *Pages from a Cold Island* is a work of non-fiction, I have in some cases, to save them and me embarrassment, changed the names of real persons, their physical descriptions, in other instances even the locations where the action occurs. Where I've used the names of known persons, famous or otherwise, the incidents described are as I remember them.

PAGES FROM A COLD ISLAND

1

At 6:30 on the morning of Monday, June 12, 1972, Edmund Wilson died of a coronary occlusion at his mother's ancestral home—"The Old Stone House"—at Talcottville, Lewis County, upstate New York, an hour's drive south from where I am putting down these words in my own mother's house at Alexandria Bay, a Thousand Islands resort village on the St. Lawrence River. The latter was a body of water well known to Wilson. In his sixty-first year he remarked the extraordinariness of the continuity that allowed him to sit yet in his mother's stone house amid the memorabilia of his boyhood, one of which was a stuffed bird of yellow cloth he had as a child bought for his Grandmother Kimball on a boat excursion down this lovely river.

Ironically, only moments before learning of his death in my hometown newspaper, the Watertown *Times*, I had been uneasily rereading *Memoirs of Hecate County* and was well into "The Princess with the Golden Hair," that section once astonishingly held pornographic by the State of New York (the Court of Special Sessions had branded the book "lascivious and salacious"). I'd reached the point where narrator-Wilson (Wilson deplored the notion of this work being autobiographical but in his concluding section, "Mr. and Mrs. Blackburn at Home," he'd invited such speculation by having his narrator write, "In those days, what with revery and alcohol and art, I carried so much of dreaming into real life and so much of my real life into dreams—as I have sometimes done in telling these stories—that I was not always quite sure which was which") learns that the object of his as yet thwarted passion, "princess" Imogen Loomis, wears—and unnecessarily, her condition being psychosomatic—a harnessed back brace. It was a symbol—attempting to show the dependency of the privileged suburban witch he is portraying—I'd once again found too trite for a writer of Wilson's sensitivity. The last lines I'd read were Imogen's cloying, "'I don't want to see you for a while. It would make me uncomfortable to see you now that you know'"—about the brace, that is—"'about me. You and Ralph and Edna Farber are the only ones who know.'" And then from the narrator: "She put her purse under her arm and left."

At that moment I'd risen restlessly from my bed. Thinking I probably wouldn't read on, I'd nevertheless laid the Ballantine paperback edition open and face down on the quilt at pages 186–187. I'd then gone downstairs, settled myself onto the black Naugahyde divan in the front room to await the evening *Times*, and without as yet having learned of his death found myself edgy and sad. In a prefatory note to the reader Wilson had written, *"Hecate County* is my favorite among my books. I never understood why people who interest themselves in my work never pay any attention to it." At the same time he had had his narrator interrupting his courtship of Imogen—when in dismay I'd laid the book down he'd been wooing Imogen for a year and had yet to seduce her—with parenthetical asides to the reader ("was I being a little maudlin?") indicating that Wilson himself, perhaps unconsciously, sensed that there were parts of the book that weren't working. He had had his narrator tell us things like "After dinner, I picked up a victoria at the Plaza and took her for a drive to the Park" (wooing indeed! Would I have to annotate the text for the kids with whom I was thinking reading it? "At the time of which Wilson is writing, the 1930s, and well into the early '60s for that matter, it was not uncommon for male in pursuit of female to make barbaric gestures such as plying her with flowers, taking her to dinner and the movies, and in general indicating to her that in his eyes she was riveted with what the antiquarians used to call 'esteem' ").

Wilson's portrait of his narrator's other "love," the Ukrainian waitress-dance-hall hostess, Anna Lenihan, a rather too obvious contrast to the wealthy Imogen, seems not to work at all. The narrator has been having an intermittent affair with Anna, and from her he has contracted a tenacious dose of the clap (no longer a disease of the underprivileged, as I can personally verify from a recent one-night stand with a lass from what one used to call "a good family"). Although he does sense the absurdity of it, as does Anna, in her utter self-awareness of her inability to manage even her own life, not to mention governing nations, the narrator amusingly and touchingly tries to bring home to her the meaning of the recent Russian Revolution and her role as a member of the new elite, the Marxist proletarian who should be thinking about dislodging her American employers and ruling!

Far more annoying, he has Anna talking of her drunken and imprisoned Irish husband Dan thusly: "'He looked terrible. He just stared at me at first, and didun say anything, like he was sore—then I talked to-um and told-um I still loved-um and everything, and after a while he calmed down. He thinks that everybody's through with-um. He's a bad egg, I know it—he's just as bad as they come. I'm afraid of-um—I'm afraid he'll cut me up— he said he wouldun kill me, because he doesn't want to burn in the chair, but that he'd do something terrible to me.'"

Still waiting for the newspaper, I thought, "No, I absolutely cannot read this with the kids. Absolutely not." As much as I wanted to work into the course—what was it to be called? "Problems of Modern Fiction"?—my unbounded admiration for Wilson, *Hecate County* wouldn't ring true for them.

"*Shit.*" And I chuckled pensively. "These kids are having oral-genital sex twenty minutes after meeting. They'll laugh my ass under the seminar table."

The Watertown *Times* arrived. As I always do, I turned it first to the back page carrying the lead local stories of the three counties—Jefferson, St. Lawrence and Lewis— served by the paper. The three-column obituary with two-column, four-inch deep artwork was displayed glaringly upper right, and I looked at both the headline and the fifteen-year-old photo a dozen times without their penetrating. Legends, myths, monuments—especially American ones—never die, and as was my habit I continued to skim for juicier tidbits, a driving-while-intoxicated, a barroom brawl or a dope bust (and both violence and drugs have come to upstate New York).

Having skipped to the interior of the paper, I found myself reading about an ex-pupil of mine who had been arrested for possession of unprescribed amphetamines. It was no surprise to find he'd taken to speed. In my seven years teaching in these nearby rural secondary schools he was one of the three kids I'd put my hands on. In front of the class he'd called me a cocksucker (we'd been reading Shakespeare and apparently his diseased mind had equated an appreciation for the Bard with a yearning to envelop inflamed penises with my oral cavity). It was a senior group, so it had nothing to do with their ears being too "delicate" for such obscenities, nor an overreaction on my part to what the hysterics who write for *Ms.* would call an assault on my sense of machismo; all that pap about the democratic dispensing of justice in our school system notwithstanding, I yet had twenty other kids in that room and refused unequivocally to let his sickness infiltrate and oppress those others. Very deliberately I'd seized a bunch of his sweat shirt at his chest cavity, yanked him from his chair, slammed the small of his back against the blackboard, and with the palm and the back of my hand had slapped him repeatedly across the cheeks. He'd wept, the tears running over the inflamed face. In truth, he wasn't a bad kid, we'd got on famously after that; but his home life was abominable, an utter desecration.

I was remembering that day in all its brilliant and furious sadness, and actually thinking of calling J. and saying, "Look, old buddy, join the Navy, or the Marines, or Vista or Action, or drive a Mayflower moving van from Portland, Maine, to Portland, Oregon—do anything so long as you get out of that pigsty you're living in!" Then it hit me. Slowly I turned again to the back page, laid the

‡   7

paper flat out on the floor beneath me, placed my elbows on my thighs, rested my now hot cheeks in the cups of my already sweating palms, and read: EDMUND WILSON, AUTHOR, CRITIC (redundant, of course, and Wilson would have used the simple "writer") EXPIRES (Wilson would have said "dies") AT 77 AT TALCOTTVILLE.

2

A month and a half before, in the last week in April, I'd flown from Singer Island, Riviera Beach, Florida, where I'd made my home on and off for a decade, to Iowa City, where to the writing students at the University of Iowa's prestigious Workshop I'd read excerpts from my new book, *Pages from a Cold Island*. The reading had gone well enough. On my return to Florida I was offered a visiting lectureship, for the fall semester only, by John Leggett, who heads the fiction section; as *Memoirs of Hecate County* was one of Wilson's two attempts at sustained fiction, I was reading it with a view to imposing on the students my admiration for him—which wasn't apparently as unqualifiedly idolatrous as I had for a number of years suspected. And I was sorry. Although not nearly so sorry as that I'd felt compelled to accept the job in the first place.

Pages from a Cold Island didn't at all work at that heady level I desperately yearned for it to work. Including moneys owed the Internal Revenue Service, I was fifteen thousand dollars in debt. I needed a change of scene more than I cared to admit. And I'd accepted the job in the hope that following a four-month respite I could return to the manuscript renewed, instantly discover a way to outflank it, and attack its four hundred and eighty pages of typescript with the inspired strategems of a Caesar. I do not mean to say the book was unpublishable. All I had to do was xerox it, put it in an envelope and mail it off to my agent. My editor had died at forty-two of a heart attack in December of 1970. I therefore had no emotional ties with any publisher, and I knew that my agent planned to submit the manuscript simultaneously to a number of publishers and that she would (rather aloofly I gathered) "permit" the highest bidder to publish it.

Following the publication of *A Fan's Notes*, I'd idly passed six months in the Village at 59 Christopher Street at the bar of The Lion's Head Ltd., a saloon frequented by writers, editors and agents, and I'd there picked up the jargon. It was axiomatic, I'd been assured, that the reviews of one's first upped the advance price on and sold one's second book and that if one had done well by the reviewers he ought with a kind of zany haste to rush into print with something new. What matter if it were a piece of crap?

"Look at Mailer's *Barbary Shore*, Styron's *Set This House on Fire*."

If one were churlish enough to point out that Mailer himself had been pleased with *Barbary Shore*, and damn the reviewers, or that Styron's second book was in fact the masterful novella *The Long March*, one was looked upon as a damp-souled literalist childishly refusing to accommodate one's hickish mentality to what everybody at The Lion's Head "knew."

Apart from my apparent obtuseness, I had advantages that allowed me to remain free from this kind of certainty. Despite some unanticipatedly generous reviews, *A Fan's Notes* had not sold well. I'd made little money; my life style of lugging my own soiled sweat shirts and skivvies to the laundromat and lunching on cheeseburgers and draft beer had altered not a whit; and I hence had not been projected into an exalted milieu in which it would behoove me to print "things" to make payments on a Mark IV Continental. Because of the autobiographical and confessional character of *A Fan's Notes*—what Edward Hoagland writing in the Sunday *Times* called "a splurging of personal history"—I knew from both my late editor and my agent (she told me this to prompt me into proving the experts wrong) that on those very infrequent occasions when my name came up at all I was summarily and disparagingly dismissed as having "shot my wad" (whenever I heard this I breathlessly sought sanctuary and with or without help did a savage job on my penis, afterwards minutely examining the semen for signs of "diminished wad") and I drew perverse gratification from the knowledge of how much comfort my *not* publishing would give to those really peculiar people (whatever else they were interested in, it certainly wasn't writing or books) who fret about such things.

After what in an introductory note to the reader in *A Fan's Notes* I'd called "that long malaise, my life," I had not published until I was in my late thirties; I was cognizant that after years of excessive drinking, three times resulting in my incarceration in insane asylums, I hadn't the zest or the wit (alcoholic sieves in the cerebrum) to produce what the boys at The Lion's Head called "a shelf"; and for these various reasons I found it easy to forelay and squelch the commercial allurements and knew that all I really wanted was to produce another book, maybe two, that would be treated as kindly as the first had. When the afternoon came that from down the bar at The Lion's Head I overheard, "Of course, had Kerouac lived in the Twenties he'd have been Gertrude Stein," I knew it was time to pack the trunk of my Nova and head its fluttering six cylinders southward. I'd chosen to go back to Singer Island. Moreover, despite my heavy indebtedness, the fact that *Pages from a Cold Island* wasn't succeeding, and that by the owner, Big Daddy, I'd been cut off from my bar tab at the hotel where I was living (truly "the unkindest cut of all"), I very much liked my life on Singer Island and dwelt in that oddly euphoric languor of a man with no place but up to go.

On my return to the island from my reading at Iowa, May had come and with it summer's relentlessly sunny squalor; but neither high heat nor oppressive moisture is noteworthy in southern Florida at that time of year. Those who make their livings there say, "Hot? You call this hot? Wait'll it *really* gets hot!" They lie. In my hometown, Watertown, N.Y., we say to February sojourners: "Snow? You call this snow? Wait'll it *really* starts snowing!" In either case it is a balming of one's predicament, a coming to terms with a milieu one has chosen for himself. Or from which one is unable to escape. Most of us seemed helpless to flee the island.

Toni was one of the hotel's regulars. Once her father wanted to take her son from her and in his affidavit alleged that the island was a "shabby resort area, the hub of Palm Beach County's drug culture, and a hothouse of whoredom, practiced both formally and informally." Toni was obsessed with the Kennedys (she told me President

marked. For years there had persisted a rumor that the actor was homosexual and with the advent of the new permissiveness there was now in circulation a story that he was "married" to a hillbillyishy male television personality, probably, I thought, one of Toni's tales gleaned from the pages of *Midnight*. Given to the new styles, Jack wore his black hair long, he sported a luxurious Mexican *bandido* mustache, and he wore bell-bottomed white-duck hip-huggers with a wide heavy silver-buckled black belt and long-sleeved extravagant-colored satiny shirts with V-necks and sleeves that bloused out at the wrists, which from me elicited, "How can you worry about your resemblance to that fucking swish and wear those fruity shirts?"

He'd spent three years in the navy and had had two years of college. At the beginning of his junior year, at that point when the bureaucratic "guidance" clerks told him he must decide what he must do and what he must "major" in, he'd dropped out. As he hadn't the foggiest idea of what it was he must do, it was only a question of time until he found his way to Beach Court where none of us knew *that* and prided ourselves on being all on a slow boat to nowhere. We employed, quite accurately but affectionately, terms like "wholly mad," "wonderfully crazy" and "a beautiful yo-yo" to describe each other. On television two days before there had been a story that in Palm Beach Gardens at the north end of the county an eight-foot tall, massive and copiously haired humanoid creature was running wild. He'd been spotted, "confirmed," and driven raving and roaring into a wooded area by a police or TV station helicopter. The year before he'd been seen in the Keys. He was thought to be working his way up the peninsula (no doubt making his way to the University of Florida at Gainesville for the summer term), and the inhabitants at the county's north end were cautioned to be on the lookout for him. In sympathy McBride had wanted to get up a posse made up of habitués of Beach Court and find the "poor fellow" before the authorities did.

"We could chip in and get him a room in the hotel next to Exley's," McBride had said.

Everyone had laughed.

"Nobody'd notice anything unusual on this flaky block."

Everyone had laughed again.

"All the reaction you'd get around here is, 'Who's the new guy in the hotel? The tall one with all the hair.'"

Some months before I'd got into a mouth-watering conversation about the blandness of the best restaurant food as against home-cooked meals with Jack's father Alex. Until a droplet of saliva fell onto the back of my hand, we had talked with an eye-narrowing and demented exuberance about roast leg of lamb—"So the skin is drippy crusty," I'd volunteered, "and you can eat it like meat candy"—mashed potatoes and lamb gravy the texture of lentil soup; sautéed peas, baby onions and fresh mushrooms mixed and simmered together; salads with great chunks of fresh tomato and cucumber and swimming in homemade Roquefort dressing; and hot apple or pecan pie ecstatically topped with fresh whipped cream. For weeks afterwards Alex had invited me to his domicile for just such a meal but as I thought the McBrides lived on the mainland I politely refused. Save when I was "kidnapped" and driven across the causeway to a movie or, between three and five in the morning, carried to drink and to listen to live music at the White Caps, a deafening place without acoustics and frequented by hotel and restaurant help when they got off work, my paranoia wouldn't permit me to leave the island ("odd things" were "waiting" for me "over there") and even those infrequent "kidnappings" became conversation pieces the next day on Beach Court.

"Exley left the island last night."

"He didn't!"

"He did!"

Then inadvertantly I'd discovered the McBrides lived right behind the Beer Barrel on Island Road. I'd at last accepted, and now they found it impossible to be rid of me. Three and four nights a week I was over there shoveling in the heavily gravied mashed potatoes with Alex and his wife Peggie, with Jack and his girl Joanne. We'd even reached that familial easiness wherein I "raced" Jack and Alex through the meal to see who would get to the couch first to watch the television movie. Whoever won invariably fell asleep during the opening credits and commercials and had on awakening to ask "What happened?" to which the reply was also invariably "Nothin'."

With Jack I now began the day's ritual.

"What's for supper?"

"I forgot to ask."

"You prick."

Pulling myself onto a barstool, I ordered a Budweiser, laid the newspapers out on the bar in front of me, took the mail from my back pocket and placed it next to the papers, then for Jack's inspection held out my hands, palms face down and suspended in the air a foot or so above the bar.

"Steady as a rock," Jack said. He shook his head in wonder. "Never seen anything like it. Most boozers come in mornings shaking like a leaf, have a couple beers, quiet down and leave. You come in here steady, have a beer, then start shaking."

This was true, and for that reason Jack read and answered my mail for me. He'd just opened the bar; the regulars wouldn't start drifting in till noon; and the few customers would be tourists who, having saved their pennies and come down from Marshalltown, Iowa, and sitting now atop the loveliest beach in Florida, would come in, drink a draft beer or two, and oddly ask whatever there was to do "around here."

Winking at me, Jack would recommend a visit to Lion Country, where the mangy lions seem always to be asleep and snoring (the management claims the animals aren't tranquilized but the one time I'd taken two little kids there not one of the beasts even conveyed the notion he might be alive and the kids had bawled); to Disneyworld, where in order to explore its inexhaustible and wondrous delights Jack claimed to go on every one of his off days but had in fact never been and probably never would be; or to Frances Langford's Outrigger Restaurant where, said obliging Jack, they offered for a buck a "mind-blowing" drink containing fourteen different ingredients called a Rooty Tooty Fruity.

"Loaded with aphrodisiacs," Jack always added. "Tell 'em I sent you."

I'd finished my first drink and the shakes had started. Having begun, the trembling would need three or four more cans to be quelled. By leaving the newspapers stationary on the bar, I found I could without embarrassment skim them and turn the pages when necessary but I was too ashamed to try and hold and decipher mail in front of strangers. By now Jack had automatically sorted out my bills and thrown them unopened into the green plastic garbage can behind the bar. The first envelope he opened was from my paperback publisher containing a fan missive, which I received at the hardly impressive rate of about thirty a year. Invariably they were from students, and save for the ones from coeds (one never knew) I almost never answered them. Long since I'd discovered that woven into the texture of *A Fan's Notes* there was a streak of hauteur I could not isolate from memory; though the letters often began on a note of rather touchingly slavish devotion there seemed always to come a time when the writer, in an abruptly paranoic turn, would say, "Actually, your book wasn't all that great; in fact there were places where it was a bunch of shit, and as you probably won't answer this anyway"—and he was right—"you can go fuck yourself!"

Today's letter, though free from this odd desire to inflict hurt, was nevertheless disconcerting. It was from a young man in Billings, Montana, who said that as the summer holiday was on us he and a dozen or so "fellow-student literati" in the Billings area had decided to seek me out ("With us," he wrote, "it has assumed the character of a pilgrimage"), sit at my feet, and let me impart the "Wisdom of Booze" to them. He promised they'd only stay "a week or so" and asked where I was and could they come.

"Throw it away."

"Answer it," Jack said. "It's friendly enough. And intelligent."

"That's all we need on this block. A dozen more Montana hippies. Fucking cowboys. They'd probably all be drinking on my tab, and I can't even afford my own drinks."

"You don't have to put a return address."

From the back bar Jack had already removed the unlined white linen tablet he used for the purpose and now held a ball-point pen poised anxiously over it.

"Okay," I said. "No address. Take this. 'Dear Mr. Smith colon paragraph I thank you and your friends for your kind words and genuinely underline genuinely appreciate your interest period However comma and at the risk of appearing a fucking liar comma I do not own a copy of my book and have never kept a single review or fan letter dash even kind ones like yours period Since I last read the book in final page proofs four years ago I have been unable even to look at it comma and I purposely live on a block among goons who either can't or don't choose to read period.' "

Jack laughed.

" 'I have chosen this seclusion among mushheads in

dumb-dumbville because whenever I find myself with some-
one who has read my book comma he seems sooner or later
to start yapping about a book that has nothing whatever to
do with me comma and I have no way of accounting for
this save for thinking that at the time I wrote it I was some
quite other person than the one I am now period new
paragraph Thank you again for your kindness period
Cordially.' "

"That's too cold," Jack said. "Can't you put them off
with something tongue-in-cheek?"

"What tongue-in-cheek?"

"Anything."

"Try this. 'New papagraph Even were I up to it I
couldn't ask you at this time as I'm leaving this afternoon for
California for the summer months period I've at last suc-
cumbed to the commercial promptings and am going out
there to stay at Playboy Mansion West capital P capital
M capital W with Hugh Hefner and his girl Barbi Doll
Benton and do an original screenplay for the latter and
another juicy blond playmate named Angel Tompkins
period parenthesis Perhaps you've been fortunate enough to
see these pulpous morsels featured in the pages of Playboy
underline Playboy question mark parenthesis Hefner tells
me that both girls quote adored underline adored my book
comma that they both yearn for some meaty roles they can
get their teeth into comma and that they've decided I'm
the guy to give them that meat parenthesis no double
entendre intended parenthesis period paragraph Hefner
assures me that Angel will be on hand in the mansion
twenty-four hours a day for consultation and collaboration
comma he further assures me that he spends two weeks per
month in Chicago on business comma and says that what-
ever collaboration goes on among Barbi comma Angel and
myself during those two weeks is quite up to me period
paragraph Certainly you fucking cowboys wouldn't ask me

to by-pass an opportunity like this question mark Cordially comma.' "

"That's more like it," Jack said.

The next letter began, "Dear Exley, You Fuck!" It was from a Bennington coed with whom I'd exchanged three or four letters. Her last two epistles had been too copious to read; she'd got the conversation away from books and me (I couldn't permit that!); from what I'd been able to glean skimming them she found college dull, dull, dull and college boys "as insipid as unseasoned summer squash"; and in my last letter I'd therefore come abruptly to the point and asked her what it was she really wanted, with Jack throwing in a few unseemly guesses of his own as to what that might be.

Together we'd told her that I was rapidly oozing into middle age, that I wouldn't seduce that many more teeny-boppers, and that if she were any good-looking and it were simply a question of getting her youthfully tender clitoris titillated she should refrain from all those excessive literary comparisons of college boys to unsalted squash and get on the next plane to Palm Beach. We told her that I'd long since abandoned youthful sexual inhibitions, would in an oral way induce from her a half-dozen orgasms before even showing her what Jack called "the frightful hog," and that between the resuscitating respites necessary to a forty-two-year-old man I would then proceed to emit on her teeth, her eyeballs, her breasts, her ass and whatever else she owned she was particularly proud of. Employing the silly-sleazy tone of "personals" in crackpot newspapers, Jack then appended a postscript to the effect that I offered "everything fancy short of accoutrements, including occasionally bringing in the second team in the person of my handsome valet-secretary, John Swinnerton McBride."

Her present response excoriated me as a filthy old man, a fact both Jack and I felt our last letter had made manifest.

‡   23

She had, however, enclosed a Polaroid colored print of herself sitting on a beach in a bikini. In an hysterical funk she had scribbled on the back of it, "Is this good-looking enough? you fucking male chauvinist pig! If it is, take a good look—'cause you ain't getting any!" She was, we had to admit, quite good enough.

"You going to answer it?" Jack said. "She's getting loonier by the letter."

"Better not," I agreed. "Sounds like the type who'd get you drunk, wait'll you pass out, then excise your scrotum with a straight razor."

Jack tore her return address from the envelope, threw the remainder of the letter into the plastic garbage can with my bills and the empty Budweiser cans, then scotch-taped the address and the colored print to the red-brick side wall for any of the regulars who wanted to pursue the correspondence.

The final letter contained a half-dozen copies of my contract and a covering letter from Margaret Mangan, administrative assistant in the Program in Creative Writing, Department of English, The University of Iowa, Iowa City, Iowa 52240. The letter was long and a number of times I had to ask Jack to read parts of it over again. Impatiently he laid the letter down and as if explaining to a child began ticking items off on his fingers.

"You've got to fill in the contracts. Right?"

I nodded my assent.

From his pinkie he moved the index to his ring finger. "You've got to send some kind of plans or prospectus for your fiction seminar." He went to his middle finger. "You have to tell her how many students up to a dozen you want to admit to that seminar." He was in exasperation at his index finger. "And you have to send her a list of the books you're going to read so she can order them and they'll be there on your arrival. It's that simple."

"Okay," I said. "Anything else?"

Two tourists had come into the bar and I asked Jack to read in silence. When I'd been at Iowa City, Dan Wakefield, another visiting lecturer, told me he'd called his seminar "The Literature of Madness," joshingly or otherwise emphasizing the role *A Fan's Notes* played in his group's discussions, which made me feel somewhat uneasy. Apparently Ms. Mangan wanted the comfort of having in her hands over the summer a paragraph or two setting forth an outline such as "J. P. Donleavy and the Black Humorists" or "John Cheever, James Thurber, John Updike, Peter DeVries and the *New Yorker* Fiction School." As I was only going for a semester, though, I didn't think I'd read anything but that which personally held me in thrall—would Miss Mangan, I wondered, be satisfied with anything as general as "Exercises in English Prose Fiction?" In idle moments I'd already begun scribbling down the names of modern (and where did "modern" begin? with Melville? with Dreiser?) novels I admired, attempting constantly and to no avail to discern a recurrent lode in them.

I had other problems. I'd never taught a more advanced grade level than secondary senior English, and though at college twenty years before I'd taken some graduate—or what we then called 500-level—courses, I couldn't for the life of me recall how heavy the assignment load had been. Moreover, whenever over the years I'd thought of the Workshop, and like every American writer I'd been made cognizant of its exemplary reputation and knew that a number of books had gone via a New York editor right from classroom to printer, I'd envisioned some very bright students from all over America coming together there to write mornings, to read, and to meet over draft beers once or twice a week to laud or belittle each other's work. And in the Workshop's brochure (which quite openly acknowledged that writing couldn't in fact be taught) I'd read while returning on the plane, I discovered the Workshop was merely a part of an overall program leading to an M.F.A. in English and that many of the students (how the hell could they do it?) were taking a full load of fifteen hours toward that master's. Hence I hadn't the slightest idea how much reading I could in fairness assign per week (one novel? two?) and far worse than anything to me were my qualms as to how known to the kids my selections would be.

For example, as one assignment I tentatively planned to discuss *All the King's Men* and *The Great Gatsby*, my "problem" being for the student "to see" that the former was "owned" by Jack Burden not Willie Stark and the latter by Nick Carroway not Gatsby, that these two had "endured" to tell and to draw meaning and moral from their tales, that this hadn't even been understood by the presumably literate scriptwriters who'd fashioned such wrong-headed movies from the books, much in the same way that high school teachers persist in believing that Shakespeare's *Caesar* is "about" Caesar.

Too, as is only natural, I very much wanted to be liked by the kids and wondered how much I'd have to pander to their taste to achieve this, though when at Iowa I'd had a conversation from which I'd extracted hope. Expecting the worst, I'd asked a student what he thought of Richard Brautigan, whose *The Abortion* I'd just tried to read and found backbench. To my unexpected relief the student had become rather light-headedly hysterical with derision and had sneered:

"He's an asshole read by sophomore sorority girls. I put him in the same maple sugar tub with Kahlil Gibran."

He then went on to tell me that in two hours he'd slapped together a pornographic parody of *The Prophet* he called *The Profit*, that an artist friend had also parodied with "marvelous obscenity" Gibran's "shitty drawings," and that by the underground press they were now trying to get the volume published. He offered a sample:

"On Love: Even as Prick inflames Itself/so shall he soggily wither/Even as he is cunt's pleasure/so is he sodomite's ass pain."

Now Jack was laughing rather dementedly at something in Miss Mangan's letter. "Jesus," he gasped. "This is too much! This is classic!"

"What's so funny?"

"She . . . she . . . wants to know . . . oh, Christ! . . . whether . . . ha! ha! . . . you want to stay at Iowa House on campus or if she should rent you . . .beyond belief! . . . a fucking farmhouse on the outskirts of town!"

"I don't see what's so funny."

"Oh, you don't see what's so funny, don't you?" Jack mimicked my solemnity. "I'll tell you what's so funny. *You* on a goddam farm. I can just see you sitting out there in your big old-fashioned kitchen, the wood stove blazing, you with your writing tablets, your vodka bottles, peeking out the windows at the November corn stalks, the wind whistling and rattling your shutters, you with your fucking paranoia waiting for the first blizzard to hit. You'd be a fucking basket case in a month. A month? *A week*. Besides," he added, "how'd you get to and from campus?"

"I'd drive. How else?"

Jack laughed scornfully. "Shit you would. We ain't even letting you take your car."

"Who's we?" I demanded. I was getting angry.

"Everybody. The whole fucking gang! Christ, you're only going up there three months. Fly up, fuck a couple coeds, stay drunk, and I'll fly up and see you some weekend. When you get back at Christmas your Nova'll still be here, sitting behind the hotel with the sun baking the paint off it, right where it's been sitting for three years! You haven't moved it in all that time, now suddenly you got visions of yourself being the proper professor, commuting from hog ranches with a goddam portfolio case on the seat next to you. *Sheeit*, man, come off it. You'll kill yourself in that car." He laughed disparagingly, then tried to leaven his contempt by saying, "Actually, we're only keeping your car to make sure you come home." He emphasized *home*.

In moody silence I pondered his words while drinking two more beers. When my hands had stilled, I rose, picked up my newspapers, the letter Jack had written for me, and the contracts—though he good-naturedly but steadfastly refused to surrender Ms. Mangan's covering letter, stuffing it into his wallet pocket and for dramatic effect buttoning the pocket and pointedly patting his behind there to reassure me of its safeness. For the next two days he used it by way of an object lesson for me. Whenever I was present he removed it from his pocket, ceremoniously unfolded it, handed it to one of the regulars and said: "Read this and tell me *honestly* if anything strikes you as weird." To a man the guys broke up at the prospect of me on a farm in Iowa.

On an oppressively hot evening a few nights later, having just finished one of his mother's superb dinners, Jack and I were standing in front of his house nursing V.O.'s on the rocks when I asked, "Are you setting me up with the guys, telling them at what point in that letter they should laugh?"

Solemnly Jack raised his right hand, the good citizen being sworn at the bench. "So help me I'm not."

"What do you think I ought to do?"

"Do what I said. Go up, have a few laughs, me and a couple of the guys'll fly up some weekend for a Big Ten game, you'll be home by Christmas and can go back to work on the 'masterpiece'!"

I thought for a moment. "Maybe I'll fly up to the St. Lawrence for a couple months, sober up, and then go out to the corn country from there."

Unhappily, Jack offered no resistance to the idea. "Nobody wants you to go, but it might be for the best."

"Thanks, Jack."

So it was decided. On going back into the house I poured myself another V.O., picked up the phone, got through to Eastern Airlines, and made the reservation for Watertown and the river.

3

I hadn't seen Bob Tompkins, who delivers the local six o'clock evening news on WWNY–TV, Channel 7, the Carthage-Watertown station, since the last time I'd visited my mother four years before. In that time long hair had become fashionable (so *de rigueur* that like Yul Brynner I'm contemplating having my hair shaven from my pate) and he seemed another person. His hair is thin, he has quite ordinary though pleasant looks, and he wears glasses that reflect the relentless studio lights. In the old days he appeared balding and eyeless, little more than a thin mouth forming and issuing mellifluously enunciated words from out a chubby and nondescript face, and I couldn't help re-marking how much character the long hair gave him, making his face thinner and sharpening his features so that he was handsome, even though—I guessed because of the glasses—his eyes still shyly, almost furtively avoided a confrontation with the camera.

Glenn Gough preceded Tompkins with two minutes of national headlines, informing us that at 6:30 Walter Cronkite would have "further details." To my chagrin he said not a word about Edmund Wilson, though I hoped that this foretold Tompkins' devoting the entire ten minutes of local news to his death. Gough mentioned that Air Force General John D. Lavelle had testified before a House Armed Services investigating subcommittee that between November of last year and March of this, he'd ordered twenty unauthorized raids against what he said were military installations in North Vietnam and had been demoted and retired for doing so. My first thought was "Splendid, and fuck the doves!"

In *The Cold War and the Income Tax* and elsewhere Wilson had for years maintained that bureaucracies were destined to be America's ruination; the civilian-controlled military was the most monstrously horrific of these bureaucracies; and if the politicians could not be made to see the wholesale homicide they were perpetrating in Southeast Asia, they might at last get a glimpse, and hopefully shudder queasily as they did so, of the elephantine unwieldiness of the Pentagon.

In my mind I'd already written and produced Tompkins' local news. In stillness we'd open with a long shot from the south or Boonville side of Wilson's white-balconied, black-shuttered stone house (the view made famous on the dust jacket of *Upstate*). Very slowly we'd dolly toward the front northeast window behind which Wilson wrote at his card table, and as we did so our voice-over would speak these words:

"Edmund Wilson, seventy-seven, one of the great men of the twentieth century, died this day at six-thirty this morning in this old stone house at Talcottville."

To my utter incredulity Tompkins' lead story had to do with a dispute regarding the tax assessor at Massena, a far northern and perhaps fantasy village in St. Lawrence County. There were two or three other local stories, then TV star Ben Gazzara was on screen being interviewed by Joe Rich, an amiable guy who'd once interviewed me.

I thought, "What the fuck is going on? Where's Wilson?"

I'd always believed Gazzara one of the most shamelessly affected actors in the business, employing all the oppressively heavy and glacially tentative gestures of Brando without in the least owning Brando's genius or sensitivity (and how galled over the years Brando must have been rendered by these legions of shoddy mimes!), so that he made walking to the sink for a glass of water appear the end of an exhausting quest, as though in lieu of approaching a nickel-plated tap faucet with a jam-jar glass he'd just dragged himself into a cloistered crypt of Tuscan marble and was reverentially crawling—stricken arm and clutched hand extended outward, breathing labored, music rising exultantly—toward a gilt altar on which sat the Holy Grail bathed in Hollywood moonglow.

For two years he'd been in a TV series called *Run for Your Life*. It had to do with a young attorney who discovers he has a year or two (the latter, I guessed, in case the sponsor decided to renew the lunacy) to live and who having nothing to lose "runs" about the earth and parachutes in free fall from airplanes, at intrepid rpm's races automobiles and speed boats, skin-dives to the formidably scary depths where squiggly monsters are thought to reign, skis abandonedly down ninety-degree slopes, confronts Mafiosi and Hell's Angels with haughty disdain, and copulates with beautiful girls who find themselves hopelessly mushy-kneed in the penumbra of his Thanatos-ridden charm. As the show served as a vehicle for the introduction of those vernally humid starlets—one wondered if the producer were also a dirty old man—of the type featured in *Playboy* centerfolds, I'd randyishly watched it a few times and always especially liked the scene where the ingenue discovered (though the stoic Gazzara never told her) that death was in the offing, which always deranged her more ever than it did Ben.

For every predicament he had one facial expression: a flickering of his long dark lashes and the petulant lowering of his lower right lip, which is meatier at that side than at the left, an expression that fell somewhere between a sage smile and a wry sneer and was meant to convey—or which Gazzara wrongly believed conveyed—everything, in this case a nineteen-fortyish what-the-hell, everybody-dies sort of thing that was so well done by Cagney and Garfield. Invariably this eyelash batting and resigned mouth shrug was succeeded by some silently protracted, poignant looks between Miss Frankheart and Gazzara; then before the fade-out came close-ups of some well-spittled, cavernous-mouthed kisses, at which point I'd celebratively shout at the tube:

"Atta girl! Atta way! Blow him! Ream him! Give him a head job that'll make that paradise he's going to look pale by comparison! Give him one that'll send him to his maker sooner than anticipated and let's make an end to this fucking nonsense!"

The New York State Democratic primary elections were to be held the following Tuesday, and Gazzara was in Watertown stumping for Senator George McGovern. He wore a pair of impeccably pressed lightweight slacks held up by an old-fashioned thin black leather belt; a pastel sport shirt open at the collar; a double-knit wrinkleless jacket of blue and white, wide candy-striped seersucker;

and he answered Joe's questions with a head-on articulation that made one see how effective he might be as an actor if he abdicated all his blowsily moody mannerisms. He naturally hoed the McGovern row and talked about the need to weed ourselves from Vietnam and concentrate on rebuilding our cities, depolluting our waterways and atmosphere, assuring equal education for all, and erasing the stigma of impoverishment emanating from our various and damnatory Appalachias. He said that what was needed in America was a "reversal of priorities," to which I'd wholeheartedly assented by thinking, "And let it begin by getting your joyless mug off the screen and on to the death of America's last preeminently civilized man!" Then Gazzara said something emetic. Asked about McGovern's proposal to erase the tax loopholes so cherished by the rich and the powerful, he not only backed McGovern but by implication suggested to amiable Joe and the rest of us out there in TV Land that as he was one of the rich and the powerful with a good deal more to lose than we, this should serve to make his proselytizing of the Senator all the more arresting.

"Ben, baby!" I shouted. "I love you! From out of your pores there sluices the milk of human neighborliness."

Ben said he had a daughter he didn't want growing up a militant revolutionist; he said that Mama and Papa Gazzara had been born in Sicily and had emigrated from there to the United States; that America had been kind to this immigrant's son and he in no way resented assuming a higher tax burden for a country that had been so nice; and though—thank the small decencies!—he didn't say so, we were definitely left to infer that he was brighter, more talented and more worthy than we hayseeds, but that if we'd take McGovern and his proposals to our bosoms he would—out of pocket!—see to it that we got a couple breaded porkchops with our evening cans of Genesee 12-Horse Ale and a new Ford Pinto every other year.

But why *really*? I wondered.

Fifteen years before in my "insane" period when for months I'd lain on the davenport reading Wilson for the first time—and I score this reading as having no less than saved my life—I'd often watched Walt Disney's kiddie show *The Mickey Mouse Club,* and I now found myself thinking of one of its stars, Annette Funicello. Some years later she'd developed an inspiring set of lungs, and in numbly touching bewilderment, her publicist—one could almost hear the poor fellow thinking, "Zounds! Annette Funicello with tits!"—had milked her booby boundary for all it was worth, almost as if he'd expected that, like Mickey, Donald and Pluto, Miss Funicello would remain forever frozen in Disney's milieu where maturity, aging and death are eternally inimical; and in trying to plumb Gazzara's motives all I could call up was the preterite, the titless and knee-dimpled Annette leading the other Mouseketeers into inquiring of the viewers their familiar and rhetorical *Why?* and in singsongy lachrymose unison shouting their own answer: "Because we *luuuhhfffff* you!"

What grated was that only days before Shirley Mac-Laine had said the same thing to Barbara Walters on the *Today* show (two days later Watertown would be visited by Dennis Weaver, Matt Dillon's erstwhile gimpy sidekick Chester on *Gunsmoke,* and I surmised that whereas national TV was graced with movie stars like MacLaine, the lesser TV people were sent out to cowsheds like Watertown), and though MacLaine was more attractive, intelligent and sincere (she'd made her opposite number, Patty Duke, who was backing Humphrey, appear an ebullient idiot) than Gazzara, this mouthing of the same "party line" made me wonder if these stars weren't being force-fed by McGovern advisers, a possibility I found reprehensible even allowing that the better part of acting is little other than an interpretation of other people's lines.

‡   35

For a flashing instant I thought of writing McGovern's top political strategist, Frank Mankiewicz, and telling him how insufferably patronizing I found this whole "star" segment of the campaign. But a man who knew Mankiewicz well had told me he was extremely well-read, devastatingly witty and unredemptively cynical (of necessity the latter goes hand in hand with the former). Politics is the art of accommodation, and I suspected Mankiewicz found the use of these people as distasteful as I and if anything would be curious as to why I hadn't exercised my simple option of turning off the boob tube. And this would have necessitated explaining my anxiety in awaiting Tompkins' obituary of Wilson, which in turn would have involved conveying to Mankiewicz my tenuously emotional "relationship" (as indeed every American writer had) with Wilson over the years, which again would have involved my setting the scene for the momentousness of his death by relating that for three years prior to its disruptively cataclysmic jolt to my languorous existence I'd lain perspiring on a white Naugahyde couch at the Seaview Hotel at the hot bottom of the world in southern Florida, would in effect demand putting down the words I'm here putting down.

Now, however, and with no little petulance, I said to the unhearing screen, "C'mon, Tompkins, get that Siciliano off the fucking camera and let's get on to Wilson!"

Of course no such eulogy as I had either hoped for, actually composed, or which Wilson merited was forthcoming. When at last Tompkins got around to Wilson he gave him three or four lines, twenty seconds perhaps, and in mentioning what he said was Wilson's most notable work— it was certainly his most "notorious"—he pronounced Hecate "Heck-it," which I thought was wrong, wrong, wrong but which I later learned from Wilson's daughter Rosalind and his publisher Roger Straus, Jr., was indeed Wilson's preferred pronunciation, no matter that I'd never heard a literate person (not that I knew that many) employ it.

The lines were a wire service handout. Late in the following half-hour Walter Cronkite gave voice (showing on a large mock TV screen over his left shoulder a still of Wilson) to practically the same three or four lines and also "mispronounced" Hecate which, though tolerable in Jefferson County, I found execrable on coast-to-coast television and later that evening prompted me to write to Cronkite. Like Bellow's Herzog I had for years been an inveterate composer of zany letters; I wrote to the famous living and the famous dead, to people I knew and people I didn't know, to anybody and everybody and nobody. More often than not these letters did not get beyond being structured mentally; sometimes they actually got written but not mailed (happily the case with Cronkite); and occasionally they were even sent, which as often as not I regretted the second the envelope swooshed irretrievably into the box. Because of my own egregious ignorance I would have shamefacedly rued the sending of what follows, but I offer it as an illustration of my murderous sentiments at what I deemed the media's gross space stinginess with the death of perhaps America's last complete man of letters:

"Dear Mr. Cronkite: Edmund Wilson was of course one of the great men of the 20th Century. That you could find it in you to give him only those brief words was deplorable. A hallmark of intelligence is the ability to draw analogies and on a day you could devote so much time to General Lavelle I thought how fitting it might have been had you mentioned that a decade ago Wilson was decrying our shameless Vietnam involvement and the ruinous, unmanageable, and tyrannical bureaucracies of which Lavelle has found himself so sad and puny a cog. At that time Wilson characterized the Pentagon as 'a great human fungus . . . which multiplies the cells of offices, of labora-

‡   37

tories and training camps' and which poisons the atmosphere of society, all of which, he went on to say, has made the present image of the United States 'homicidal and menacing.'

"What was unforgivable was that in mentioning only a single work in Wilson's *oeuvre,* an aggregate of some twenty volumes, you mispronounced Hecate. Now it is true that for metrical and stress reasons this witch in Shakespeare is called 'Hek-it,' but among the modern literate and educated"—oh, my, Frederick!—"she is called 'Hek-a-tee.' Presently I am fifteen thousand dollars in debt, I understand the not very difficult method of employing a dictionary, and if you will agree to pay me twenty thousand dollars a year I will, working with you only a few minutes a day before your air time, assure you that before the cameras you can proceed with impunity and without fear of humiliation or before millions of viewers making yourself an insipid vulgarian."

Oh, my, indeed! though I must say I hold my last line as applicable: "For a paltry twenty thousand I cannot of course assume responsibility for what you, your writers and editors deem newsworthy; in that regard you'll have to go on bearing the burden of being your own jesters."

Mentally I'd composed this during the remainder of the "news"; when I heard Cronkite say, "And that's the way it is, June 12, 1972," I rose, ascended the stairs, sat at my typewriter and put the words down. Then rising, I stripped naked, dropped my clothes into a pile in the middle of the room where I stood, crawled into bed and there remained for twenty-two hours, smoking cigarettes, staring at the ceiling, sleeping fitfully, finishing *Hecate County* and rereading *Upstate.* When in hunger I at last got up, dressed and descended the stairs, another day had gone and I turned immediately to page four, the editorial page of the

Watertown *Times.* The lead editorial was titled EDMUND WILSON. Wilson would have liked it. It was not well done, and I guessed that in trying to praise such a literary colossus the writer had choked up, resulting in sentences like "He [Wilson] possessed an agility with many of the tongues of the world." Yet I couldn't help thinking that Wilson would have been touched—perhaps profoundly so—precisely by its awkwardness. From the time in 1950 when Wilson "became rather worried about the family house in Talcott-ville" he had, with one or two exceptions and in order to flee both the interruptions and the temptations of the summer literary community at Wellfleet on Cape Cod, come "home" for months at a time to work and, as Alfred Kazin has elsewhere suggested, had made a real attempt to go "down" among the farmers, the truckdrivers, the waitresses, the drugstore clerks—the "mechanics"—of Lewis County and had not only enjoyed the experience (this comes through on every page of *Upstate*) but had been oddly humbled by the experience. At a point when his exasperation was such with America that he'd all but given up, he relates his and an elderly friend's having a blowout south of Boonville: three different drivers pulled their trucks to the side of the road to volunteer their aid; one of them changed the tire; and when Wilson and his elderly friend offered the man money, he scorned it, pointing out that they could one day help him. It was the neighborly gesture Wilson believed no longer existed in America.

No, I hadn't any doubt whatever that Wilson would have been touched by the editorial writer's stutteringly upcountry attempt to put his ghost on its way. What would have dismayed Wilson possibly to the point of one of his infrequent oaths was the five-column UPI story immediately adjacent to his eulogy: B52'S GREATLY EFFECTIVE AGAINST NORTH VIETNAM IN A WAR THAT PLANE WAS NEVER DE-

SIGNED TO FIGHT, and written in a tone of such gung-ho admiration that the writer might well have been on a quarter-century bender and had for the first time sobered up since last covering our invasion of Normandy in 1944.

> A North Vietnamese battalion is camped in a mountain valley, the men chatting as they empty their rice bowls. The sky seems still and empty.
> Suddenly, bombs are exploding everywhere as rice bowls, timber, trucks and human limbs are sent flying in [*sic*] an instant hell.

are the lead paragraphs and the make-up of the editorial page is such that the last two lines fall like this:

EDMUND WILSON   human limbs are sent flying in an instant hell.

Irony is in fact so rampant on the page that it calls for nothing less than Wilson himself to shape and give it meaning. "PROTECTING NAVY PERSONNEL" is the second editorial. It has to do with the Navy Department establishing a program to bring sanctions against merchants who are bilking sailors. The *Times* wasn't sympathetic and thought the program highfalutin. In the old days of World War II Watertown had been overrun—once we'd had the better part of three divisions here—with soldiers from Madison Barracks and Camp Drum (Pine Camp then) and if a local merchant had a reputation for screwing GI's the military police simply descended on the offending establishment and slapped OFF LIMITS signs on it. The *Times* concluded: "They didn't need a fancy-sounding 'Preventive Consumer Awareness Program.'" Wilson would have liked this upstate disparagement of yet another bureaucracy.

The penultimate editorial (the last was READY FOR ACUPUNCTURE?) was called REMEMBER THE IRVINGS? It

40   ‡

said that though it had seemed an eternity since Clifford and Edith Irving had pleaded guilty to federal conspiracy charges for their parts in the Howard Hughes "autobiography," they now must pay the piper and were on Friday surrendering themselves for sentencing. "And what has Irving been doing in the meantime?" the *Times* asked. "Rushing to complete a book [sic] about the book [sic]." What, one wondered, had Wilson made of Irving? and what would he have thought of their being lumped together on the same editorial page? One couldn't be sure, and the beauty lies in imagining the quirky insights that through his old-fashioned, flawless and luminous prose he would have projected upon the reader. He might, for example, have extolled Irving for his cleverness, ingenuity and industry and used the occasion to damn the publishing business for wanting to bring out such a book in the first place and even gleefully lauded Irving for conning the industry out of three-quarters of a million dollars for a manuscript which to Wilson wouldn't in any case—perhaps as a curiosity—have possessed any merit whatever.

In over fifty years of relentless dedication to his craft, he couldn't have failed to see in what paltry esteem— Cronkite would have given more time to Irving's death and on Friday did in fact give more time to his sentencing— he was held by the general public; certainly in order to forbear and keep putting down words in a society that honors Irving with a *Time* cover story, which Wilson had never had, and makes wealthy writers of Jackie Susann and Harold Robbins, Wilson had had to have cultivated an amused though doubtless jaundiced eye with which to view the literary parade. One likes to think that at the end he would have been amused by his and Irving's name coming together on the editorial page of upstate New York's most distinguished newspaper.

From Wellfleet on Cape Cod Wilson had come "home" to Talcottville for the last time on May 31, two weeks before he died in the stone house he had known for better than the three score and ten years meted man by either the Bible or the actuarial charts. For twenty-two days of the June month his arrival would usher in, it would rain, often torrentially, and at the time of the coronary occlusion that ended his life the waters of the Black River were already rising ominously toward the cresting that would result in the flooding of thousands of farmland acres of his beloved Lewis County. Listening to the unending rain, I thought of Shakespeare's Calpurnia admonishing Caesar:

"When beggars die, there are no comets seen; The heavens themselves blaze forth the death of princes."

Certainly no man of such *succès d'estime* had ever loved Lewis County and its inhabitants as Wilson had, and in a perversely obstinate way I insisted to myself that the "high skies" Wilson had remarked and loved were for him "opening up" in some awesomely profuse farewell.

For me the rain had a profound immediacy. On the street in the village I'd run into a man I hadn't seen since high school. He had gone on to make money as a house contractor. Moored a block directly behind my mother's house in a slip at the Bonnie Castle docks he kept his thirty-eight-foot Hatteras. To rehash old times we'd gone aboard and for hours had rhapsodically remade the past and drunk from his well-stocked whiskey cupboards. When we were reluctantly leaving, he'd abruptly handed me an extra key to the boat's cabin and told me that as he almost never used the boat—he reminded me "our" northern summers were so minimal that when he could he often worked seven days a week and that a contractor's owning a boat "hereabouts" was nothing more than a gesture of the most absurdly reckless vanity—and if as a change of scene I wanted to come there and "write" I should feel free to call the Hatteras and its whiskey cupboards mine.

Until the death of Wilson and the continuation of the rains I hadn't even remembered being given the key. Then out of an aggrieved need to be alone, I took to going to the Hatteras daily, sitting in the leather booth at the mahogany table in the galley, the waters of the St. Lawrence gently provoking the hull beneath me, the sluicing rain almost atop my head at the cabin's roof above me, sipping vodka on the rocks, rereading novels I hoped to discuss at Iowa, and seeing Wilson everywhere, he having become for me a kind of appallingly referential mania whereby once as I was reading Anthony Burgess's *The Doctor Is Sick* I actually had an auditory hallucination—of the kind Wilson had suffered in his last years—and swore I heard him say to me, "That novel won't do at all!" (Unable to deny my Workshop students the dazzling Mr. Burgess, I finally settled on his *Clockwork Orange.*)

This mania reached its culmination when I was on the boat reading Nabokov's *Pale Fire.* Although there was no question I would read *Pale Fire* with my group (unlike *Hecate County*, about which I still hadn't made a decision), I was trying now in perhaps my sixth reading over the years to determine at how many levels I ought to try to discuss it without risking turning the kids from Nabokov and wondering, too, if the prose wasn't so luxuriously brilliant that the kids would feel their own talents trifling by contrast (on reading *Lolita*, which surrenders its meanings more readily than *Pale Fire*, no less than Graham Greene uneasily remarked the paucity of his own prose by comparison) and in self-belittlement find their fingers constricting themselves above their typewriters' keys. I myself understood *Pale Fire* at about half the levels Nabokov would have liked it understood (from the half-dozen meanings—two of them major—that had revealed themselves to me and hadn't to my knowledge yet been detected by the critics, I'd long ago decided that in plumbing *Pale Fire*'s layers the academics had as much work cut out for themselves as they had had with *Finnegan's Wake* [Kinbote's wonderful spelling]).

Suddenly, without ever in my life having seen Wilson, I was struck with the wild notion that Nabokov's corporeal model for his "shaggy"-headed, downhome and aging poet John Shade was Wilson! By that time most of the reminiscent and eulogizing obituaries of Wilson had been published, into some of which there'd been woven physical descriptions as well as Wilsonian mannerisms, and when I now found Nabokov's mad Kinbote giving Shade Wilson's walking stick or cane, his "wobbly heart," his "severely rationed" liquor; when of Shade's walk Kinbote describes "a certain curious contortion of his method of progress"; when he puts into Shade's mouth trumpeting and comically grammatical pedantry like "I cannot disobey something which I do not know and the reality of which I have a right to deny"; when in his unconsciously hilarious index Kinbote lists under *Shade, John Francis* "his exaggerated interest in the local flora and fauna" (I'm thinking of Wilson's amusingly resolute quest for the Lady Showyslipper orchid in *Upstate*), everything about Shade began to seem "peculiarities" perfectly interchangeable with statements made about Wilson in the eulogies of his friends.

Beyond the admitted mania of Wilson's lurking all about me in those days, reading Nabokov could hardly fail to call up Wilson. Well aware of their celebrated feuds over *Eugene Onegin* and Wilson's by no means *that* uncomplimentary portraits of "Volodya" and his wife Véra in *Upstate* (both of which feuds, frankly, were carried to distasteful extremes suggesting both men were playing games), I thought that so gratuitously injecting Wilson into

Nabokov's novel resulted from nothing more than the guilt I felt that so hard by his death I had determined to read *Pale Fire* and hadn't yet decided on the Wilson fiction. Yet I couldn't escape the fact that at the time Nabokov was composing *Pale Fire* the two men were still on cordial terms and visiting one another, that even the births of Shade (1898) and Wilson (1895) were but three years apart before the turn of the century. What prevented on my part another reading of *Pale Fire* in demented search of EW in the being of John Shade was suddenly remembering that of *Pale Fire*'s two most perceptively brilliant critics, one was Mary McCarthy (the other was Andrew Field who asked Nabokov if Robert Frost were the model for Shade and received the evasive reply that Nabokov knew nothing of Frost save "Stopping by Woods on a Snowy Evening"), who had been married to Wilson and would certainly have remarked similarities between Shade and Wilson.

When at last I abandoned this fruitless Wilson-Shade equation it was just past six-thirty, still raining heavily, and I'd missed supper by an hour. I snapped on the overhead lights in the cabin, poured myself another vodka, and tuned to Walter Cronkite on the Sony TV on the table next to me. Instantly I was hit with a news bulletin that called forth something from out of my immediate past, I turned off the Sony, let my head go to my crossed arms on the mahogany table, and for a long time—until well into darkness and the roaring stillness of the rain's cessation— underwent the worst crying jag I'd ever had. It was awesome, an expression of some consummate grief compounded of I know not what and into my mouth came first the words of another Nabokovian creation, the pathetically comic émigré Pnin:

"I haf nofing left, nofing, nofing," words I abruptly found myself transposing to "He won't haf nofing left, nofing, nofing."

4

Prior to leaving Singer Island I'd wanted to repay the McBrides for their many delightful *soupers*. For Alex and Peggie, Jack and Joanne, Big Daddy and his wife, and the rest of the gang, I persuaded my friend Steve LaRosa, the Seaview's night bartender, to fix Italian sweet sausage smothered in butter-fried bell peppers, rigatoni and marinara sauce, hot garlic bread, and great bowls of salad with chunks of tomato, fresh mushrooms, anchovy, Bermuda onion, and Italian dressing garnished sumptuously with Parmesan cheese. With the meal we drank three quarts of imported Chianti, and with mock passion everyone kissed me on the mouth and gave me ribald cards and obscene offerings of farewell, Toni's being a paperweight representation of a naked Caspar Milquetoast caught in a rain barrel; when one slid the clockwork barrel upwards there sprung alarmingly from beneath it the meatiest, rawest (it looked venereal) and most potently terror-inducing prick in the consummately sinister flowering of its manhood, and for the first time one comprehended the anomalous and hubristically impertinent expression on Caspar's face.

Except for Mr. and Mrs. McBride, who retired early, we drank and talked through the darkness and the dawn until it was time for my seven A.M. flight to New York. Sure that in the off-season of early June, a seven A.M. flight would be practically passengerless, we had selected this one with a view to easing me gradually from the idyllic quiet of the island into the harsh clatter of the world.

With what furious vengeance the world imposes itself on apostate "monks"! On the flight every blessed seat was taken, and I found myself next to a garrulous, bejeweled and chain-smoking mom and her teenage son, a fat slob she was delivering from Palm Beach to Montreal for the summer holiday, to the custody of his father, her ex-husband. Fatso ate his thick, pielike, caramelly and pecaned sweet roll, then his mom's; and when he eyed mine, I passed it to him and ordered a double vodka on the rocks. At that time of day the stewardess had no booze on her dumbwaiter and, looking pointedly at her watch, then at me, she went, the cheeks of her ass bouncing with chagrin, to the pantry and fetched me two miniature red-labeled bottles of eighty-proof Smirnoff. No matter that I feigned reading *The New Yorker*, that I was drunk and sad and tautly strung at my departure from the island, that I was already depressed surrounded by these "weirdos" on their inconceivably worldly errands, selling and seeking and visiting and journeying and fleeing and being summoned, Mom had aches to impart and her mouth fluttered like a whippoorwill's ass all the way to New York, while I sat stunned, hot with wrath and grief, wanting to say:

"Oh, lady, give my a break. A few months ago I was in Rome and never saw the Colosseum! A quart a day I've been doing, my brain cells are so pickled I can't even understand a movie. I've just come from months of sticking my prick into strippers with names like Zita the Zebra Woman, with a normal body temperature and an IQ of about sixty-two point five. The bartender next-door has to answer my mail for me, I shake so badly I can't hold the letters! Gimme a break, I don't wanna hear."

I was going to hear. Although her husband had remarried, neither he nor the incumbent Mrs. (what sounded like) Bas-Thornton—after the family in the Hughes classic, "the third Mrs. Bas-Thornton, I might add" —were at all reliable, and at every summer and Christmas holiday since the divorce Mom had had to fly to Montreal, rent an efficiency apartment, and daily telephone Fatso— his name was Eugene—to assure her much-tried heart that he was being properly fed (properly fed!) and that his father wasn't giving him bourbon, which, she said, Mr. Bas-Thornton drank from sunup to sundown.

"Ha!" she cried. "Sundown doesn't tell the half of it! At sundown he's only just getting started!"

The court had awarded her what seemed to me a painfully generous three hundred dollars a week in child support and alimony, but for all the trouble it made her shuttling between Palm Beach and Montreal, she at one point had returned Mr. Bas-Thornton's checks and gone to work as an interior decorator—with phony self-effacement: "My racket"—only to be told curtly by the court that whether or not she returned the money she still had to comply with the court's order and deliver Fat Eugene to his father as the court had directed. Throughout this Eugene remained still and immobile as stone, in the awful embarrassment of Mom's gratuitous revelations feigning a deep sleep in the tight economy-class seat between Mom and me, only occasionally bringing up his obese fingers to lap unctuously at the sweet buns' sticky remains. In repose he looked a baby whale gargantuan enough to put a gleam in the eye of the late Mr. Barnum.

When the plane landed at La Guardia, I waited until the New York City passengers had disembarked and only those going on to Montreal remained, then took my yellow London Fog jacket from beneath my seat, rose, put it slowly on, with great deliberation zipped it up, and spoke the words I had in my mind been articulating for the past hour:

"Why don't you get off here, return to Palm Beach, go back to work as an interior decorator, and let this pathetic outsized fellow go on to his father by himself? He's reached an age when he ought to be having his first bourbon with his father. And if the kids in Palm Beach are anything like they are across the inlet on Singer Island, where I live, and I understand from a Palm Beach detective I know they're more promiscuous, he ought at his age to be fucking himself cross-eyed."

In shock Mom's face had begun to fall away, the way the face of an alcoholic coming off the wagon after many months can be seen with each drink to disintegrate before one's eyes. Although Eugene's right eye, the one hard by his mom, was yet riveted in his rigidly faked sleep, his left was now comically and orbitally bugged out in recognition and horrified incredulity.

"But take a look at what you're doing to him. He's so repressed he's eating himself into oblivion. His features aren't even distinguishable in his lardy face. In fact, his head looks like a bowling ball of soggy dough."

Then I added, "Nice listenin' to yuh." Then I left.

At La Guardia I was dopey drunk, had hours to wait for my Allegheny Airlines connection to Watertown, and as I was up to no more of the world's woe I decided to "hide" in the men's room until I needed another drink. At a drugstore I bought the *Daily News*, a blue plastic traveler's razor good for a shave or two, an extra stiff green toothbrush in a plastic case holding a miniature tube of Pepsodent, a 39-cent pocket comb, a small jar of Squibb glycerine suppositories, and two large styrofoam containers of black coffee. Then I went to the lavatory and for a quarter checked into a stall. First I dropped my chinos to my knees, bent over and inserted two suppositories. Pulling my pants back up, I lifted the lid and started sticking my middle finger back past the uvula. The small of my back on the right side was throbbing, my liver was quaking with excitement, I knew I'd have no difficulty vomiting. I didn't, puking up the remains of the previous evening's farewell supper. Both the marinara sauce and the Chianti gave the vomit a nauseatingly rich pink, as though I were hemorrhaging. That done, I replaced the seat, again dropped my pants and sat, where I sipped the scalding coffee, read the *Daily News* and waited optimistically enthroned to pass whatever my system had digested.

As I always did, I laughed riotously at the newspaper's editorials. Those who disagreed with President Nixon's Vietnam war policies were called "die-hard doves," "sniveling carpers," "twittering defeatists," and "puny peaceniks," and as always I had an overwhelming urge to seek out the editorial writer and buy him a few drinks. So unrelentingly nasty was his tone that for years I'd been certain he didn't believe a word he wrote—nobody bright enough to construct a grammatical sentence could believe it—and that he knew his loonily Olympian derision was doing more for peace than any march on the Pentagon. I had even fantasized a romantic image of him. Certainly nobody in the

Daily News offices ever saw him. He was an inch over five feet, crabbed, wasted, and he chain-smoked nonfilter cigarettes that left nauseous stains on his fingers. Winter and summer he wore an Army-issue wool khaki greatcoat whose hem brushed his shoe tops, and on awakening each noon he gathered up his ball-points, his yellow lined tablet, his *Thesaurus* and the morning newspapers and went to The Lion's Head on Christopher Street, took a spartan wooden table in the back room and ordered black coffee and two ounces of top-shelf brandy, Hennessey or Martel. After a half-hour of diligently perusing the newspapers, with the aid of his *Thesaurus* he wrote his editorials in fifteen minutes, sent them by messenger to the *Daily News*, and passed the rest of the day pacing himself on imported St. Pauli Girl beer and writing unpublishable poetry about the childhood he'd imagined he'd had in Crosby, S.D., remembering always the afternoon he'd had a single beer with Dylan Thomas in the White Horse Tavern.

Today's editorials mentioned both Hanoi and Haiphong, and I was abruptly struck with how geographically knowledgeable the military had made my generation: El Alamein, Anzio, Bastogne, Iwo Jima, Pusan, Hué, ad infinitum, any of which could be instantly located on a globe. Aloud I pronounced Haiphong. *Haiphong.* For some reason the word had pharmaceutical sexual connotations for me and I never saw it without thinking of a pessary.

"Insert your haiphong, darling, and let's fuck."

Within forty-five minutes I needed some more vodka to get me through to Watertown. At the sink in the outer room I gave myself a splotchy shave with liquid soap and my plastic razor, washed my booze-swollen face till it went from white to pink to red to white again, using all the toothpaste in the miniature tube scrubbed my teeth until my gums bled, as I did so swallowing mouthfuls of the diluted paste to allay what I was sure was a disgustingly abhorrent breath. Then soaking my head with water, I combed my hair, threw everything including the unused suppositories into the disposal and was, as they say, ready to meet the day.

Even at eleven A.M. the first bar I looked into was jammed, and I sought another. Travelers all have stories and I could not bear to hear another. Too, I owned the cunning of the boozer, I knew my speech was impaired, talk would reveal that drunkenness, and I'd thereby run the risk of being cut off. The next bar was also crowded save for a single space against a far wall, and I made a direct line for that space, thinking that if anyone started talking with me I could turn my back on him and address myself to the blank wall. What could be ruder than that? With a painfully jaunty articulation, as though it were the most natural thing in the world at that time of day, I ordered a double vodka on the rocks with "just a splash of tonic—no fruit."

"Hello, hello, hello," a voice said, loudly, not so much as if I were deaf as if I shouldn't be dumb enough to try to avoid what it was he had to share with me.

I moaned.

"You're from Florida!" the voice exclaimed. "Me too! Just missed my flight to Tampa, gotta wait for another!"

I took a large swallow from my drink. I did not look in his direction.

Explaining that as soon as I'd walked in the door and he'd detected my tan, my canary yellow jacket, my beige chinos, my pastel blue and plaid-banded porkpie hat, and my torn and dirty white deck shoes worn without socks, which he'd noticed when I lifted my foot onto the bar rail, he'd known I was "a beach rat with sand in my shoes" and with an awesome abruptness he'd suffered the worst pangs of homesickness he'd ever undergone. To myself I moaned again, and felt somewhat dizzy; he was going to tell me everything! To gain entrée to my heart he bought me a drink, then he talked.

In Florida, where he'd been since the end of World War II, he owned and leased to contractors all sorts of heavy equipment. He'd married there, raised children, and made himself a lovely home. Over the years he'd tried to observe the familial decencies with his brothers and sisters on Long Island, but he'd long ago "buried the folks," he no longer recognized Babylon as that quaint village in which he'd grown up in the Thirties, his trips back to the island (on which out of boredom his wife had long since ceased to accompany him) had grown increasingly less frequent, and on this particular visit he'd found his brothers and sisters so caught up in their own lives that he felt a stranger among them and had cut his visit short.

"When you walked through the door," he said, "it hit me like a shovel full of shit in the face that *Florida* was my home and has been for a quarter of a fucking century!"

He sighed. To keep returning to Babylon, he said, and a past that had ceased to exist the day he'd left it in 1946 was sheer fatuousness and for the first time he could hardly wait to board the plane "home" to Florida.

"When I saw you, it hit me like *that*," he repeated. For emphasis he snapped his fingers, startlingly.

Well, now! I turned to him. When I looked into his large dark eyes they were lambent and moist with the appeal that I share with him this long overdue revelation. He was a tall, trim and very muscular-looking guy with a full head of straight, well-barbered black hair; almost disarmingly exquisite of feature, one was sure that in youth he had been pretty but time and sun had done their work giving him a striking masculinity. He was definitely Latin. Although he wore clean and oiled work shoes, finely pressed khaki trousers, lightweight blue zipper jacket, and appeared poised to mount the throne of a diesel-powered bulldozer and move mountains of earth, there was something so inflexibly correct about his dress, there was in his exquisitely manicured nails and a kind of atrophy in what had obviously once been very powerful hands, a suggestion that it'd been a long time since he'd done anything but lease his equipment. An exemplary guy, he bought me another double and for a long time we talked about the nontourist Florida from May through October. We agreed that one learns to live with the dazzling sun and the oppressive heat, remarked how little one needs in the way of clothing and never feels imprisoned in the cumbersome attire of northerners, said that if one's palate were up to it he could live forever, sans funds, on dolphin, pompano, snapper, snook, and crawfish; delighted in the memory of the first long chilling draught of beer following an afternoon of fishing or swimming; and most of all, with something like fluttering hearts, recalled the easy lethargic pace of the native Floridian.

"A pace," he said, wagging his head in wonder, "a guy can live with." He was silent a moment. Abruptly he wafted his blue-jacketed arm to include the customers of the entire bar. "Look at these jokers!" he cried. "Eleven o'clock in the morning! You call this living?"

"Sure don't."

With the drinks he was growing heavy and inward with nostalgia. When from his wallet he suddenly showed colored Polaroid prints of his snow-white stucco ranch house, his flagstone-patioed blue pool overlooking the green sea of the Gulf, and his thirty-foot, teak-decked Chris-Craft moored at a wooden dock on a canal which ran just north of his well-manicured yard, I said, "The heavy equipment business must be booming."

This disarmed him. "Huh. You know, I hadn't thought about it but it wasn't the way it looks from these pictures. I bought the property in '46 for nothin'. Then I built—well, just a house; then additions as the kids came; then the pool when they were big enough not to drown; then when I'd educated them and could afford it, I bought the Chris-Craft. I built the house, the pool and the docks myself. Yeah, I hadn't thought of it but I suppose the joint is worth a shit-load on today's market." He sighed. He studied the prints. "I love it, fuck if I don't. Though there's way too much room now that the kids are gone. You keep the rooms thinkin' there'll be big reunions and stuff like that at the holidays. And there are for a year, two. Then they go."

Now he produced prints of his progeny and with a tortured fondness studied these, shuffling and reshuffling them like a deck of cards. His oldest son was an engineer in Vancouver, his youngest an ensign in the Gulf of Tonkin, and his "baby" daughter Lucia was studying for a master's in language arts in Florence, Italy. "I send her to Syracuse University and she ends up in Florence. 'Why Florence?' I cry, already thinking how much dough it's gonna cost me. She knows the old man is mush in her hands, she turns on the charm, she says, 'Cause, Daddy,' "—he imitates her affected lisp for me—" 'Florence is part of Syracuse University.' Cha ever hear such bullshit?"

"I think she's telling the truth," I said. "I don't know how tenuous the connection is, but I come from near Syracuse and I know I've heard before there's some connection between the university and some school in Florence, some exchange program or other."

"Connection, smonnection!" he cried. What he deemed his foolish generosity as a father was causing him proud pain. "She's probably over there banging some greaser, will come home eight months with bambino, and expect me to set the Guinea up in a pizza palace."

Certain he was Italian, I was as always nonplused that ethnic groups could so comically demean themselves and yet wouldn't allow it from outsiders.

"I don't mean to be impertinent but I took you for Italian."

"Of course I'm a wop! Venetian. My grandfather was a custodian at the medical university at Padua. It was either the same thing for my father, or America. He chose America. I'm first-generation, my kids second, and I haven't worked since the day I was discharged in '46 so some stupid broad of a daughter can bring home some ginzo and start all over again. Why can't she marry a guy named—" He paused. He was working himself into a state. He said, "*Come si chiama?*"

I laughed. "Exley. Fred."

He was knocking himself out, this guy was. "Why can't she marry a guy named Exley?" For my amusement and edification he sorrowfully pursed his lips and theatrically brought himself to the brink of feigned tears, woefully shaking his head.

"If she married *this guy* named Exley, it'd cost you more than a pizzeria. That's how spoiled *americani* are. I'd want a joint called Casa Lucia sitting among eucalyptus trees on a bluff overlooking the Gulf of Mexico, with nothing but imported Chiantis and a penthouse apartment above the restaurant. If she brings home her greaser, as you call him, he can sleep on an army cot in the pizzeria—you can tell him he's guarding the ovens—and he'll still think he's got it knocked up. Wait'll he and Lucia present you with a couple of grandsons, take him deep-sea fishing in the Gulf, and give him a little help falling overboard. When he cries for help you can stand in the bows playing the thick-skulled Calabrese—you won't be Venetian after all—saying, '*Scusa, scusa, non capisco italiano. Non capisco.*' "

Abruptly I was standing there in the bows, leadened and stricken with a heavy stupidity, shaking my head no and over and over again repeating *non capisco*, and as that luckless and fantazised son-in-law—and poor maligned Lucia! if she was banging anyone, for all we knew she was banging an Oxford man named Winston—went down for the third time I gave him a tentative, limp-wristed wave of farewell.

This guy and I laughed like hell, uproariously, and so goofy drunk was I that for the rest of our conversation I slipped in and out of the giggles.

Twice I'd asked him where he was from in Florida, and twice he'd evaded answering by saying only "the west coast." The west coast of Florida is eight hundred miles long. Now I demanded, "*Where* on the west coast?"

He smiled sheepishly. "Can't say. Don't even ask me. I can't tell anybody with a straight face."

"Try."

He mumbled something I didn't catch.

"What's that?" I was insistent.

"*Panacea*," he snapped. "Panacea! I ain't shittin' yuh!"

Wide-eyed with mirth, I said, "P-A-N-A-C-E-A?"

"Panacea," he repeated glumly. "Ain't that awful? Ain't that the height of fuckin' pretension?" He groaned. He shuffled his feet in a silly little soft-shoe. In mock horror he furiously encased his cheeks with the palms of his hands, a *mamma mia* thing. Again we laughed uproariously.

Then it was time for him to catch his plane and we shook hands very enthusiastically. With his free hand he reached across to me and in the warmly intimate Italian way squeezed the humerus muscles of my right arm just below the shoulder. So I did the same to him. He told me to look him up when I got back to Florida.

"At Panacea!"

We laughed again.

He said, "Goddam, good fellow, I enjoyed it, *really* enjoyed it. And you know something? I'm goin' *home. Home, Exley, home.*"

Then it was "take care" and *"ciao"* and "luck, man, luck" and *"andante presto"* and "You'll be okay" and *"buono fortuno"* and "seein' you" and *"arrivederci."*

And what I had heard that day on the Sony in the cabin of my friend's Hatteras, spoken in the mellifluous tones of Mr. Cronkite, the news that forced my head to the table, released in me this awesome pent-up grief, that had me paraphrasing Nabokov's Pnin and over and over dumbly repeating *he won't haf nofing left,* was that the hurricane called Agnes, which afterward would wreak such havoc as it flowed northward and spent itself through the Carolinas, Virginia, into Pennsylvania and New York, had entered the republic from the Gulf of Mexico. It's point of entry and the place that had taken the full brunt of its winds had the improbable name of Panacea.

I once had a friend suffering from ulcerated colitis. Eventually it reached the point where he could not drink two bottles of beer and trust himself to get to the men's room and get his pants down on time. He went from specialist to specialist, was put on one diet after another (cereals and other foods that linger in the intestinal tract) and was invariably told the same thing: an operation was necessary. Still in his mid-twenties, and a gifted athlete on the local semipro level, he could not abide the thought of having his lower intestine removed, having a surgical sphincter created in his side, and a lifetime of draining his stool into what he called "a fucking perfumed fucking feces bag." When he'd lost fifty pounds, when in their prognoses the specialists had graduated from cautious phrases like "it looks suspicious" and "it's possibly precancerous" to the flat-out fact that he was toying with his life, and when at last during a city league basketball game he evacuated in his gym pants, he got the message and scheduled himself for surgery.

One Sunday noon his wife called me and said that the

following morning he was checking into Strong Memorial Hospital in Rochester for the operation, that at the moment he was out somewhere having a final drunk, and that as I understood would I find him and stick with him. I found him at Canale's in the Sand Flats, the first bar I went to. He was on his second beer.

I said, "Okay, pal, I'm your man. We're gonna hit every bar in Watertown, get drunker than a coot, then I'm gonna buy you the biggest dish of spaghetti and meatballs in Canale's—garlic bread, the works. But the first thing you're gonna do is switch to whiskey. Giving you beer is like feeding Epsom salts to an infant."

"Deal."

In my car we'd come up out of The Flats, turned right on Massey and swung into Holcomb Street, had just turned left at the country club at West Flower Avenue, and were traveling east through what in our naïveté we used to call "The 400 Section." It was a brilliant sunny day in late spring. We were going to begin at the Cold Creek Inn southeast of the city, hit all the places on the outskirts and in gradually contracting circles work our way back to the heart of town and Canale's for pasta. To keep up his courage my friend was regaling me with what a bunch of preposterous quacks the specialists were, reminding me of all the dough he'd spent just to be told to eat "cream of fucking wheat," and because I knew he needed his raving I didn't bother to remind him that every one of those specialists had told him that surgery would sooner or later be necessary.

"You know what finally convinced me?" he demanded. "It wasn't taking a big dump right in my pants during a basketball game. Not by a fucking long shot. It was this. The last joker I went to told me Loretta Young had had the same operation. Jesus, Ex, I laughed right in the bugger's face. *Loretta Young?* I mean, that's pulling out all the stops. What? Not Joe DiMaggio, mind you, not Wilt

Chamberlain—*Loretta Fucking Young*! I mean, if that sappy bastard is gonna throw poor Loretta at me he's desperate—I mean, *desperate*—and I gotta be scared. Right? I mean, butter wouldn't melt in that broad's armpit. Now every time I see her bouncin' downstage to the front of the boob tube in one of those chiffon gowns of hers I start yakkin' at her. 'Who you kiddin', Loretta?' I say. 'I know all about you.' The last time I was yakkin' like that my bride started bawlin' and threw a full fuckin' bowl of popcorn at me!"

We were both roaring with laughter when suddenly, and this was a cry I'd heard a dozen times before, he bellowed, "Oh, shit! Potty time!"

With desperate urgency I jammed the brakes, mumbling as I did so, "That fucking beer."

Outside the car, he could not go to his right as there was nothing but the open expanse of Ives Hill fairways jammed now with golfers, so he went hurriedly round the back of the car, quickly crossed the street to the front lawn of a large white-shuttered brick house, and next to a high hedge separating that house from its neighbor dropped his pants and the flow began immediately. Solemnly removing a package of Kleenex from the glove compartment, I jogged across the street, stood in front of him, and as well as I could protected him from the view of passing motorists. From the property next-door a man holding a croquet mallet stepped through the hedge and said something about "drunken bums." When I said that though a good case could be made for our bumhood we weren't drunk and that what was happening obviously couldn't be avoided, his anger refused to be abated and he pointed out how abhorrent this was in front of his and his neighbors' children with whom he was having a Sunday afternoon croquet game. All popeyes and indignation he was.

"I'm calling the police."

I was on the verge of telling him to do anything he damn pleased, call the FBI for all of me, but that he better go back on his own property before I grew irritated and knocked his teeth out when a little boy about five, whose croquet mallet was as tall as he, stepped through the hedge. With great and touching dignity he looked at my squatting friend, then at me, then at his father, then back at my friend, and with the marvelous ingenuousness and directness of children said, "Are you sick, mister?" to which my friend and I laughed in unison, my friend with a weary and heavy exhaustion saying, "Sick to be sure, kid. *Sick to be sure.* You and your daddy go back and finish your game, I'll be okay."

Then I handed him the Kleenex, then his pants were up, then we were in the car and gone, laughing, and I know of no way of equating those days following the news of Hurricane Agnes and Panacea other than in equating my state to that of my friend's malaise, save that in lieu of lower intestine my tear ducts were ulcerated. It was as though I'd touched the lodestone of some universal grief and found it infectious, and though the death of Edmund Wilson was certainly tied up in it and the memory of that guy at La Guardia, it had nothing whatever to do with self-pity: it was as though my entire being, at times over which I had no control, were ridding itself of some putrefaction of grief, were eliminating the soul's sick fecal matter.

One afternoon in the lounge of Cavallario's Steak House in the Bay I was drinking and talking with two attractive young couples from Syracuse, and one of the men told an incredibly funny story. In general the tale reflected how little the word *fuck* has come to mean in our society; in particular it had to do with a guy who couldn't employ two words without one of them being *that* word; in that the story had a rising crescendo of punch lines, each funnier than its predecessor, it was the hardest kind to tell; the

young man who told it was very gifted, as he'd have to be
to get away with it in mixed company; I'd started roaring
even before he'd got to the first of the punch lines, and
presently I was hysterical, ready to go under the table and
roll tummy-huggingly around the carpeting and plead with
the guy to refrain.

"Whoa! No more, no more, I beg you."

But then an unsettling thing happened. Before he
reached the end of the joke I suddenly detected that every-
one at the table had ceased laughing and was staring in
open-mouthed and shocked dismay at me and that, like my
buddy's molten stool pouring forth from his diseased body,
grief was again erupting from me. Furious with aggrava-
tion I bolted upright, spilling my drink on the table, fled
the lounge and, head down, rushed breathlessly past the
moored cruisers to the end of the village docks, repeating
over and over, "He won't haf nofing left."

And though I had never learned to pray there was
something of the devotional in my ramblings. I invoked
the Spanish god of storms, Huracán. "Hey!" I cried. "Listen
here, just listen to me: don't let it be that stucco house, that
patioed blue pool, that teak-decked Chris-Craft. No, no,
no." It was too much like the irony of classical tragedy, or
the irony of the world in which we live from the stench of
the womb to the rot of the shroud, the good man coming to
terms with his lot only to discover it is already too late. And
so addressing myself to this prick Huracán I said, "If you
could have seen his face, you wouldn't do this thing. You
see, after a quarter of a century his presence exuded the
exaltation of the ultimate acceptance of what his life had
been, that life so vividly and humbly illustrated in those
colored Polaroid prints of what he'd made for himself.
'Home, Exley, home,' he'd said and I know you are not
wanton enough to erase all that. He won't haf nofing left."

But as the days passed and Agnes moved her monstrously dumb and hideously brutal way up the coast, and on the colored screen there came the bewildered, drawn and haunted faces of those in her wake, I came at last to accept Agnes's evil whimsicality and grief was with me always, it ballooned in me, weighed me down, I carried it like a knapsack bulging with iron skillets. It came on me with the abruptness of my friend's relentlessly uncontrollable shit. I'd be taking my first bite into a porkchop of what looked an altogether delicious supper, and frantically straight up from the table I'd come, out the screen door and into the backyard where, dropping into a chair of the umbrellaed lawn table, my head would fall to my arms, and always now there was this *he won't haf nofing left.* Like a man possessed or LSD-high on grief, I was up and down the stairs a thousand times a day, all day I fled between house and Hatteras where I'd have two quick belts of vodka, in some oddly insane way hoping that the fury of my movement would prevent these terrifying "bowel" movements.

But have I not strained the reader's credulity to the breaking point—nay, to the point of inviting his rightful scorn, his sneering mockery, his derisory hilarity—by asking him to believe that these days of immoderate grief "had nothing whatever to do with self-pity"? to accept that this daily deluge was utterly divorced from any tears I was laying at the feet of my drunken and absurd self? to swallow that my "nobility" was of such stunning grandeur that this unseemly woe was brought on by nothing other than the death of EW, a man I'd never known save through his writings, and the tragedy that had likely befallen that funny self-proclaimed wop with whom I'd passed a couple loony hours in an airport bar? Knowing that the reader, like me, grew up in the penumbra of seven-foot-high images of Mr. Clark Gable and Mr. Duke Wayne and was educated to the notion that such unmanliness lent itself to nothing short of damnation, I of course invite his mockery. I might apologize by saying that as an "unstable" man I was obviously under-going a "breakdown" during those endless days, then offer the reader some marvelously pointed psychological explana-tion to which he'd be able to nod his noggin wisely and say, *"Ah, I see. I understand."*

But I shan't. In the first place, I haven't for years seen any validity whatever in the Freudian voodoo and cannot read the most obvious psychological maxims without my nose plugging and wrinkling in the most exorbitant distaste. In the second place, there come moments with every writer when he yearns to address his reader familiarly and say something he constantly fights against saying. Due to a vow I made twenty-odd years ago when I was just out of college, had just taken my first job in New York City, and was living in a lonely Y.M.C.A. room, the effort will prove doubly strenuous for me. Having very little money to do the town, I spent most of my free time reading the newspapers (there were seven then!) and there was a certain sports columnist, Jimmy Cannon, who on occasion—and though I admired him immensely—used to drive me mad! In these particular columns Jimmy'd invite his talentless and closeted reader to step into the shoes of the mighty.

"You are Joe DiMaggio, the son of an immigrant San Francisco fisherman," Mr. Cannon would begin, "and you are the greatest center fielder who ever played in Yankee Stadium, and you are married to Marilyn Monroe, the heartthrob of a nation."

It goes without saying that, lying on an iron cot in a bleak Y.M.C.A. room, with three bucks in my pocket to last me until payday, I'd take heated umbrage with Jimmy and talk right back to him, aloud.

"Nah, nah, Jimmy, Joe DiMaggio I ain't. The greatest center fielder who ever played in Yankee Stadium I ain't ever gonna be! And about as close as I'll ever get to Marilyn Monroe will be to get that fouled handkerchief hidden

under the clean shirts in my dresser and do a savage number on my prick while looking at the latest *Life* photo of Marilyn!"

For that reason, and to this day, I've never been able to address the reader with the familiar "you" and write a line like "You are driving down Route 66 and you look across the wide green pastures to your right and you see the moocows grazing lazily in the sun" because I've invariably imagined my reader saying, "Nah, nah, Exley, I ain't driving down Route 66 and I don't wanna see no fucking moocows grazing lazily in the sun!" Be that as it may, let me say here and now, and at last put to rest my fatuous hangup, that of course those days were excessively compounded by the most reprehensible self-pity.

And fuck *you*!

One day on the Hatteras I was well into a fifth of vodka, rereading Walker Percy's *The Moviegoer*, when I had what I thought an inspired notion. At the glass booth on the docks I charged the call to my home phone and after the usual hassle with the operator at last got through to a policeman in Panacea. Drunkenly I explained everything.

"Conceded it sounds crazy," I said. "Saying the guy's a friend of mind and not even knowing his name. But he is, my *compari*. Look, don't hang up. How big can Panacea be? Yeah, the heavy equipment business. An Italian guy. Lives right on the Gulf there, a white stucco house with a pool. Three kids, all grown, the oldest boy is up in Canada, the other an ensign in the navy, and the baby daughter Lucia is over in Florence bangin' some greaser—no, only kiddin', she's over there studyin'. Yeah, I can appreciate that you've had a bad storm down there and how busy you are, that's what the fuck I'm callin' about. Just give me the fuckin' guy's name and I'll call'm. Just wanna make sure everythin's okay."

The policeman hung up on me.

I told the operator I'd been cut off and got through to him again.

Sore, he said, "You're drunk, boy, get yourself some sleep."

He rang off again and I made my way slowly back to the Hatteras. I drank all night and well into the morning. When I awoke later in the day, and I do not remember how I got home much less into bed, I opened my eyes once again to Mr. Walter Cronkite (it was as though he'd summoned me up from drunken slumber) and as I focused on the screen there leapt from among the colored shadows another image from out of the past, that of my "friend" Ms. Gloria Steinem. My days of grief ended as abruptly as they'd begun.

5

The Democratic primaries were over and South Dakota's Senator George McGovern held a substantial enough delegate lead to appear a first-ballot Presidential nominee at the upcoming Miami convention. In Washington the party's platform and credential committees were meeting to draft a platform and entertain challenges to the seating of those delegations that did not appear to have honored the Democrats' new guidelines for a representative corpus of women, blacks, chicanos and young voters in the proportion that they in fact existed in a state. The "nonpartisan" Women's

National Caucus was hovering churlishly in the wings making their demands known.

Ms. Steinem had come to town in a huff.

One of the women's demands was that the convention be co-chaired by a woman (in the colossal nit-picking of their unisexually prone minds they wanted their selection called a "chairperson"); and a ghostly memo which was never put forward and which McGovern called a "misunderstanding" had come to light whereby the McGovern high command had apparently suggested appeasing the women by appearing to go along fully cognizant the convention would be chaired by Larry O'Brien. Aides of Alabama's Governor George Wallace were, among other things, telling the platform committee that the bussing of schoolchildren solely for the purpose of integration was neither financially viable, politically practical, morally right, nor in fact legal. The women's caucus demanded women be granted total dominion over their reproductive means and insisted the platform adopt an "abortion on demand" clause (an astute pundit had written that all the McGovern claques were saying "gimme this and gimme that," a far cry from John Kennedy's "ask not what your country can do for you" motif) and it now appeared that the McGovern forces were backing away from this sticky issue.

Ms. Steinem wore a long-sleeved black jersey turtleneck and big round raspberry aviatrix's spectacles, and though the color on my TV was poor she appeared to have abandoned the bleached blond strands which habitually fell over and triangularly framed her high cool brow. I smiled. When I had complimented her on the loveliness of her hair and asked her if she tended it herself, instead of graciously accepting it for the harmless compliment it was, she had, to my uneasiness, used the occasion to ascend her platform. A woman named Rosemary—"Sister Rosie," she'd called her

—was her colorist, the best in Manhattan, but in a man's game Sister Rosie didn't get credit for so being. Looking at her now and smiling, I wondered if poor put-upon Rosemary, carried round the bend by the discriminatory practices of all those fag (were these the men to whom Ms. Steinem was referring?) hair stylists in New York City, hadn't finally in a swoon of oppression gone off the deep end and taken a jolly leap from the heights of the Pan Am building.

"I love you, Gloria. I worship and adore you."

Directly Ms. Steinem began debasing the language by saying something to the effect that she'd come to Washington—I had a movie idea: "Ms. Steinem Goes to Town"—to join hands with her "black brothers and sisters." Again I smiled tentatively, sadly. Did Gloria really believe that keeping company with the black Olympic decathlon champion Rafer Johnson—"Shit," I thought, "half the women in America would do the same!"—gave her some privileged insight into the black soul, made her a Daughter of Islam? She doubtless did and seemed not in the least to understand that when the black revolution came it would be she above all who got that splendidly milky and columnar throat slit first. In the same way William Styron so acutely has Nat take a fence post and bash in the chestnut-haired head of the lovely, betaffeted Miss Margaret Whitehead (she who above all in her young, innocent and ignorant way had intimated a comprehension of Nat's plight), there was nothing the black loathed so much as the presumption (if we could give him nothing else, he demanded the right to the uniqueness of his suffering) of an intimacy with his humiliation, abuse and degradation at the hands of a white America. Obviously referring to Governor Wallace and his ilk, Gloria said that all the pressures being brought to bear on the platform committee were erupting from the right and she'd come to the Capitol to rectify that. Failing to do so, she implied she would withhold her support from the Democratic Party.

Oh, my!

Her performance was restrained to the point of being coldly mannered, brittle, arrogant, slightly nasty, and not altogether fair. Her lovely head was incapable of admitting that in the primaries Governor Wallace had taken his views to the people (which *she* certainly hadn't), had been nearly assassinated and rendered paraplegic in the process, and that in fairness to the delegates he'd picked up his views had every right to an airing. Nor could she admit the historical reality that in any close election, which if the Democrats won (and at the gut level I knew McGovern hadn't a prayer) this was certain to be, no Democrat had ever won without a heavy Roman vote in the cities and that "an abortion on demand" clause was suicidal, not to mention that there is now and will always be a continuing philosophical and legal debate on whether or not the fetus has rights.

At the moment I could not isolate what it was—though unlike Ms. Steinem I wasn't sure of anything and stood abjectly poised to admit it might be the obvious emasculatory fear—but as I had been when I'd last seen her I once again found myself afraid of as well as for her. Her posture was so vulnerably rigid that one suspected the slightest well-placed jab would cause the collapse of her entire spinal column and that behind that moisturelessly cool and beautiful mask there were harbored unspeakable grievances, mean furies and aborted passions, and I knew that if she represented the New Democrat, I could not in conscience vote for McGovern. Since I'd last talked with her she'd apostrophized into her thinking a reverse sexism wherein she'd begun to elevate women to a plateau both beyond and quite apart from the concerns of men, she had equated women's role in marriage with that of whores, and she appeared either to be seeking headlines (a very real possibility) or to have become tetched. And how unworthy, unmanly and self-indulgent she made me feel, with my wretchedly unbecoming grief at Edmund Wilson's demise and my lunatic calls to Panacea. Her very presence was a stinging reprimand and summons to get off my ass, to cease from my unseemly jerking off, and to enlist myself in her and McGovern's holy cause.

But, alas, I couldn't.

From a young academic at Oberlin College I'd once been sent a note and a student's term paper on *A Fan's Notes*. The paper was brilliant, hilarious and totally derogatory. Taking as his vantage point the fact that my narrator had thrown away all of the Sunday *Times* save for the sports section, the student said that nobody could seriously approach a protagonist who wasn't interested in "significant things like world events." Proceeding from there, and in a wildly funny and sardonic way, the student had destroyed my narrator for what the student considered my narrator's monumental self-indulgence. In his note the academic told me the boy was an electronics engineering student, had an IQ "off the charts," and that though he wrote splendidly and the paper was obviously worth an A, how did one "teach" such people?

On my post card in reply I wrote, "One doesn't."

And the discomforting thing about Ms. Steinem, and all the Steinems of the world, was her similarity to this boy: her cocksure capacity to make one feel unworthy in the face of her concerns, this haughty need to make her concerns my concerns. She reminded me of those students who so diligently perused school issues of *Time*, boldly underlining everything, and got their A's in what we used to call "current events" while I had dreamt of dry-fucking cheer leaders. There was a kind of rigidly terrifying single-mindedness about these people which I frankly considered uneducable and I knew that, were I to save my soul, I couldn't under any circumstances permit them to make their obsessions mine.

Let Ms. Steinem go to Miami, run hand-wringing and weeping up and down the aisles of Convention Hall and imagine herself caught up in historical events of great pith and moment, I had my own "selfish" griefs to allay. I would go to Talcottville, talk with the few people who had known him, and find some way to help put the ghost of Edmund Wilson on its way. Yes, I thought, let history judge whether the wiser course was to have petitioned Elizabeth I to engage the Spanish Armada in the Channel or to have wept at the bier of Shakespeare. If one could draw any consolation from Steinem's troubled performance it was that she was still embarked on her "temporary aberration" of proselytizing the women's gospel. She had told me that speaking at universities and what she called her "whole public bag" was merely a temporary aberration (she had used that expression three times), that her real work was writing, and that when she felt she'd contributed everything she could to the movement, she would go back to that real work. At the time I hadn't been unkind enough to say that she'd better hope her temporary aberration lasted forever, but watching her forbidding performance on TV I had, if for nothing else, to be thankful that she was still in this public limbo and that we were therefore being spared her prose.

In December I'd interviewed Ms. Steinem at the Sonesta Beach Hotel on Key Biscayne in Florida. I'd gone to her a troubled, "wounded" man, my life a shambles. When in early September I at last accepted that *Pages from a Cold Island*, a book on which I'd been working for four years, was a bad book, I decided to go to Europe. With brown supermarket bags and heavy blond cord I tightly wrapped the four hundred and eighty pages of yellow second sheets that comprised the manuscript and deposited the excessively neat (with scissors I even trimmed the excess cord) package into the trunk of my gray-green Chevrolet Nova parked in the windswept sandy lot behind the hotel, where for three years it had sat in dumb anticipation, the relentless sun having baked its paint lime-white, the elements having rusted out its fenders from beneath. In stolid sadness I packed my bags, took a Shawnee Airlines dozen-passenger Beechcraft to Nassau, a Bahamas International Airways flight to Luxembourg. Thence I flew to Rome. I'd never been to Europe before and wasn't in fact in any shape to go any place—perhaps to the loony bin.

I had to go. As I've said, except on those infrequent occasions when by friends I was "kidnapped" and driven across the causeway to the Riviera Theater on the mainland, I never left the island, and even these outings were disastrous. At an interval of eighteen months I had on two Saturday nights been taken to *The Godfather* and *The French Connection* and sitting among full-house weekend crowds I had understood not a word of what was taking place on the screen. It was something more unsettling than the dialogue and the understated sound tracks with which the writers and the directors had attempted to catch the idiom of characters caught up in a society given over entirely to a sleazy verbal shorthand. What had proved so ignominious was that on both occasions I had found myself next to perfectly attuned young couples who had caught everything and had on cue roared and moaned and gone rigidly breathless throughout the films while I had sat in exasperation, tilting my head to the right and to the left, in suppliance leaning forward toward the screen, feeling as dense and unresponsive as lard and older than Methuselah; and to imagine that I, who couldn't even understand a movie, was ready to leave the idyllic stillness of that room

‡ 73

and hike jauntily on the Appian Way, stand in humbled awe before the Colosseum, or reverently explore *San Pietro in Vaticano* indicates the extent to which my book's failure had deranged me. In fact, I understand in retrospect I'd never do anything like sightseeing in Rome. I suppose I thought if I came at last to lie retchingly drunk beneath tables of the sidewalk cafés on the Via Veneto, if I could create that ultimate torpor and sloth, those epiphanies might come. I could then flee back to Singer Island prepared to outflank the manuscript now imprisoned in the hot tomb of the Nova's trunk, and thereupon deliver a "masterpiece."

In Rome I was for ten days the guest of Ed, an American novelist my age. Like me, Ed had published one interesting novel which seemed destined to be his life's output. Where Ed got his money I don't know, nor did I ask, though he appeared to have plenty of it and worked all the angles besides, including having on retainer of twenty-five dollars a month a Roman overseas operator who between midnight and eight permitted him to make calls to the States. Each day at Ed's apartment we were drunk on vodka by one P.M., at which time we enthusiastically endorsed the Roman custom *fare la siesta* and snored until five, then cleaned up and went to the Trattoria Maria on a lane off the Via Veneto and ate antipasto and spaghetti *al burro* or *con salsa di vongoli*, then went back onto the Via Veneto to Harry's American Bar, got drunk again on Irish whiskey, and in English talked nostalgically with other Americans about professional football, which we all missed and all agreed made the autumn an execrable time to be in Italia. On returning to Ed's apartment we drank espresso and grappa and talked about our "work in progress" until two in the morning—eight at night on the eastern seaboard at home—and then using Ed's bribed operator we telephoned people we knew in the States. Nobody seemed surprised or awfully pleased to hear from us, and when I was asked, as I invariably was, what I was doing in Rome I always said either that I hadn't the foggiest notion or that I'd come to see the Colosseum but that nobody'd tell me where it was. Ed and I were doing nothing we couldn't as well have done from the bar of the Village's Lion's Head Ltd. had we been able to bribe a New York City operator.

At Harry's I struck the acquaintance of a wealthy, Vandyked, Oxford-educated Maltese of thirty who owned apartment houses in London, Paris, Rome, the South of France, Jamaica, Trinidad, and Valletta, Malta, where he lived but was only able to get a few days a year. He hadn't when I met him been home for nineteen months. He was having a torrid and, I suspect, sick affair with an American starlet who had come to Italy for the spaghetti Westerns. I can't imagine what she was doing to him, but he was so enslaved he daren't leave her for the few hours necessary to fly to Malta, and as he saw I wasn't doing anything he suggested I go there, live in his apartment, and spy on his manager who he was sure was screwing him. He would give me a letter to the manager admitting me to the apartment— he described it as splendid with wrought-iron balconies overlooking the Grand Harbor—and said I was welcome to all the whiskey in his plentifully stocked cabinets. He said the matter of checking on his manager was easy. He drew me a map of his various properties, including alleys leading into the courtyards behind them, and told me all I had to do was wait until dark and check the lights coming from the various apartments. His manager claimed the buildings were running to only sixty percent occupancy, and if lights were coming from all the windows he was obviously not only going to need a new manager but the present one would be food for Mediterranean fish. For an Oxford man, he made the threat ring paradoxically and sinisterly true. Detecting my reluctance, he picked up the bar phone at Harry's, charged the calls to a number in Rome, and in his

Oxford accent made loudly impressive talk to both his grocer and liquor dealer in Valletta. He told them I was to be his guest in Malta and that they should give me anything I needed and bill him for it.

"You are set, dear Frederick. What do you say, chap?"

I went. I stayed for eight days, had all my clothes cleaned and laundered, repacked my bags against what I was sure was going to be instant flight, and checked on nobody, not to mention the manager. Each day I sat from sunup to sundown in my jockey shorts on the wrought-iron balcony, watched the yachts and the naval ships maneuver in the Grand Harbor, and drank vodka and Schweppes quinine water. The only volume in my host's library not dealing with money or sex (the same thing, in a way) was *History of the Wars of the French Revolution*, a ten-pound tome I laid at my feet on the balcony and read cover to cover, hunched over with my drink and turning pages with the big toe of my right foot. When I completed it, and I cannot now remember a single notion put forth by its authors, I thought about going to India to the Vindhya Hills north of the Narbada River to seek out a holy man about whom I'd read, but as I had no idea how to get there I flew instead to Barcelona and for a week walked all day and well into the night looking for a shaded park or *avenida* of which I'd once seen a photo. Hemingway was said to have sat on a bench beneath its trees and thought long thoughts. When the *calles* of Barcelona all became familiar and began to repeat themselves in my mind and I still hadn't found the park or *avenida*—or if I had, hadn't recognized it—I flew back to Luxembourg and used the other half of my ticket to return to Nassau.

In Nassau I stayed four days, and on my last night there got the worst beating of my life. At the piano bar of the Anchorage Hotel up the street from where I was staying at the Sheraton British Colonial, I'd met a Bahamian charter boat captain and his stunning girl friend, a wealthy American of nineteen from Medford, Oregon. The captain was a Conch. In the parlance of south Florida and the Bahamas a Conch or Conchy Joe is an interbred person, mostly white, who for reasons known only to himself hates blacks with a near-deranged passion, and he and his family, as they have done for generations, make their livings from the sea. Conchs are stoic, formidable, uncommunicative, terrifying in anger. The captain had the same name as a family I knew on Singer Island, and since I knew them to be originally from the large Long Island in the south Bahamas I asked him if he was from there.

When he said that he was, I said, "I know some of your cousins stateside."

"Got nothin' but cousins, mon."

That was almost the extent of the conversation, his odd American paramour being even less communicative than he. Thus the next day proved an unsettling surprise. While the Conch was "fishing a party" from St. Louis, she came to my hotel in her eighteen-foot custom-built Donzi with twin 427 Holman Moody engines and at a hair-raising seventy miles an hour took me to a small out island to water-ski. We water-skied for an hour, dropped anchor in a cove, waded ashore, and lay down face up on a blanket, whereupon, as abruptly as a belch, she took down my bathing suit and with her mouth engaged me. She did this all day long, and did the same for the next three days. She'd absorb the load, lay back, leaving her hand on my exposed genitalia, then after a time begin all over again. She wanted to do nothing else. Whenever out of the most rudimentary considerations of politeness I'd query her about her past, she'd hatefully sneer, "Medford, Oregon—what's to know?" And though I suppose that she was, I'm not much given to the literal use of "insane." If I confronted the malaise with a quart a day I had to concede her her right to confront that same malaise in her own way and admit the simple possibility that she was, as the kids say, "doing her own thing." Daily she had me back at the Sheraton British Colonial by four, I'd shower, shave and dress, then go to the hotel's Whaler sidewalk café fronting on Nassau's lovely harbor and drink V.O. until dark, whereupon I'd retire in anticipation of the next day's ogreish pleasures.

On the fourth evening I decided to see the town, and after inquiring of a cab driver ended at Tommy's night club. Between strident calypso sets of the steel band, I talked with Tommy, the owner. As an American married to a Bahamian he was under the black government allowed to own a business. When he pointed out his wife manning the cash register at the far end of the bar, without thinking I said, "She's a Conch, isn't she?" to which he shook his head in wondrous admiration and said, "You better believe a Conch. You cross her she'd cut out your gizzard and feed it to you."

At one point late in the evening I mentioned my strange girl friend. Tommy moaned and said, "You're not foolin' round with her, are you? She's crazier than a shithouse rat. They ought to run her out of the Bahamas."

"We've been going miles away to one of the out islands."

"That don't matter a shit," Tommy snapped. "She tells 'im about it. She gets her jollies watching him and his two black mates stomping the shit out of her quote lovers." He repeated, "She ought to be run out of the Bahamas."

Tommy called his wife down from the cash register and said something to her. She looked wide-eyed at me.

"Oh, no, mon, you stay with us tonight and get out of the Bahamas tomorrow!"

I graciously and stupidly declined her kind invitation, believing her disposed, as was the novelist Robert Wilder, to romanticize the violence of the islands. When I turned

78   ‡

into the long front walk leading to the entrance of the Sheraton British Colonial, the girl was there on the well-trimmed lawns with the Conch and his two black mates and whether or not this was part of the game in which she got, as Tommy said, her jollies, she at least feigned concern for me and bellowed at me to hightail it. Thinking they wouldn't be stupid enough to start anything in front of the Sheraton British Colonial (its very name has the ring of empire, what?), I kept walking, head down and very purposefully. When the Conch grabbed me by the arm and said something to me, I yanked my arm free and said, "Fuck you, Conchy Joe." When he knocked me onto the lawns, I stayed there hoping he'd think me more hurt than I was. The last thing I remember was their starting to kick me.

When I awoke in the hospital, I had a minor concussion, I had lost a tooth, my entire torso from beneath the armpits to the waist was tightly swaddled in adhesive covering two cracked ribs, my scrotum was swollen and throbbing terribly, and in it they had cut a small incision and inserted a tube to let the blood and pus hemorrhage into a kind of diaper they'd put on me. Even though I was all doped up, I had to get out of there and knew a hospital was the easiest place in the world to get out of. I summoned the hospital authorities, lied by telling them I hadn't a farthing, and they let the police take me to my hotel for my bags, thence to the airport, where I caught a Shawnee Airlines Beechcraft back to Palm Beach. When I got to the Seaview I discovered I'd been gone a month to the day, assuredly a lunatic's "grand tour," and I now went to bed for another month and in tall frosted cylindrical glasses labeled *Islander Room* drank triple vodkas and grapefruit juice and read magazines cover to cover.

Toni changed my bandages, my sheets, the records on my Garrard turnstile, fluffed my pillows, and from McDonald's fetched me Big Mac hamburgers with the works.

The swelling in my groin refused to deflate, and a serious infection set in. Three times I had to return and get the scrotum draining "healthily," and each time I was given ever increasingly potent drugs. Insisting I should be in the hospital, the doctor told me antibiotics could not properly do their work until I abstained from booze. But I didn't stop drinking. Toni was with me and heard what he said, so she refused to go to the bar for me and whenever I needed a drink I had to fetch it myself. On those occasions I had because of my crotch to walk with my legs wide apart as though I had an unseemly load in my pants. The regulars at the bar all laughed at and jeered me, mainly because I'd refused to say a word about my month away from the hotel or tell them what had happened to me. We had become too much the family, and everyone at the hotel believed he should have easy access to everyone else's most cherished places. Especially was this true of Toni. That anything as "juicy" as my being beaten up had occurred and she did not have a single detail made her absolutely rabid with frustration and her posture became nastily self-righteous.

"Whatever the fuck happened to you, I'm sure you deserved it!"

Then on the same day, lying abed with a pillow between my thighs so I wouldn't press them abruptly on my wounded nuts, I enthusiastically read three articles about Ms. Steinem: one a cover story in *Newsweek,* one in *Esquire*, and one in the Palm Beach *Times*.

Dick Boeth, whom I'd known in Chicago in the Fifties when he was a contributing editor for *Time*, did the *Newsweek* piece. Except for allowing that Steinem didn't write as well as Updike, he had her dedication to the women's movement so selfless as to be saintlike and even suggested the possibility of her one day being our first woman president. Writing in *Esquire*, Leonard Levitt was not so kind.

He not only said she couldn't write, and quoted her attempting to prove it (she wrote easily as well as he!), he implied that her present eminence was in no little part derived from association with the appropriate guys at the appropriate moments: with Thomas Guinzburg, president of Viking Press (publisher of Joyce, Steinbeck and Bellow!) when she had allowed to be printed one of those how-to-move-among-beautiful-people nonbooks called *The Beach Book* (with, for Jesus' sake, an introduction by John Kenneth Galbraith!); with President Kennedy's amanuensis Theodore Sorensen when she'd become interested in politics and its tandem power; with black Olympic decathlon champion Rafer Johnson when with a logic best understood by herself —and a logic that would certainly get her laughed and whinnied off the platform of any Harlem gathering—she'd begun to equate the plight of women with the plight of blacks.

When I later asked her about these ungentlemanly suggestions of Levitt's, instead of answering me she attacked Levitt by saying she'd heard that in order to get the *Esquire* assignment he'd told the magazine's editors he was an ex-paramour of hers; she understood that because of the piece's uncompromising nastiness Levitt's wife had left him (To join the movement? I'd wondered, trying to keep a straight face); and that though the attorneys of *New York* magazine, for whom she wrote a political column, found the piece "definitely actionable" she'd decided against pursuing a suit.

Noblesse oblige, I thought.

In that same political column Gloria had made Mrs. Richard Nixon, the first lady of the land, appear a sniveling, carpish, monumentally self-pitying shrew; that Gloria had even contemplated a suit against Levitt and *Esquire* made me uneasy and seemed to me, though I dared not say so, "frightfully feminine" and at utter variance with how reporters played the game. On the day I read these contradictory pieces in *Newsweek* and *Esquire* I also read in the Palm Beach *Times* that Ms. Steinem was coming to town to speak to a local women's professional group. By then I had already determined I must meet her.

6

Pages from a Cold Island didn't work because it was so unrelievedly desolate that despite its humor I was sure the reader couldn't turn back the final page (allowing he got that far) without wondering whence I'd mustered the will to put together its four hundred and eighty pages of typescript. And in Ms. Steinem—and I'd all but leapt from the bed in exaltation when the possibility began to form itself in my mind—I'd seen the metaphor to lift the pages from the gloom in which they wallowed. The book was a reminiscence; and the *cold* of the title, applied to Singer Island where 80-degree-plus temperatures are not uncommon, apostrophized my being, not the weather.

In those pages I'd put down one American's journey through the Sixties and especially his reaction to what historians call "the great events." If I had entered the Sixties more given to dark derogation than to joyous celebration, I'd at least been an articulate, relatively hopeful creature. But I had crawled out of the period on my knees, a simpering, stuttering, drunken and mute mess. The obscene decade had begun with President John F. Kennedy's "ask not what your country can do for you" and in the late summer and fall of 1969 had ended at Chappaquiddick. At that numbing moment following the assassinations of the brothers Kennedy and Martin Luther King, Jr., when I'd at last come to accept that there existed no desecration left capable of unmanning me, Senator Edward M. "Teddy" Kennedy had fooled me and for nine hours had left the body of Miss Mary Jo Kopechne to float about the back seat of a car among the currents beneath the now-famous wooden span at Martha's Vineyard. I'd then gone back to bed, had pulled the sheets above my head, now and again had sneaked out to drink vodka and to put down bleak words, and had come at last to lie there with swollen balls reading about Ms. Steinem in the glossy magazines.

Struck with the parallels of our both having been Depression babies, having come from impoverished homes, having managed to get the semblance of an education, I was intrigued and baffled by what it was in her character that, having been shaped by the same events that had shaped me, had yet allowed her to come out of the putrid years so splendidly, refusing to lead a disappointed life. I wanted to know how she could rise mornings, erect, trim, courageous, unquestionably beautiful, not lacking a kind of nobility, and with an unswervable commitment go forth to do her duty as she saw it, while I'd come out of the years badly whipped, cravenly, running to a quitter's obesity and had come at last to lie on that bed at the Seaview Hotel at the hot bottom of the world on Singer Island, drinking myself to death, my balls ballooned with life's hurt.

Two days before reading about Steinem I had almost, in fact, and for the second time in my life, committed suicide. Next-door at the Beer Barrel I borrowed Yogi's .22 Magnum pistol—on what pretext I don't recall. Then I telephoned the poet Jim Dickey in South Carolina and told him I was "taking the deep six." I apologized to Dickey because he had been instrumental in getting me ten thousand dollars from the Rockefeller Foundation and I thought I owed him the courtesy of knowing that neither he nor Mr. Rockefeller was going to see any manuscript for the moneys. I said goodbye, so did Jim.

Jim said, "I'll be seein' yuh, boy, yuh heah?"

Then I stepped into my closetlike shower and for perhaps an hour let scalding waters cascade over my aching body, as I slowly and painfully removed the tape still clinging to my rib cage. When I'd dried myself, I wet the towel thoroughly and swaddled my head tightly with a view to making as little mess as possible. Then I picked up the Magnum, stepped back into the shower, and closed the glass door behind me. Whether I stood there five minutes or five hours I can't say. Like Charles Dickens who later in life could never recall how long he'd been in a blacking factory when at twelve he'd been put there to work, the experience was so traumatic I could not begin to estimate the time.

I do know what saved me. At some point I began to laugh, riotously. Suicide presupposes that something is being eliminated. With a silver-inlaid shotgun Hemingway blows away the back of his head, and when the world recovers it finds itself able to remark, "What a man!" But what precisely was being eliminated in my case? Certainly not a man. Whatever I was eliminating was so inconsequential as to make the gesture one of trifling and contemptible ease and I began to think how much more felicitous the act would be if I sobered up, as best I could healed my mind and body, then erased some bone and tissue that at least conspired to resemble the human. Only then, I thought, might the gesture take on a certain flair or style. When I returned to the outer room and seated myself on the white Naugahyde couch, I understood for the first time how close I'd come. Still laughing, I found my hands shaking so severely that I could not for a long time unswaddle the towel and for the next two days I suffered fits of trembling compounded by alternating flashes of extreme heat and cold. Then in stricken absorption I read about Ms. Gloria Steinem.

With Ms. Steinem my overriding desire was to discover who she was apart from her cause. If she consented to see me at all, I knew that in my approach I'd have to feign embracing a concern for the movement and I cared not a jot, an iota for Women's Liberation. With Emerson I held that one speaks to public questions only as a result of a weary cowardice that has so debilitated his energies he is no longer able to do his own work or rest easy with the painful prospect of articulating his own demons. Over the years I'd read the Ms. Friedan, Millett and Greer and had agreed with almost every tenet they had put forth. Nonetheless, in his *Prisoner of Sex* Mailer had been right in taking Millett to task. Of all the women's writings and manifestoes, hers had resounded with a nasty vindictiveness, and though in reading her I hadn't known what had so distressed me until Mailer articulated my concern, he was right in implying the Millett mentality was incapable of understanding D. H. Lawrence, Genet, Mailer himself, and most of all Henry Miller with his joyous, hilarious, rowdy and utter adoration of the cunt.

What was disappointing in Mailer was that in bothering

to dignify Millett with an answer he'd allowed himself—one always does!—to be lured into Millett's own brand of nit-picking and pettiness. No intelligent person could read Mailer's *An American Dream* without understanding that Deborah Caughlin Mangaravidi Kelly was into analingus. Mailer was amused that Millett had confused analingus with sodomy, when in fact the former is embraced by the latter; and if Norman believes he could put his tongue up the bum of the University of Iowa's Homecoming Queen, or vice versa, in the window of the Iowa Book and Supply Company in downtown Iowa City and get arrested for anything other than sodomy, it is Millett who should have been gloating. But gloating had begun to characterize the battle, with too many mindless points being scored, and the prospect of entering the arena bored me beyond comprehension. Least of all did I understand the women's grandiose glee at the "discovery" that an arousal of the clitoris was essential to orgasm—understand what Ms. Germaine Greer has called "clitoromania."

As though posing for a Bayer advertisement in their antiseptic white denim jackets, with their electrodes and massagers and vibrators and dildoes and surrogate partners, looking—not voyeuristically, one is assured, but scientifi-cally—through their glass partitions at those desperately sappy yokels straining so mightily, touchingly and dement-edly to pop each other's gonads, Masters and Johnson could not be taken seriously by decent or civilized people and I didn't in the least understand why women held it ominous for men that these quacks had unequivocally estab-lished the clitoris as the female orgasmic organ, a Lilliputian prick. I'd never believed anything else. To be sure, this was ignorance on my part (having out of boredom been unable to complete my reading of Freud, I hadn't known he'd plumped for the vaginal orgasm), but up in the cowshed of Watertown we'd known forever about the "button" or the "man in the boat" and that a man bent on giving a woman pleasure must approach this cute little bugger with a certain worldly and heady enthusiasm. In fact, the first time I had anything resembling an affair I learned to my contrite humiliation that there need be no clitoral stimulation whatever and that a woman's orgasm could result from nothing more than the willingness of her heart.

In the Forties, in Watertown, we got our sexual educations as corner boys standing in front of the Y.M.C.A and Whelan's drugstore on the public square and listening, slack-jawed and bug-eyed, to the "older" guys. Especially do I remember Dong. At eighteen Dong stood six-one. A championship swimmer, he swaggeringly carried a lithe and muscular one hundred and eighty pounds. In an age when the brush cut was universal he wore his curly blond hair in something very like ambrosial locks. Dong dressed always in expensive shell cordovan shoes, finely pressed tan gabardine slacks, and spotless lightweight jackets on which he left the zippers at half-mast exposing his navy turtleneck sweaters. Like so many swimmers Dong had matured early on and at eighteen it was already said he'd seduced half the women of our fair northern and chaste city, not entirely excluding the possibility of one's aunt, sister or—Lord forbid!—mother.

When we acolytes crowded round, Dong had a way of rocking pensively on his cordovan-shod feet, crossing his strong arms snugly at his massive swimmer's chest, and among imparting his sexual wisdom nuggets to us expectorating little BB's of spit between the small gap of his upper front teeth. Dong had an absolute passion for what he called the button or the man in the boat. Looking straight ahead but aware of our vacuous breathless attention, Dong told us if we really desired to drive women mad the thing to do was get the clitoris—Dong never of course called it anything as grand as that—between the front teeth and ever so tenderly roll it back and forth between the jaws. Letting his cowlike brown eyes fall dementedly cross-eyed to the bridge of his tanned nose, as one loonily hypnotized or demonically in thrall to the urgency of his art, Dong made his tenderly gnashing motion and in dumb hilarious imitation we all followed suit! Our sex educations! Then Dong spat between his teeth. He shook his head wearily. At eighteen, Dong was heavy with the responsibilities of life's sexual lore. Then Dong spoke.

"She'll pass out on you and shit the sheets." Dong pondered his own wisdom for a moment, then turned to me. "Do you know how to take a pulse, Exley?"

"Pardon, Dong?"

"You have to take their pulse all the time you're doing it or you might lose them entirely."

Again Dong spat between the gap in his front teeth. Oblivious to the passers-by and to his splendidly pressed gaberdines, he now dropped spread-eagle on his knees to the foul pavement, again assumed his loonily four-eyed face, again made his tenderly gnashing motion, and as by implication he always did at such times he reached up now onto that grand envisioned bed and cupping his thumb, index and middle fingers showed us how during the engagement to keep a constant check on the girl's unquestionably explosive pulse. From his knees Dong now looked forbiddingly up at us. "Don't forget," he said menacingly, "if you lose her, she'll shit the sheets on you and you know where that'll end up!" Now Dong screamed. Whhheeeeeeeeee!!! He made a face of excruciating pain, shuddered violently, and with furious hands frantically brushed the imagined feces from his face. Now, rather solemnly, we all spat between our teeth. Those of us who had no gap in our front teeth spat right through them.

Although I'd fucked before, I had my first affair in the summer of 1950, when I was a sophomore at USC. I was twenty, contracted double pneumonia, and after ignoring it for days was at last taken by ambulance to the Queen of Angels Hospital. For seventy-two hours I recall hardly anything but being wakened every three hours to receive a shot in the buttocks, after which I'd roll over and go back into the feverish chatter that had become more or less my condition. When finally I began coming out of it—and I remember having to be told where I was and how long I'd been there—I struck the acquaintance of the nurse on the graveyard shift who gave me my penicillin at midnight, three and six A.M. Her name was Gretchen, she was thirty and married to a top sergeant in the First Marine Division, then fighting in Korea.

I do not know how it started with Gretchen and me. I had been at the brink of the abyss, so to speak, I owned that peculiar and exaggerated affection for life people acquire having just looked into a tear in the heavens and seen nothing, nothing at all, and in brimming desperate gratitude to everything and everybody on earth my hands started going unctuously out to Gretchen and I touched her on the hands and on the wrists and on the forearms and on the hips and on the waist—there was on my part this terrifying need to make human contact and I felt myself as helpless and cuddly as a bunny rabbit. Presently Gretchen and I were kissing. This led to a more refined and passionate kissing. One night Gretchen grew alarmed at the immediacy of my state and obliged me with a rather bored hand job. From that night on, without any discussion on the matter whatever, Gretchen began obliging me with fellatio, on some nights having to relieve me on the occasions of all three of her penicillin ministrations.

On the day I was discharged from the hospital, Gretchen began a week's vacation at her beach house, a quaint little dump on stilts at Malibu, and she asked me to come along, rest up, and make sure I was okay before returning to classes. She was going to use the week trying to rent the beach house, getting her clothes in shape, and packing. She had taken a job at the Tripler Army Hospital in Honolulu, and though she would still be thousands of miles from her Marine sergeant—she called him Dicky— she drew comfort from knowing she'd be at least that much closer to him and I recall her constantly dreaming aloud of being reunited with Dicky in idyllic Hawaii when finally he came back from Korea.

As I say, I'd fucked before but my partners had invariably been my age and as inexperienced and as inept as I and hence neither the girl nor I had anything against which to measure the worth of our performances. Worse, this was at the very top of that monstrously oppressive decade that for some reason has now become sentimentalized into The Quaint Fifties, and I remember that all my relations with girls up until this point had been furtive, deceitful, disappointing and shoddy. It goes without saying that Gretchen was different. Since she was nineteen and still a student nurse, she'd been married to her Marine and had had all sorts of other men besides, affairs Dicky condoned when he was off on his various tours of duty. Dicky's only real condition was that he not be subjected to the details.

"Dicky said I could fuck anybody I want so long as the guy wasn't military and so long as I spared him the mush."

To say that in 1950, at twenty, I wasn't shocked— utterly so—by the worldliness of Gretchen and Dicky's connubial arrangements would be so much nonsense, but as it was I who was now installed in that rickety stilted beach house and the legatee of Dicky's sophistication, copulating with the wonderful impunity of knowing Gretchen had been ordered by good old wordly and heroic Dicky not to bother him with anything as mundane as my name—

especially my name!—I couldn't help accepting their relationship as an eminently sensible and fair one and for a week Gretchen and I took her dresses to the cleaners, her skivvies to the laundromat, interviewed people who wanted to rent the beach house, lay on the sand, ate, slept, showered, and copulated. It was the first time I'd been to bed with a Woman, with a capital W, and as I badly needed assurance of my manhood and prowess and as Gretchen was wonderfully kind and sexually acute and loved the language of fucking—as opposed to the endearments of what we had in that long-ago time straight-facedly called love—she never ceased giving me that assurance.

To my initial horror, which I soon overcame and easily fell into the deliciously obscene and forbidden language of sex, Gretchen, doubtless having received her training at the hands of a Marine sergeant, said things like, "Come back to the beach house and fuck my face," or, "Forget about cooking those fucking hamburgers now; get into this bed and diddle my ass off." Astride Gretchen, breathing like only a twenty-year-old still in the drooling masturbatory state and trying to cleanse himself of his pus-infested pimples can breathe, which is to say like a wounded boar, *uh, uh, uh, uh,* among this awful, adolescent and embarrassing bleating I whistled out frightfully breathless things like *"Am I okay?"* and *"Am I all right?"* and the wise and wonderful Gretchen assured me I had the most marvelous, unique, adorable prick in Christendom and was besides the greatest—oh, hyperbolically!—she'd ever had.

Alas. On the last night Gretchen and I spent together we had a long earnest talk and Gretchen set me straight not only as to her generous white lie about my bacchanalian expertise but to all sorts of other sexual matters from which Dong and Mums had sheltered me. Cautioning me not to take what she had to say wrongly, least of all personally, Gretchen assured me that what she had to tell me would in time future hold me in good stead or post position. She then proceeded to tell me how childlike every man she'd ever had was in his asinine need invariably to seek verbal affidavits as to his genius in bed and how astonishingly little he understood that though atmosphere, penis size, and performance all counted for something to a woman, compared with her need to be attracted to her partner all these things fell into some twilighted area out yonder there in that land bordering on indifference.

Gretchen said that as a fifteen-year-old high school sophomore back in Grand Rapids, Michigan, she had lived next-door to the star senior fullback. Because his mother had made him do so out of courtesy, he had at every high school dance asked her to dance once and once only, and that though the jock had been as indifferent to her as if she'd been an ugly-bugly pain-in-the-ass cousin, Gretchen's attraction to him had been so overwhelming that that single dance had never failed to induce in her such profoundly embarrassing orgasms she eventually began lining her panties with toilet paper before even starting out for the dance.

"Let me tell you something, Exley. My relationship with Dicky is such that he doesn't even have to touch me. Say, if I go down on him? He comes, *I come*. Sometimes repeatedly. That's attraction!"

I did not say, "Carrying your thesis to its logical conclusion, Miss Gretchen, I'd guess that if you just thought long enough and hard enough about such activity the results would be the same" because at twenty I did not preface my remarks with portentousness like "carrying your thesis to its logical conclusion." Even so, in my awkwardly ignorant way I did manage to make my way through to this point.

"But of course, Exley! You're marvelous! Not only could I do so, I have done so. Many times!"

Gretchen paused. Her voice took on an air of furtiveness. *"Can I tell you something awful?* The first three days you were out here with me, I didn't make love to you, I made love to Dicky. You know what changed all that? It was the day we did all the errands getting ready for my trip, how you did three baskets of laundry for me while I drove to the airport for my ticket, made arrangements to sell my car, and picked up my dry cleaning and all. I mean, when we got home and I saw how neatly you'd folded up everything and all, I started thinking what a douche bag I was for using you in this way and from that moment on I made love to you, not him. I mean, if a guy is nice enough to wash your crumby bloomers for you, you ought to be generous enough to fuck him and not somebody else. You know what I mean, Exley? Let's face it, Errol Flynn you're not, Exley. But that doesn't mean a goddam thing to a woman. You know what I'm telling you, Exley?"

I have put all this down by way of saying that if at twelve or thirteen, up in the cow country of Watertown, I had from the suave bemuscled Dong learned all about the button or the man in the boat and how to make a woman go into a death coma and evacuate her bowels, and if at twenty I had had that week with Gretchen (and I here must add not only that I wept profusely on putting Gretchen on the plane to Oahu and her Dicky, but that in many ways my quarter of a century of life since that day had been a pilgrimage in search of some other, some unattached, some Dickyless Gretchen) and been the heir of her earthy wisdom, I did not twenty-five years after the fact need to be told by Masters and Johnson or the ladies of the movement the clitoral function or that a big prick—least of all my rather sorry specimen—was not in the least necessary to their well-being.

If Gretchen had given me nothing else, I was ready to concede a woman the right to employ the pharmaceutical equipage of the good doctors, to take into herself a huge rubberized and pimpled dildo strapped to the crotch of a broad-shouldered bull dyke, to put her pet Great Dane Hamlet to work if that's what turned her on, or, like Gretchen herself, simply to define mentally the limits of her sexual paradise and by steadily envisioning that Elysium to think herself through to shuddering orgasms. As long as she did not try to tell me she was into something special, as long as she would allow Gretchen and me the right to wet our pants at someone's being kind enough to do our laundry for us, I was buying everything she was telling me.

In my reading of Friedan, Millett, Greer, et al., I'd spent ninety percent of my time nodding my head in a vigorous accord that I was nothing less than the chauvinist pig and the scum to whom and to which they made constant and biting reference. Behind me someplace out there in the republic are two ex-wives—and I take this occasion to salute them both wherever they are. Hi, Fran! Hi, Nan! How's it goin'?—who had left me for many of the reasons these women had so corrosively articulated and for that reason I bought not only the obvious, boring and neo-proletarian tenets like equal pay for equal work and state-sponsored day-care centers for the children of working mothers but even the trickier mental areas like a woman's right to abort herself any bloody time she chose or her right to eliminate her female function utterly by having her fetus nourished in a bell jar. At least women were thinking in a grandly bold and adventurous way, and though I was sure it was this kind of boldness that sent men to an early grave, I'd be damned if I'd deny a woman the right to conquer or be vanquished on the epic scale, whether she croaked in the process or not.

No, though I'd have to approach Ms. Steinem as though I really cared a shit about the movement, I was in fact so in accord with her that I did not see any hope of getting a middlingly interesting dialogue going on a subject that was not only as obvious as dammit to Gloria but equally as obvious to me. What I wanted from Ms. Steinem was something quite else. We had as I say both been born to the Depression, had gone through the public school system under what one used to call straitened circumstances, had managed to fake our way through to something resembling a "higher education" and without any evidence to the contrary I stood prepared to bet that ninety-nine point nine percent of our contemporaries who had managed to escape similar milieus had in reaction to those dark uncomfortable beginnings ended up in Old Greenwich, a member of the Round Hill Club, and a devotee of P.T.A. meetings. Well, Steinem had not, and I had not, and other than the obviously metaphorical comparisons of female with male, beauty with beast, dutifulness with hedonism, courage with cravenliness, sobriety with drunkenness, and so forth, and so forth, I thought if I could look right through that lovely placid mask and understand why Steinem so *cared*—and as I've indicated it made no difference to me whether her cause was Women's Liberation or the Women's Christian Temperance Union, only that she *cared*—I might then introduce her into the pile of desolation I called *Pages from a Cold Island*, stacked now as neatly as ever on the dementedly waxed thirty-two-by eighty-inch door, and thereby lift the pages into those heady regions I felt worthy of offering to my peers.

In *Newsweek*, Dick Boeth had written that Gloria gave freely of her time to the disaffected women of the republic. He said she was scrupulous about answering her mail and had even been known to take women's long-distance calls and to those lonely grief-wrought souls patiently dispense advice over the wires. Dick did not say what kind of advice Gloria was dispensing. In her classic *The Female Eunuch*, Ms. Germaine Greer had written that one of a woman's profoundest fears was of discovering she had a twat as big as a horse collar, and I thought that if Gloria were accessible enough to take the time from her busy schedule to assure a lady that this did not make her a "bad person"—that is, if Gloria were all that approachable —I'd just call her up and cry, "Gloria, baby! Fat Freddy Exley here! Listen, O magnificent woman, never mind that nasty Leonard Levitt in *Esquire*, or even my brilliant acquaintance Dick Boeth in *Newsweek*, I'm going to put you in a book, yeah, real hardcovers, six ninety-five, the whole smear! You with me—you incredible creature from the ethereal regions?"

If Ms. Gloria Steinem were approachable, she did not prove to be so with me. It did not of course hurt or surprise that she'd never heard of me. Aside from some generous gestures extended by my peers, and a certain limited and somewhat dopey cult following among university students, my royalty statements and present indebtedness told me more than I wanted to know about my following. Still, I could not guess I would be approaching Elizabeth Taylor Burton and in fact honestly believe I could have been through to Mrs. Burton quicker than I got through to Gloria. In my days as a publicist I'd once set out to ask John Wayne a favor regarding a charity we were promoting and in which we'd heard he was interested. Beginning without even a telephone number for him, I was through to him in seventeen minutes (I timed it) and found myself batting the breeze with the Big Duke himself. "Can't help yuh out with a personal appearance, kid, but if yuh give my little gal here your address, I'll see yuh get yuhself a check."

The girls around Gloria in the offices of *Ms.* were a most formidably haughty crew and said things on the phone like what-is-it-you-want-with-Ms.-Steinem? in a lofty tone that suggested who-are-you-that-you-have-the-audacity-to-approach-Queen-Gloria-directly? I of course refused to

‡ 97

tell any lackey what I wanted with Ms. Steinem. It was going to be difficult enough explaining to Ms. Steinem what I wanted, I'd be damned if I'd risk an as yet unarticulated notion being further garbled in translation, and on follow-up calls I continued to be informed by the ladies that I'd have to put what I wanted in writing. I was assured that my note would be brought to the attention of the Empress. The girls felt confident that Gloria might even get back to me. Still I refused to put anything on paper, still I continued to make a pest of myself. On my fourth call over a period of days the palace guardess rose up in indignation and went right for my balls. She said that Ms. Steinem had never heard of me, could not imagine what I wanted with her, and unless I complied with her wishes and did as I was told there was not a prayer of our getting together. By this, the last call, I'd become so bored and amused with the whole preposterous charade that when the girl came out with her half-whining, half-nasty but-what-is-it-you-want-with-Ms.-Steinem? I came within a hair's breadth of employing the vernacular of that long-ago darling Gretchen.

"Oh, I don't know, my dear. I haven't as yet decided what I want with Ms. Steinem. It may be as simple as that I'll want to fuck her face for her."

On hanging up, I drank a couple more vodkas, then abruptly thought of a new tack. It occurred to me that I knew two or three writers in New York who knew Steinem, if not well at least well enough to act as intermediaries. I called the first guy collect. He was rich and famous, and whenever I know a writer to whom providence has been gentler than it has to me, I always call collect. This particular guy, a prince, never even waits until he learns who's calling. As soon as the operator identifies the call as a *collect* one—"Mr. So and so? Would you accept a collect call from . . ."—he issues a heartfelt groan, mumbles an irate shee-it, and to the blameless operator says, "Yeah, I'll take the goddam thing. It's either that fucking Exley or that fucking Cecil." Although I see the guy whenever I'm in the city, and though most of the time I am of course fully cognizant of who that fucking Exley is, I keep forgetting to ask the rich and famous writer who that apparently equally impoverished fucking Cecil is. My friend wasn't home, and to my red-faced embarrassment his wife accepted the call.

"If that's *that*"—that *that* had rather a bite to it— "Exley, I'll take the damn thing myself."

We exchanged pleasantries, threw a couple funnies at one another. She told me the rich and famous writer was in London working on a screenplay, here appended a battery of ironically pointed ha's—Ha! Ha! Ha!—by which I gathered she meant that among creating epic scenes for The Big Screen she had no doubt the rich and famous writer was getting his spermatozoa drained by Cockney starlets. I then came to the point of my call. As though I'd wrecked her day, she moaned.

"Aw, Exley. Whadda you want to do that for? What happened to *Pages from a Cold Island*?"

I explained that the Steinem bit was going to be a part of *Pages from a Cold Island*; was going to raise the manuscript to new and glorious heights. "Aw, Exley, no it won't. You won't like Steinem, she won't like you. And if you don't like her, you won't be kind. Let me tell you something. This chick is not only very nice but vulnerable as hell. For all that worldly crap about her bedding down with all those famous men, she can't be unaware that she's carried a great head and a lovely body a hell of a long ways. I mean, it isn't as though she were Germaine Greer or Mary McCarthy who could fight you toe to toe, son, and kick the shit out of you, now is it?" She paused. With no little wariness she said, "Look, Exley, are you just trying to fuck Steinem or what? I mean, I'd rather do my damnedest to arrange something as grossly unlikely as that mating as anything as manifestly preposterous as you have in mind."

She wouldn't under any circumstances lift a finger to bring Ms. Steinem and Mr. Exley together, but she would give the word to the rich and famous writer on his return from London. "I'll bet he won't call her either. He'll just laugh. He'll think the booze has finally destroyed your brain cells completely." I then called two other writers I knew, Joe Flaherty and Jack Newfield, and a week later, at nine in the morning, I answered the phone and it was Gloria. She was nice. She apologized for the trouble she'd put me to and agreed to see me on one of her upcoming swings into Florida.

Ms. Steinem and I did not get together on the occasion of her visit to Palm Beach. I had taken too long to make contact with her and by then her speaking engagement was already upon us and I was in no shape to meet her. My ribs were such that I could now breathe, my balls no longer looked as if I were suffering elephantiasis; but I was still on a bender and because it had become apparent to me that Ms. Steinem took herself as piously as the saint Dick Boeth suggested she might be, I thought I'd best sober up, reread the gurus of her movement, and everything I could find by and about her. On the phone Steinem had suggested she'd still like to know in some detail precisely what I had in mind and my last gesture before going on the wagon—because I was too drunk to put it in writing—was to talk my ideas onto a thirty-minute cassette tape and mail the tape off to her.

I was so smashed I don't vividly recall what I said into that recorder, but I remember enough so that even thinking of it in retrospect forces the blood to my face, causes some embarrassed aw-shucks gulping, and an incipient vertigo takes over. Steinem and Mailer were rumored to be friends.

He claims it was she who planted the seeds of his political ambition by asking him to run for mayor of New York City (though how she could reconcile this with her whole philosophical outlook escapes me), and for that reason I thought I'd pull a Norman (which ill behooves me, which ill behooves any of us!) and on the tape I came across almost as full of shit as he is. With great solemnity I began by setting forth my portfolio (it consisted after all of one fucking book!); I gravely related the difficulties I was experiencing with *Pages from a Cold Island*; and I then really went as batshit as Norman talking about the Proustian-Tolstoyan-Joycean novel he is one day, one day, one day going to lay at the public's feet, leaving all his peers for dead, and told Steinem that the next time I came to Fun City people would be pointing me out and breathlessly exclaiming, "See that fat gray-haired guy down the end of the bar? He's one of the best writers in America!"

As it happened, the tape made no difference at all. Steinem was too busy to listen to it—she had one of her lackeys do so and report its contents to her—and at last we agreed to meet on a morning in early December at the Miami airport. In league with Ms. Dorothy Pitman Hughes, a black advocate of state-sponsored children's day-care centers, she was the night before addressing the student body of some rinky-dink sounding college up in the redneck country of northern Florida. The following morning she was coming on to Miami for a fund-raising dinner in George McGovern's behalf and she told me if I wanted to meet her plane she'd give me the time between her arrival and the moment she'd have to take a nap and primp herself for the night's festivities. A Ms. Joanne Edgar—Steinem's secretary, I gathered—assured me it'd be the longest interview Ms. Steinem had ever granted.

I said, "Golly."

By that time the dingbats on Beach Court had got

thoroughly caught up in my zealous yearning to engage Ms. Steinem. What little business I still had with the outside world was conducted over the phone on the back bar. These conversations were invariably overheard and known all over the Court by nightfall, and now that I was once again sober, swimming and taking the sun, and my demeanor had taken on a certain sad-eyed dopey earnestness, the gang, partly out of affection, partly out of lack of anything better to do, began planning the whole outing as though they were planning their prepubescent son's first journey to dancing school.

Because she was sure I'd wear what she called my "foul fucking Bermudas," Big Daddy's wife went through some cardboard boxes in my closet and found some white shirts, a pair of gray wool J. Press slacks and my black wing-tip Florsheims and had the shirts laundered, the slacks pressed and the shoes reshod. Diane Rent-A-Car (we called her that to distinguish her from Diane the day barmaid), one of the cocktail-hour regulars who managed an automobile rental service, had read in Levitt's *Esquire* piece that Steinem owned all kinds of hang-ups as to what was and wasn't seemly and in this regard cited Levitt's saying that in order to receive some corny award or other at Harvard Gloria had refused to arrive there in anything less than a great long limousine (Gloria later denied this, as well as every other contention of Levitt's), and for that reason Diane wouldn't hear of my meeting her in my lime-white beautiful Nova. Because it would take "a fucking week to clean the fucking empty Bud cans" from the car's interior and "the rusty fucking fenders" would doubtless fall off as I was suavely trying to tool Gloria from the airport's parking lot, Diane put at my disposal a chauffeur-driven electric-blue Buick Electra!

McBride's reaction was the most touching of all. He spent days staring at me over his twitching *bandido* mustache, shaking his head with heartfelt rue at my abhorrent sobriety, and when he at last came to believe that my mission was what I said it was and not, as he kept insisting, to show Gloria "the frightful hog," he began stuffing my shirt pockets with twenty-dollar bills and telling me to buy Gloria a nice lunch poolside at the Sonesta Beach Hotel. McBride always summed up his notions of a nice lunch with the words:

"Champagne, the whole mother-fucking smear!"

The night before the long-awaited meeting I packed a little overnight bag, quite as solemnly as I'd done a little satchel when at eleven my father told me he'd had enough and to get ready as he was taking me to reform school. In it I put my cassette recorder, a half-dozen virginal tapes, the questions I'd neatly typed up on yellow lined paper, the various Bibles of the movement I'd reread in preparation for Gloria, and a handful of ball-point pens. I had decided that McBride's champagne poolside lunch would take much too much of my time and in my refrigerator, wrapped snugly in cellophane against their morning's packing, I had made two of my favorite sandwiches for Gloria and me, tuna fish, hard-boiled egg and chopped onion, all whipped lovingly up together with mayonnaise, a dab of mustard and salt and pepper. When I'd taken the ball-points from my desk I noticed that I still had Yogi's .22 Magnum pistol and for a moment I thought of packing that. If my confrontation with Gloria turned into a nasty business (and I had no reason to suspect it might not), I thought I could remove it from the bag, level it at what Gloria herself calls her "old stone face," tell her to disrobe and pull a Henry Miller on her—say, use her for a wheelbarrow by walking her naked body around the suite on her hands while I gripped those creamy-white thighs as the barrow's handles.

The last thing I did before retiring was go down to

Zita the Zebra Woman's suite. Zita was currently the featured stripper downstairs in the Islander Room. I'd known her intimately, as they say, for years, and I asked if before the show started she wouldn't give me a little fuck to assure my getting a nice comfy sleep. Zita adamantly refused, saying I had spoken nary a word to her in the week she'd been back at the hotel and she could not abide me if this is what I was like when sober. Without any ado whatever I reared back and with all my might gave Zita a resounding open-handed crack on her left cheek, and instantly we were sinking in the bedding and copulating like madmen.

Zita had once tried to get me to tie her to the bedpost and flail her with wet towels while she hung her weeping head and lisped, "Hurt me, daddy, hurt me: Zita's been bad, bad girl."

Although I refuse to go that far in the service of anyone's fetish I had come to see that the one piece of eloquence Zita understood was a fierce boot in the ass and right up until the time there came the knock on the door signifying fifteen minutes until show time Zita and I had a most exemplary, exhausting and animal-like fuck.

I was of course testing my balls. If Levitt's implication that Gloria's sexual inclinations ran to the rich, the famous and the powerful were true, I thought that by the time we got done with the heady business of *Pages from a Cold Island* she'd obviously be able to see that though I was totally unknown now I'd one day be famous and that during the nappy-poo she told me she'd have to have in preparation for the night's festivities she might be kind and invite me to lie with her, as they say in the Testaments. Who knows? Certainly my homemade sandwiches would show how domesticated I was and perhaps afterwards she'd want to take me back to her New York apartment to "make a nice home" for her, keep the place tidy, hand-wash her raspberry trousers, and when she came home from a hard day at the office have ready for her a nice hot dish of lasagne. Better still, one of the last things I'd done in preparation for Gloria was skim the inaugural issue of *Ms.* If nothing were going to come of *Pages from a Cold Island*, I thought she could add me to the editorial staff and I could sit around the office floor with the girls in their overalls as the weighty editorial decisions were made and play a sort of devil's advocate, swigging warm beer from the bottle, belching, scratching and farting.

On the editorial page under WHAT IS A MS.? I'd read: "In practice, Ms. is used only with a woman's given name: Ms. Jane Jones, say, or Ms. Jane Wilson Jones. Obviously it doesn't make sense to say Ms. John Jones: a woman identified only as her husband's wife must remain a Mrs." As I laughingly read this and thought I could have prevented that kind of simplistic lunacy from slipping through, I skipped to the back of the magazine, came across a lengthy interview with a lesbian, and the first question and answer my eyes fell on were these:

"When you first realized that you were possibly getting involved with a woman, were you afraid or upset? *No. The strange thing is that the next morning, after I left, I felt a fantastic high. I was bouncing down the street and the sun was shining and I felt tremendously good. My mind was on a super high.*"

Certainly what was needed here was more than warm beer swigging, scratching and farting and in my role of scurvy advocate I now heard myself saying, "Now look, girls, let's not get carried away—let's not let this sneak through and make something of it it isn't. These broads are popping each other's nuts, pure and simple. You know what I mean, pure and simple? Look, let me illustrate by telling you the story of Zita the Zebra Woman and me."

It was while dozily daydreaming such heady dreams of glory, with the pungent odors of the Zebra Woman still upon me, that I fell asleep. Presently it was morning and, seated next to my chauffeur, a bespectacled bepimpled teenaged clod named Bill, I was in my electric-blue Buick Electra wheeling down the Sunshine State Parkway toward my ill-starred meeting with Ms. Gloria Steinem.

7

But listen: I fell totally, dizzyingly in love with Ms. Gloria Steinem almost immediately, when she had not been five minutes disembarked from the twin-engined Aztec which had brought her down from out of those heady blue skies of southern Florida, and by the time we reached Sonesta Beach Hotel on Key Biscayne, in Tricky Dicky Country, I'd settled down to the sad, graceless and pedestrian state of being once again severed from love.

Gloria's hair was coifed in its usual way, flowing black-sepia with those blond strands that fell over and triangularly framed her lovely cool brow. Here were her big round raspberry aviatrix's spectacles resting on those great high cheekbones that seemed somehow so much more striking than other cheekbones; and when she offered her hand, said hello and smiled and I had a glimpse of those big even white teeth I was visited by angels who whispered to me that something quite like heaven would be to put my tongue in Gloria's mouth and just loll around on her back fillings for about a half-hour before even moving up those marvelous ivory monuments up front. The gang's having attired me in J. Press slacks and Florsheims proved an egregious error, for Gloria had on a pair of crumby-looking raspberry suede cyclist's boots, raspberry corduroy breeches, and a short-sleeved navy blue cotton sportshirt that laced up the front in little x's, Kit Carson style. She carried a floppy old canvas and leather grocery bag, ballooning with correspondence and manuscripts, and this together with a somewhat anemic pallor, a real tiredness about the eyes and a sagging untoned thinness reminded me again of how incredibly busy she must be.

One of the articles pointed out that Ms. Steinem's penchant for trimness bordered on the pathological in that her cupboards were forever bare and she seldom deigned to eat. As one given to a sloppy self-indulgence I'd forgiven her that on the theory that any kind of dedicated commitment, which Gloria certainly owned in abundance, must begin with a commitment to one's own person; but looking at her now I saw her thinness lacked the toning of exercise. There was a kind of pinched droopiness about it; she looked as swayback as a weary but splendid race horse, so vulnerable my heart went immediately out to her and I could hardly wait to feed her one of my tuna fish, hard-boiled egg and chopped onion sandwiches (later I tried to feed her both of them but she politely and adamantly demurred, in her forceful way informing me she'd discovered the war against FAT was a war in which one had to be ever vigilant, pretty much I gathered like the one against chauvinists, and though it may have been my paranoia I thought at this point she gave my tumtum a rather ironical and scrupulous going over, and I sucked in like a madman). With some trepidation I volunteered to carry her grocery bag and Gloria graciously handed it over and smiled wisely, her way of saying that her commitment to liberation did not extend to eliminating the petty little gestures we pigs felt it necessary to make to maintain the lunatic tenor of our machismo.

When we started down to pick up Gloria's suitcase at the baggage station, I stepped onto the escalator first, attempting boldly to lead the way, stumbled rather badly, and when I at last managed to recover myself I turned to find Gloria standing ramrod straight on the step behind and above me, a queen descending to the nether regions to view her fallen subjects. To account for my stumbling, I said to that incredibly lovely face up there above me, and I was as precious as a cherub at confession, "I'm sorry about my awkwardness. It's just—you know, you know—that I'm so intimidated, you know, being with you and all."

Then if possible I became even more nauseating. I smiled with a weakness verging on illness, batted my big baby brown eyes at her, and gave her a helplessly feeble shrug by way of eliciting her utmost in pity. Gloria looked straight down at me and with deadly serious and sympathetic earnestness said, *"Don't be."* And, oh Lord, I score that as the moment I fell head over heels in love with Ms. Gloria Steinem! What can I say of the simple eloquence of that "Don't be"? It said that though she could see how queasy I'd been rendered in the face of her beauty, her regality, her nobility, her grandeur, that though she could certainly appreciate that I was one of life's jerk-offs where women were concerned, she was reassuring me that she would do nothing immodest to set my blood aflame and send me back to the island, say, with the pimpled clod Bill tooling the electric-blue Buick Electra in the front seat and I doing a savage number on my weary and wounded genitalia in the back seat. For that assurance I gave her a shy smile of heartfelt thanks, then turned away from her and we descended into the nether regions in screaming silence. For some reason all I could think of was what Gloria would have made of my "becoming male timidity" had she seen me twelve hours earlier knocking Zita the Zebra Woman ass over tea kettle onto the bed, then mounting her among the ruined bedding.

At the electric-blue Buick Electra Gloria wanted to be democratic and sit up front with my "friend" Bill, but with a flick of the wrist I wafted this suggestion off by pointing out that friend Bill was in fact "my driver." When Gloria seemed to linger still, as though even the prospect of sharing a seat with a chauffeur did not throw a stalwart liberal like herself off stride, I held my ground and insisted she get into the back seat. Although her present proximity to Bill couldn't be avoided, I hadn't wanted her within a country mile of him. Coming down in the car I'd asked him why he wasn't in school. Bill said he'd dropped out earlier that fall; and when I asked him whatever for, Bill had snarled, "The fucking niggers, that's what for."

That fall the Palm Beach County school system had gone to full-scale integration. In some of the most abandoned patterns of which I'd ever heard they were busing kids from one end of the county to the other. Every other day a racial incident at one school or another was reported in the newspapers, and all the way from my island to Miami I had sat in thrall to Bill's hair-curlingly hateful diatribe about the "fucking niggers" beating him up and taking his lunch money, and so forth, and so forth. Rendered downright timid by the extent of Bill's inordinate rage, and sad and sorry that a man so young—a boy, really—could be so consumed with loathing, I found myself studying him out of the corner of my eye and wondering if his problem had anything really to do with blacks.

I don't know what it was but Bill seemed to own that peculiar pimply surliness which so magnetically attracts the cruelty of his fellows (a cruelty that seems always to be abstracted from the literature, movies and TV shows about teenagers) and he reminded me of guys up home we had, as kids, pounded on just to work up a sweat. For all that, though, afterwards I found myself wishing we had sat up front and that for Gloria's benefit I'd lured Bill into his quaint spiel on the "fucking niggers." The trouble with Steinem and her pals changing the world from coffee klatsches in Fifth Avenue apartments, and all those fatuous Harvard sociologists drawing their impressive diagrams in the cubicles of the department of Health, Education & Welfare, was that they seemed touchingly oblivious that the Bills of this world, both white and black, even existed and seemed obsessed with the puerile notion that things were as simple as wishing them so (McGovern's whole campaign was permeated with this youthfully demented naïveté); and if nothing else I made a mental note to have Gloria tell Frank Mankiewicz, whom she was meeting that evening for the fund-raising festivity, that the money they'd be raising to help McGovern in the Florida primaries might better be employed to courting the delegates of McGovern's home state or flushed down the toilet bowl.

I never that I remember got around to giving Gloria this message. By then I was already into my opening sally. In my rather monastically disciplined preparation for Gloria I'd found myself, with a single reservation, stricken with admiration for her and wanting to put that exception behind me directly I now addressed myself to it.

"Look, Gloria, let me say at the outset that I'm perfectly prepared to accept Dick Boeth's verdict on your sainthood. If in my reading I've acquired any qualms, it's that I gather you are, well, without humor about yourself or anything regarding The Movement."

"Oh?" Gloria seemed surprised.

In his articles on the radical chic Tom Wolfe had written of a party for Cesar Chavez's migrant laborers Gloria had organized and held out in Gatsby country on the lawns of an affluent Long Island estate. To raise money for Chavez, Gloria had invited some beautiful people to mingle there among the grape pickers and Wolfe had described the lovely women standing about in their Gucci shoes, the breezes whipping their Pucci dresses, imagining their well-pampered pussies being penetrated by the pricks of melon pickers and Gloria had blasted the piece as "destructive." Now, thirteen hundred miles' distance and no few months in time from this odd fete, I asked Gloria if she didn't think the incongruity of the scene lent itself to a certain hilarity; if in fact Wolfe might not have straight-facedly described the scene and permitted the hilarity to take care of itself. Alas, Gloria most certainly did not think so. She had worked "damned hard" on that party and with no little chilliness now repeated, *It was destructive.*"

At this point I slid rather glumly down in the back seat of the car. If Gloria's subtlety did not allow for incongruity in that ludicrous gathering I hadn't a prayer of getting an appropriate response to my next question. I had meant to ask Gloria if she did not see the probability that when the revolution she was so tacitly promulgating came it would be she and her Gucci-Pucci pals who got lined up against the wall and had their well-coifed heads blown off first; ask if she didn't see the reprehensible condescension in her friends with their checkbooks offering these chicanos a warmth, camaraderie and love that cost them nothing, nothing, nothing whatever—well, perhaps an afternoon of whiffing the sweat of laborers and the energy it takes to write a check. And if Gloria herself did not see the incendiary condescension inherent in such commingling, would she not allow the possibility that some of those young chicano turks had seen it and marked it well? Going further down in my seat, I did not of course bother to ask these things.

Gloria's name had been linked romantically with that of Henry Kissinger and in chagrin Gloria had summoned reporters, held a press conference and told the assembled newsmen that she wasn't then and had never been a girl friend of Dr. Kissinger.

"Look, when I read that I was perfectly prepared to ignore your name's being linked with Dr. Strangelove. But other than it's being a rather unlikely romance, I don't understand the kind of gravity that would allow you to feel the need to make a public disavowal of this quote affair."

When I'd first read Gloria's announcement I'd literally cringed in embarrassment for her. All I could envision was some chain-smoking, whiskey-drinking twenty-year veteran of the city room being sent by his boss to a press conference and having arrived there being met with Gloria's earthshaking, "I am not now or ever have been a girl friend of Henry Kissinger." What was his reaction? Incredulity? Hilarity? Fury? Stupefaction? Had Gloria been a man, she might have got out of the conference with her limbs intact, but I suspect that within days she'd have been removed from the scene in a strait jacket, drooling, and what I was now trying to suggest to Gloria was that I thought the missionary rigidity with which she approached matters left her hopelessly vulnerable.

"One must fight fire with fire," Gloria said.

By the time we reached the Sonesta Beach Hotel I had of course long since given up hope of Gloria's relaxing her right-on posture and had turned to the books I had so diligently reread. Because Gloria and Mailer were said to be friends, I was surprised to learn she hadn't read his *Prisoner of Sex*.

"He does some job on Sister Kate Millett."

"I've heard. Norman wouldn't have if he'd known her. She's really nice. I mean, Norman likes me and he'd never do anything like that to me."

This remarkable piece of naïveté really set me back, and I was about to point out that if Mailer's book was without merit otherwise he had brilliantly documented Millett's embarrassing misreadings, her shoddy scholarship, her facility for lifting lines from context to score points they were never meant to score. I was going to say further that had Gloria written *Sexual Politics* not only did I doubt Mailer would have spared her but that friendship or no she wouldn't have deserved sparing, when abruptly Gloria was laughing in a strangely unsettling and nerve-racking way.

"That's good! That's really good!"

Turning uneasily to her, I said, "What's good?"

"*The Prisoner of Sex*! I mean, that title is so classically apt. I mean, Norman *really is* a prisoner of sex!"

There was something so oddly childlike and gleeful in her tone that I did not know what to say. Bewildered, I said, 'Well, I guess we're all a little of that."

"But nobody," Gloria assured me, "to the extent that Norman is."

By then we were at the hotel and from the electric-blue Buick Electra gathering our gear to go up to Gloria's room for our "interview." For the life of me I don't know why I didn't then and there profess illness, go back to my island, get drunk with Zita, and have a ball. I guess I stayed partly out of courtesy, partly because I can't help being a creature of somewhat frayed hopes, partly because I believed my life style with women was a shambles and thought I might yet take something from Gloria to abet me on my farcical journey in search of my destiny or salvation or whatever preposterous thing I imagined myself in search of.

I of course held no brief for Mailer, but one could see that in *The Prisoner of Sex* his reference to Steinem had been made as one to a friend, and I felt that whereas I was under no constraints to give Norman a few happy verbal knocks on his pompous noggin, it didn't become Gloria to do so and I wished her laughter in pointing out Norman's "enslavement" to sex hadn't been so—well, catty. Who the fuck wasn't a prisoner of sex? And once again I found myself thinking of toppling Zita the Zebra Woman onto the ruined bed. Once again I remembered falling asleep to the heady dreams of "lying" with Gloria. And had I not, but a half-hour before, been told by no less than the angels that I ought to shove my tongue in Gloria's appetizing mouth and loll around on her fillings for a while? Had my eager tongue got that far it wouldn't have stayed itself in those acidic backwaters and certainly would have gone on to the more deliciously forbidden areas of that heavenly creature! Were Norman and I the only prisoners? If not certainly with the likes of me, did not Gloria move among other men with an appraising eye, thinking that that one might be okay, that this one was a real drool? Perhaps not, perhaps not, and by the time we got to the room and I'd solemnly set up my tape recorder I was feeling somewhat catty myself and spoke to her with a wooden jollity.

"One of those articles said you had small boobs. You aren't too grand in the fucking jug department, are you?"

But I could not pursue this nastiness. Quite angry, Gloria tried to come back with The Movement's cliché reply. She tried to say, "I wouldn't ask you how big your prick is, would I?" but, oh Lord, gentle reader, she couldn't bring it off, she stumbled on the word *prick*, delicately and stutteringly substituted *penis*, the blood rose becomingly in those lovely cheekbones, and I smiled apologetically and thought, and I was sincere, *I like this girl. I really do like this girl.*

I have the tapes, three hours of them, and I take this opportunity to tell any surly insatiable masturbator out there that if he sends me five hundred dollars in care of my publisher I'll mail them off to him. To their erotic qualities I cannot attest, but my dopily unemotional voice can easily be erased from the tapes, and the dedicated joint whacker can use the wonderfully modulated tones of Ms. Gloria to help him, as the crooner says, "make it through the night." Because Gloria and I never finished the "interview" I have never bothered to listen to them. Of course, as I say this, it occurs to me that I have shamelessly teased and provoked the lustful-souled reader into believing there would be a confrontation on The Epic Scale between Gloria Wonderful and Monsieur Frederick.

Such was not the case. Nor do I blame Gloria. She wasn't much on her answers, but then I was a dreadful interviewer. Confronting each other over a narrow table, weary and enchanted eye to raspberry aviatrix's spectacles, the intimidating hum of the tape recorder between us (something I later learned a trained reporter, realizing how much it discomfits his subject, would never use), Gloria and I were not a happy "mating"; and, in fairness to her, she had every right to expect I'd ask the moronic chauvinist's questions like whether she scorned the new butterscotch, strawberry douches in favor of good old Ivory soap and hot water. But I've already said I cared not a mouse's turd for this nit-picking and had been struck by the likeness of our backgrounds, how much she "cared" and how little I did. With all my heart I wanted to know why she did, and to understand that it was essential I discover *who* she was.

In reading about her one of the things that had hit me most jarringly was her remarking the similarity of her childhood to that of Augie March. As it happened, and as I have elsewhere related in *A Fan's Notes*, *Augie March* had at a certain time in my life been a Bible of mine, a volume I perused until the binding came off and the pages fell out, a novel I identified with to such a terrible and distressing degree that even now I remember everything about Augie's tyrannical Grandma-"boarder" Lausch, sitting among her bric-a-brac, her fart-blowing pooch Winnie at her feet; Grandma Lausch lording it over all, with great cunning teaching Augie's simple Mama the grave art of conning the charity institutions out of free spectacles, and so forth. And I remember Augie's older brother Simon, even as a teen-ager secretive, crafty, ballsy, funny, hard as nails, hand-some, and utterly in thrall of, rhapsodized by, The Ameri-can Dream. And always there was the idiot brother Georgie who, on reaching his manhood, was on Grandma Lausch's orders "institutionalized," after which Grandma refused to exit from her bedroom to say goodbye to him, to come out and witness "what she had wrought." At the Army-Navy store Augie bought a little Gladstone bag for Georgie and with the keys taught him how to lock and unlock it, "that he might be a master of a little of his own, as he went from place to place" (I quote from memory!). In damp snow Augie and Mama had taken Georgie to the idiot farm on streetcars, changing from car to car in the filthy and melting Chicago slush. At the institution, Georgie, seeing himself among his own kind for the first time, "wagging their weak noodles," and realizing that Mama and Augie are leaving him, sets up this tremendous, this overwhelming, this heart-crippling wail until Mama "took the bristles of his special head between her hands"—I numbered that scene among the great scenes in American fiction!

Thus it was that on the publication of *Herzog*, when in order to make "hamper space" for his new "baby," Bellow committed infanticide on *Augie* in an interview in the Sunday *Times* by implying the book was a youthful and rhetorical indiscretion, I wrote him one of my "mad" letters, furious in composition it was, which, happily (for I regard Bellow as one of our *genuine* Nobel candidates), I never mailed.

Years later I at last got to meet Bellow at a cocktail party at a chic apartment on Chicago's north side. As I knew he was going to be there, I was ready for him and was going to do it to him good for that "unforgivable" interview. But the apartment turned out to be on about the hundred and ninetieth floor, and it had floor-to-ceiling spotless glass walls making it seem as if one could take one petite step off the end of the rich wall-to-wall carpeting and come, *whoooossssssh*, face to face with his Maker. An upstate yokel, and a raving paranoic into the bargain, I got instantly dizzy and fled immediately to a couch where I found myself seated next to Bellow's date. By the time I had a couple vodkas and with them the courage to maneuver, other guests had begun to crowd Bellow. He looked distraught and cornered, and when at length I got to him to do my "eloquent" number I found that all I had to contribute was some idle and horseshit literary gossip.

Be that as it may, I asked Gloria to tell me about the similarity of her childhood to Augie's. I don't recall her answer specifically but I'll try to suggest the substance of it by drawing an analogy. In my senior year at USC I was summoned to some phony-baloney's office and told that as an English major I'd failed to fulfill the second semester of a sophomore survey course covering the Romantic poets through Auden and Dylan Thomas (the first semester had of course covered Beowulf to Pope). When I explained to the bureaucrat that as a senior I'd already had all the material on a considerably more complex and heady level, some of it in graduate-level courses, and that my taking the course would be an extreme waste of time and money, he said, as one always did in those long-dead, tyrannical and good-riddance days, that I either fulfill the university's "requirements" or fail to graduate.

I then went to the professor, an elderly woman who by the students was rumored to have got her Ph.D by counting the *thous* and *thees* in Shakespeare, and asked her if I could, under the circumstances, circumvent the three-cut-per-semester rule and come to her class for examinations only. She said no. So it was that I spent an entire term, on Mondays, Wednesdays and Fridays, at eight o' fucking clock in the morning, listening, dopily and dreamily, to this wan soul talk in ritualistic phrases about material I'd already had presented to me. The one thing that made the semester memorable was falling madly, utterly, hopelessly in love with an absolutely stunning ash blonde who sat to my immediate left, Miss Diane Disney, the daughter of none other than the genius Walt! When I discovered this fact, I found it utterly precluded the son of a lineman approaching her "romantically"; but when a couple of years later I read in the society pages of the New York newspapers that she had married a USC tight end, I smiled sadly and decided that "the poor little rich girl" had no doubt been more accessible than I and about a hundred other "haunted" guys at USC had imagined. In any event, I wish now to tell her, across all these years, how much I worshiped her from "afar," notwithstanding that in our close-cramped seats our elbows and toes brushed each other three gloomy mornings a week.

Prior to discovering who Diane was, I had detected that the professor pandered shamelessly to her—And what does Diane think of this? And what does Diane think of that?—and one day, when we were discussing Byron's *Prisoner of Chillon*, I recall the exchange as something like this: That summer Diane had done her "grand tour" of Europe, the fact of which the professor was somehow aware, and she now asked Diane if she'd seen the castle at Chillon on which Byron had based descriptive aspects of his poem. Indeed Diane had. The professor then said that in his poem Byron had given either a very scant or a very elaborate description (I always thought Byron an old fraud and hence don't remember the poem) of the castle and asked Diane to give us her reminiscence of that structure as compared with Byron's. It was a stupid question, unfair to my adored Diane, assuming as it did that a stunning nineteen-year-old coed would run around Europe taking notes to check against the works of famous poets! Diane red-facedly pondered the question for many moments, trying to call back the castle at Chillon, then offered the line that has endeared her to me forever:

"Oh, it was a *real* castle all right!"

Lord, dear reader, how I chuckled over and brooded on that line for days afterwards, thinking that in fairness to my lovely Diane, and compared with those castles created by her genius papa, wherein Snow White, Prince Charming, Grumpy, Dopey and all the other guys mucked about, the castle at Chillon had indeed been a *real* castle! And though, as I say, I don't precisely remember Steinem's response to my suggestion that she parallel her life to Augie's, and though I would continue to prompt her and learn that in the Steinem household there had been embarrassing "boxes of stuff" piled in the hallways or someplace, and that the Steinems had once had a welfare tenant upstairs or downstairs or someplace in their house, a guy who with charming regularity used to get smashed and beat the bejesus out of his bride, for whatever reason I vividly recall that Gloria's initial response to my query summoned up the long-ago Diane and it was as though Gloria had said:

"Oh, I had a *real* childhood all right!"

Although we continued to talk and to laugh, to go through the motions, I guess that for me the interview ended with something Gloria said a few moments later. The break-ups of both my marriages had been dreadful affairs (none of those cool, suave, lightly ironical, *New Yorker* magazine partings for Exley); and though I get along jolly well with one of my exes now, the situation with the other is still and always will be horrendous—ghastly, man, *ghastly* —and probably a lot closer to my reader's predicament than that sophisticated drivel novelists contrive. In reading about Gloria I had sensed that no matter how much she "had it together" in most respects, like me she had had difficulties sustaining relationships with the opposite sex. Having been asked in interviews about some of her past partners, she had not been altogether kind. About the famous and brilliant director Mike Nichols she'd been quoted as saying she'd mistaken his "head for a heart," and she now admitted that she had indeed said that but that she and Mike were still "close" and that he had in fact called her up to sympathize with her over the "cruelty" of that particular piece (not likely, *not at all likely*, I later learned from a man who knew Nichols well enough to have spent days on Nichols' sets watching him make his movies). I then went through the names of all the other "famous" men with whom Gloria had been "linked," as Louella used to say. There was old "Ken" Galbraith, and "Teddy" Sorensen, and the great alto sax Paul Desmond, and Herb Sargent, and Rafer Johnson, and—well, to Gloria they had all been merely "friends," which, it goes without saying, had me gritting my teeth, biting my tongue and repressing a terribly naughty-boy urge to ask Gloria if she fucked her friends.

I was saving one guy, Thomas Guinzburg, who seemed to me such an ideal mate for Queen Gloria, and about whom I'd heard many nice things, until last. Guinzburg owned one of the half-dozen most prestigious publishing houses in America; he was wealthy; he was said to number among his friends and entertain at his town house dinner table the rich and the famous from the theater, the movies, the literati, and so forth; and above all, and for which one will forgive him, he had thought enough of Gloria to have allowed to be printed, under the Viking imprimatur, her *Beach Book*. I wanted to know what the problem with Guinzburg had been.

On the morning that President Kennedy left on his trip to Dallas, Gloria had been in Sorensen's White House office and from the window had watched the President walk across the lawn and board the helicopter that would take him to the airport to Air Force One and to his eventual destiny. On learning of his assassination two days later in New York, Gloria apparently went into some kind of catatonic withdrawal, some epitomy of grief beyond us lesser Americans, and that was the day she knew she and Guinzburg couldn't hack it. Gloria thought Guinzburg took the assassination too cavalierly. Now Gloria raised her right eyebrow into an ironical arc above her raspberry aviatrix's spectacles, smiled tolerantly, and with wry condescension said, "Tom Guinzburg should have been a sports reporter for the *Daily News*."

Ye fucking gads, dear reader, where could Gloria and I go from there? One must understand that the dream of my life—*the dream of my fucking life!*—was to be a sports reporter for the *Daily News*! I'd have a lovely and loving wife named Corinne; three sons named Mike, Toby and Scott; two boxers, Killer and Duchess, with bulging muscles under their fawn coats, and black ferocious masks, and like all boxers they'd be big whining slobbering babies who couldn't even sleep when they were denied access to the boys' beds. I'd have a split-level home somewhere on the north shore of the island, say, at Northport; and just at that moment I was up to here with Corinne, the boys, Killer and Duchess, my boss at the sports desk would telephone me and cry, "Hey, Ex, don't forget you got to fly out to the coast and cover the Mets' five-game stand with the Dodgers." And off I'd wing, to stand in the press box, a paper cup of Coors beer in my hand, the klieg lights dissolving the faces of the crowd into one another, cheering like mad for Seaver and the guys; after which, renewed, I'd fly back to the loving Corinne, Mike, Toby and Scott, Killer and Duchess. *A sports reporter for the* Daily News? Had Gloria's humble beginnings in that crummy Polack section of East Toledo been just a dream on her part, and had she sprung full-blown out of the mists, sitting in her present eminence as she sat before me now, imagining that with all that arm-raised, fist-clenched, "right-on" horseshit she was up to something infinitely grander and more noble than my dream of Corinne, Mike, etc., etc? From that moment on, though words continued being spoken, the interview was over. At the end of our time together she accepted my as yet unasked questions, said she'd take them back to New York with her, work on them at her earliest convenience, and mail them off to me. We then had a distinctly uneasy parting.

Early the next morning I telephoned to thank her for so graciously giving of her time. She was wonderfully kind and said she couldn't recall having had such a stimulating day in ever so long. She also told me I'd left my jacket in her room. Having with the loonies on Beach Court got caught up in the spirit of shining for Gloria, I'd gone over —yes, actually left my island when I didn't have to!—to J. M. Fields, a mammoth discount house in Lake Park, and bought a mustard-colored lightweight zipper jacket. It cost $5.95.

"Keep it, Gloria. One day you'll be trying to tell people I gave it to you and they'll tell yuh you're full of shit!"

Gloria laughed. She reassured me I'd be getting her answers to my questions soon, and we again said goodbye. I hung up the phone on the back bar. In that spirit, and mindful that I still needed her cooperation, I called a florist connected with Western Union, sent her a bouquet of whatever it was the girl recommended, and to accompany the flora dictated a suitable sentiment. From Ms. Steinem I never got the answer to the rest of my questions.

When after many calls over a period of days I at last got through to her she was profusely apologetic, explaining she'd been overwhelmed giving birth to *Ms.* Then abruptly she did a distressing thing. Invoking what she called one of my "Lion's Head friends," whom she never identified, she used that "friend's" words to accuse me of drunkenness, irresponsibility and sloth, all of which I'd have happily pled guilty to had she asked, and she then went on to say that her lack of diligence in getting back to me had been motivated by my "friend's" persuasiveness. Aware of how precious I'd been with my tape recorder, my neatly typed up questions, my homemade tunafish and chopped egg sandwiches, I said, "Was that your impression of me?" By way of an answer Gloria apologized again and said she'd finish the questions and get them to me by the end of the Christmas holidays. She never did, of course, which lends real credence to that mean cliché about things working out for the best. Had Gloria honored her bargain, I'm certain I'd have had her moving in auras I never saw her moving in.

To say that Gloria and I had a "distinctly uneasy parting" from the Sonesta Beach Hotel requires exposition. Ms. Steinem and I had been talking the better part of four hours into the tape recorder, and as time was running out and Gloria had to take her nappy-poo and primp herself for the night's festivities, I was quickly throwing the used questions onto the floor so as to be hurriedly prepared to ask the next one. When she could go on no longer, we rose and she kindly began helping me pick up my notes and get my gear together. We had as I say been talking and laughing a long time. The abrupt silence seemed embarrassingly charged, and to fill it I decided to relate something I'd been undergoing the past days.

Toni had been rendered absolutely paranoid by the flurry of her sire's affidavits (although I suspect he never intended to take her son from her) and in fear she took the boy and departed in the night for God only knows where. Around my pad Toni had been immediately replaced by an even odder companion I will here call Gabrielle. An astonishingly beautiful twenty-two-year-old, Gabrielle was a recent magna cum laude Stanford graduate and a lesbian who was being kept in one of the pads on the Court by a broad-shouldered bull dyke my age. As is the case with almost every homosexual I've known, Gabrielle was miserable and when the dyke was out working days had taken to hanging about my place keeping me company, typing the questions I was preparing for Gloria, hustling us cheeseburgers and coffee, and listening to my FM radio and playing my Brubeck collection on the stereo (though Gabrielle grew to love Brubeck I can't describe how antiquated I felt when I learned that until then she'd never heard of him). Gabrielle came from a wealthy ranching family out in New Mexico or Idaho or Arizona or some such place, and her father's brother, "good old Uncle Willie," had introduced her to a prepubescent sex, having induced her to an oral stimulation of his penis and to the packing of that penis with cow manure (one for Krafft-Ebing!). For motives neither Gabrielle nor I understood—fear, I'd guess—good old Uncle Willie had stopped molesting her when her menstrual cycle began, and though she'd never had anything to do with a man since that time she found her present predicament every bit as oppressive and degrading as the one with good old Uncle Willie. What should she do?

Without batting an eye I suggested she immediately move her gear into my closet and take one of the twin beds in my bedroom. I said as I was feeding her most of the day anyway I saw it as no extra hardship, and that at twenty-two she might do well to get her lovely ass in a bikini, lay on the beach for six months getting a tan, and determine what direction she wanted her life to take.

"Christ," I said. "Look at all the rinky-dinks your age all over the Court. Many of them are as bright and as educated as you. They're just puffing a little of the evil weed, sucking up some apple wine, and waiting for some sign from this ludicrous world we've made for them to live in. You could make friends with them. It wouldn't hurt you a bit to do the same thing for a year, two, three if you're enjoying yourself. Shit, in that scurvy group you'd be Queen of the Court."

Gabrielle laughed. "I know. Every time I go next-door for breakfast some of those apes are drooling in my scrambled eggs." She now eyed me warily and said, "If I did move in, what about sex?"

To this I laughed, rather scornfully I'm afraid. "Cut the shit, Gabrielle. My bed is a foot and a half from yours; if you decide you want to try, all you have to do is hop over. But don't let your hot little pussy get nervous worrying about my needs. Anytime I pick up a piece of ass I'll let you know in advance, and you'll have to take the couch out here. Anytime you want to grab Chick or one of his muscular lifeguards across the street, you let me know and I'll bunk down in here. But look, if you're genuinely serious I'll be damned if I'll relinquish my bed to a broad, so don't ever bother to ask."

Gabrielle grew very solemn. "I want it understood that I could never have sex with you."

Well, sir! I knew I had twenty years on Gabrielle, that I was getting gray, chubby and sloppy—but then, never is an awfully long time and I laughed and said, "C'mon,

Gabrielle, *it is you we're worrying about*! My frightful hog can take care of itself!"

"But that's what I mean," Gabrielle emphasized. "I didn't at all mean it the way it sounded. Seeing some of those girls or whatever they are you hang around with, I'd be afraid to do anything with you—afraid you'd give me some awful disease that'd make my eyebrows fall out."

This was on the evening before I was scheduled to meet Ms. Steinem. Gabrielle and I offered each other eager hands by way of agreement. I promised that the day following my return from the interview I'd help her move her gear, and that if necessary I'd knock the dyke on her ass in the emotional scene that would almost certainly ensue. We shook hands again, Gabrielle left, and I went downstairs to woo Zita the Zebra Woman.

Early the following morning I was hurriedly shaving —pimply Bill was already leaning on the horn of the electric-blue Buick Electra in the courtyard below—in preparation for meeting Steinem when Gabrielle came in, made me a quick cup of instant coffee, and said, "I've changed my mind. I'm going to stay with Sappho."

"I'm sorry. What happened?"

Gabrielle then pointed out to me (in the *Newsweek* cover story I'd given her to read!) that no less than the girl I was going to interview accepted lesbianism, that our society was reaching the civilized state where there wasn't going to be any stigma attached to it, and Gabrielle felt she ought to acknowledge being what she was and learn to live with it.

"That's nothing but that New York City liberal horse-shit! Every noble soul accepts cancer as a part of life until he himself contracts it." In very measured tones I pointed out to Gabrielle that Steinem's acceptance did not constitute endorsement, that as far as I knew Steinem herself was quite wonderfully and healthily heterosexual. "Look, Gabrielle, Steinem's got it all together and that makes it easy for her to be tolerant. People who are happily straight just don't worry about other people's sex life. I mean, I don't care if a guy wants to fuck the exhaust pipe on his Volkswagen, it's nothing to me. And I don't give a shit either if you want to continue in your life, but I don't think you do or you wouldn't have been laying it on me since the day we met. And incidentally you know, don't you, that all men don't force little girls to suck their cocks? I'd feel a hell of a lot better if you stuck to our agreement."

Gabrielle adamantly refused. We shook hands. Gabrielle asked if she could continue to hang around my pad and by my pal. I said *sure*. What the fuck else could I say? Apparently not all that pleased with her own decision, Gabrielle then wept quietly. Then she accompanied me down to the car.

When Steinem and I were getting my gear together in the hotel and I was trying to tell her something of this—and as I told her I attempted to put it on a kidding level by accusing her of very possibly beating me out of a luscious piece of ass—I also pointed out she'd reached an eminence and influence where she ought to consider very carefully what she "accepts."

"But she's a lesbian!"

It was a good deal more unnerving than Steinem's apparently being unable to "see" what I was saying. In her tone there was an overwhelmingly nasty irritation with me that quite honestly made me somewhat afraid, an accusation and a rebuke that I was not man enough to accept aberrations for what they were—I who had spent three years of my life in and out of state mental institutions and knew I'd come to see and tolerate more aberrations than Steinem'll live to see!—and that under no circumstance did I own the sympathy or the necessary zeal either to comprehend or to be a part of her Holy Cause.

By far the brightest, the most literate, the most articulate, the most tolerant (and the only one with a sense of humor) of these women is Ms. Germaine Greer. Reading the "Newsmakers" section of *Newsweek*, I laughed uproariously at her admission of having fallen quite hopelessly in love with a "very elegant" man "of some note" and her further admission that if at thirty-three she could make "a crass fool" of herself "over a tailor's dummy" The Movement needed all the help it could get. As I read this all I could do was entertain suspicions of what Greer would have said had I told her the same thing I tried to tell Gloria and I found myself imagining, "But, my dear chap, you should have removed this Gabrielle's bloomers, given her a superlative fuck, and had done with it." And instead, and against any expectations whatever that it would turn out that way, I left the Sonesta Beach not only distraught at Steinem's pipe-backed stridency but sorry, sad, afraid, hurt.

Prior to seeing Steinem on television so loftily excoriating the Democrats' platform and credentials committees, I'd seen her one other time on the tube. As it happened it was on a morning when Gabrielle and I were making love. For as it turned out Gabrielle did move in with me and we had a lovely, loving idyll for a time until, as I knew she would, she took up with those alienated youth on the hot bright streets beneath me, took up with people more appropriate to her age, her needs, and the destiny I so wanted for her. There came an urgent knocking on the door. I called and asked who it was, and was told by Big Daddy that on Channel 5 at that very moment I could see "that Women's Lib gal you interviewed a few weeks back." I dismounted, rose, flicked on the TV, and sure enough there was Steinem with Dinah Shore, she of the chiffon undies and whose boyfriend was Burt Reynolds, *Cosmopolitan*'s centerfold. Gloria proselytized Women's Liberation, plugged *Ms.*, tap-danced a little soft-shoe with Dinah, then stood about in a somewhat awkward sweat as Dinah whipped up a layered and sumptuous-looking ice-cream cake. Gloria was, I thought laughingly, right where she ought to be. In exasperation Gabrielle said, "Are you going to watch Steinem or are we going to finish what we started?" I laughed again, flicked off the tube, and we finished what we started.

And as I now lay in my bed, in my mother's house, at Alexandria Bay on the St. Lawrence, which I like to think of as the cold top of the world, I found myself saying to the television, "Oh, dear, dear Gloria, *relax, do relax.* They say your man McGovern is the most decent man in the Senate. I suspect he is, and yet every time you and those disaffected souls he's surrounded himself with open your mouths you bury the poor slob that much deeper. We yokels don't understand your smugness, your certitude, the militant, celery-like curves of your spines, and what we don't understand makes us afraid, turns us off, and worse, will end with that benighted yo-yo Nixon's getting into a position of power." Then suddenly I thought, Look, Gloria, you want to do something meaningful with your life? Get Friedan and the rest of those meatballs, rent a bus, pack some picnic lunches, go to Wellfleet on the Cape, bow your heads at Edmund Wilson's grave and pay homage to one of the century's great men! Do anything but what you're doing. What I'm imploring of you, dear, dear Gloria, is that you help me see your man McGovern as a man for whom I'd interrupt my love-making. You won't do so until you and his followers become a lot less brassily strident, until I detect in your demeanors at least a tacit admission that, like Ms. Germaine Greer, you too are becomingly vulnerable and might yet find yourselves the victims of love.

8

Kramer's Pharmacy is at Boonville, New York, in the northernmost part of Oneida County. Across the street and but paces to the northeast sits the lovely, white-columned limestone Hulbert House, the hundred-and-sixty-year-old hotel I have in fantasies dreamed of buying, restoring to some kind of rustic splendor (fourposter beds, Boston rockers, Franklin stoves, and pine washstands with wash basins of milk glass), settling comfy down (doubtless with, as McBride has said, my writing tablets and vodka bottles) at a great old pine harvest table near the mammoth limestone fireplace in the dining room, and thereupon letting the world go by. And the world would go by.

South of Boonville the main highway, Route 12, veers to the east and goes round the village so that the traveler gets no glimpse of Boonville other than the backs of some houses and commercial buildings fronting the highway at what—because the village is so small it might all be deemed outlying—one hesitates to call "outskirts"; as much as we'd like to, we cannot dignify the village with "outskirts." If, however, one bears west and enters the village proper and proceeds down Main Street and passes the Hulbert House, he can turn hard right into Schuyler Street and in a matter of moments he is out of Boonville and traveling north on Alternate Route 12D.

Almost immediately he will have left Oneida County and passed into Lewis County, then almost as quickly he will have moved up and into Talcottville, where if he is not speeding to get to—well, as an example—Alexandria Bay and the Thousand Islands resort area, where I'm playing necrologist and putting down this "elegy," he will be able to get a glimpse of Wilson's stone house. From the rise on which the stone house sits, the road dips almost immediately, crosses the very narrow bridge spanning the Sugar River, then rises up the twisting and treacherous northern approach to the bridge. If the traveler safely negotiates this unfortunate twisting rise he comes to Locust Grove and Potters Corners (here the road to the west leads to Constableville, where Wilson often dined at the hotel in the Parquet Room) and up into Turin, where they ski and where Wilson, in the off-season when the skiers weren't in rowdy residence, often drank at the Towpath Lodge and chatted with its owners, Klaus and Mignonne Heuser. From Snow Ridge one motors to Houseville and up into Martinsburg (all I ever think of moving through these hamlets is interminable and harshly inclement winters and illicit sexual mores among towheaded inhabitants), and at the latter one begins a miles-long descent into the idyllic, shaded, brick and clapboarded village of Lowville, the county seat of Lewis County, where one again picks up the main Route 12 north to Watertown, Lake Ontario, the Thousand Islands, and Canada.

Save by natives like myself this alternate route isn't much traveled, and I suspect few have traveled it for my motive: hoping to see a car in Wilson's front yard and thereby draw sustenance from the knowledge that Wilson was once again in residence and still putting down words. To upstaters the alternate route—we call it the "high road" —is known to be four miles shorter, a good deal less patrolled by state police, and hence in our journeys to and from Utica, where one picks up the New York State Thruway and comes together with what I've always insisted is "the rest of the world," we feel we can make better time and travel with immunity from speeding tickets. As I am most familiar with the road I have often traveled it at a breakneck and lunatic seventy miles an hour, braking only at the hamlets, the insidious approaches to Sugar River, and at Wilson's stone house.

On a brilliant blue Sunday morning in early July, three weeks after Wilson's death, I was standing in front of Kramer's Pharmacy in Boonville, leaning my elbows on a parking meter, and looking across the way at "my" hotel, the Hulbert House. At nine-fifteen the sun was already relentless, the humidity oppressive, and I was upset by a number of things and growing more uneasy by the moment.

Driving down from Alexandria Bay I had stopped at Wilson's stone house, empty now, and to my sorrow had discovered Wilson had at long last lost his battle with the State of New York. For a number of years he had fought the State's attempts to eliminate those treacherous ap-

‡   133

proaches to Sugar River. To do so entailed building an elevated widened span across the waters and for the bridge's southern approach it would be essential to take a large piece of Wilson's sloping front lawn. Wilson had retained counsel to put his case. Over the years I'd read some pieces in local newspapers about the controversy, and I'd been told by John B. Johnson, editor and publisher of the Watertown *Times*, that in a majestic snit Wilson had once come to his Watertown offices and tried to get him to enlist the rhetoric of his editorial pages in behalf of saving Wilson's lawns. I don't know what briefs Wilson's counsel invoked, or the case Wilson put to Johnson. No doubt Wilson took the position that America On The Move could goddam well stay on the main road where it belonged; probably Wilson felt the already harassed taxpayers' dollars were being used to duplicate a perfectly good main highway; perhaps, with Johnson, Wilson even became chummily provincial by pointing out that the alternate route was used only by natives—that is, used by "us," Wilson and the rest of us.

But Wilson had lost this, perhaps his penultimate battle; the State had forced its right to eminent domain; and on this hot Sunday morning on the soft scarred earth above the Sugar River the bulldozers sat at Sabbath idleness. To accommodate the bridge's southern approach a large section had been taken from Wilson's front yard. The stone house now sat somewhat astonished-looking almost atop the highway, and workers had built a white cement curb nearly as high as a cottage's picket fence on the east and north sides of the house. In *Upstate* Wilson had rued the hoodlum motorcyclists and snowmobilers cutting kitty-corner across his yard and ruining his ferns, and if for nothing else one had to be grateful that the curbs would now prevent this. The house looked run down, its trim badly needed painting, and I knew if the house were to be saved someone—how I wished it could be me!—would have to spend considerable money and begin immediately. From the amount of work already completed on the bridge's approaches and the tons of earth moved to support them, it was apparent that in the last days of his illness Wilson had to put up with not only the rain but the noise of the bulldozers. It was a pathetic irony. It couldn't have escaped Wilson that the bureaucracies he had fought all his life could not be thwarted in their "missions" (what one would give for his dying words on those bulldozers and that white cement curb!). In the end, at Talcottville, not only couldn't Wilson flee that America with which he had been on distressing terms for so long but in the name of a concept he deplored, "progress," that America had brought its earthmovers and concrete within spitting distance of his doors.

In my pilgrimage south to bid Wilson adieu—from what I'd read every other writer in America was going to Miami to rub elbows and sip martinis with Ms. Steinem and Mr. Mailer and to articulate the cause of Senator George McGovern—I'd come to Boonville to meet Mrs. Mary Pcolar (puh-KÓL-ar), Wilson's last great "passion." During the week Mrs. Pcolar worked at Kramer's Pharmacy. It'd been there she'd first met Wilson a dozen years before, and she'd suggested the drugstore as our obvious meeting place. But it was now approaching nine-thirty, and she was already half an hour late. I was wondering if we'd understood each other correctly, and recalling what the state had done to Wilson's yard I was growing more restless by the moment. To kill time I bought the New York *Sunday Times*; in the book review I read Wilfred Sheed's nice reminiscence of Wilson; in the back of the review in "The Last Word" Wilson was himself represented by a piece he'd written for *The New Republic* in 1928, "The Critic Who Does

Not Exist." In it he called for some enlightened criticism of contemporary writers, a chore that at his death he himself had not undertaken for years. It was too hot to read in the car, so I read sitting on the cement steps leading into the pharmacy. On finishing these articles I got up, brushed the dirt from my pants, balanced the fat *Times* on the convex top of a mailbox, and placed my elbows on a parking meter and waited.

Almost everyone who entered the store came out with the Sunday newspapers, but only a few had the *Times*, most of them having bought the Rome and Syracuse papers and the New York *Sunday News*. One woman with LE tags signifying she was down from Lewis County pulled up and parked, went in, and came out with the *Times*, three or four crossword-puzzle magazines, and a carton of Pall Malls, obviously literate and in for a leisurely day.

I said, "There's a wonderful piece about Mr. Wilson on page two of the book section."

Startled, she said, "Pardon?"

I repeated myself, adding, "You know Mr. Wilson— *the writer* from Talcottville."

To my embarrassment the woman said, "Oh?" Then she giggled self-consciously.

Up and down the pavement behind me a stupendously moronic-looking girl kept walking back and forth, back and forth. She had on dirty beige hip-huggers and a cerise tank shirt under which she wore no bra, allowing her sturdy, youthful and provocative tits to sway back and forth. Her hair was lank with dirt. She was cross-eyed. Her comings and goings behind me were so aimless, and so obviously did she have great pride of hip movement and such devoted affection for her own swaying, pulpous tits, that one couldn't doubt she was the town fuck and an idiot into the bargain. For years I'd been cognizant of her in these upstate

136 ‡

villages, the girl who ripens at eleven and by thirteen has the farm boys taking her out into the pastures, settling her on her knees among the cowpies, and jamming their up-country throbbing pricks into her jaws.

To me there was something obscenely inappropriate about her, something that clashed hideously with the "sacredness" of my pilgrimage, and I tried to concentrate on "my" hotel across the way. But the Hulbert House also looked run-down. I thought that if I were ever coming into that mysterious patrimony that would allow me to restore it, I'd have to come into it soon, and in exasperation I walked across the street, turned my back on the hotel, and watched the front door of Kramer's for Mrs. Pcolar. In *Upstate* Wilson had included a picture of her, her husband George, and her children. I'd studied the picture and was sure I'd have no difficulty recognizing her. It was getting on to a quarter to ten, the sun was high and the humidity stifling, abominable for that time of morning in that part of the country. And I was tired, anxious and irritable.

In a big styrofoam container on the back seat of a borrowed Pinto I had provisions for a magnificent picnic and I prayed the heat would not wreak its despoliation. The night before I'd filled two Mason jars with water and put them into the freezer but that morning discovered the expanded ice had cracked both of them—and these ac-cursed jars had been sold for precisely this purpose!—and to keep my delectations cool I had to settle for the cubes from a single tray (naturally only one was full) dumped into a plastic bag. Unable to sleep but a wink (I'd been as nervous as if I were going to meet The Great Man him-self!), my picnic got altogether away from me. To pass the hours from two A.M., when I gave up all hope of sleep-ing, I prepared four big chicken breasts with Shake 'n Bake only to discover that this took less than forty-five minutes. In the pantry I then found two boxes of premixed ingredients, one for banana bread and another for a chocolate marble coconut cake. For the bread, one had to add a splash of milk and two medium-sized bananas. I put in six small bananas, then mixed up everything in the electric blender for an hour until the texture was as lubricious as a cheerleader's cunt. As both the bread and the cake demanded the same oven temperature I could have baked them simultaneously, but to kill time I did them separately. On completion the bread looked a masterpiece.

I put it on the sideboard to cool, then went eagerly —a little dementedly, I think—after the chocolate marble coconut cake. For this I had only to add milk, but I found two tins of shredded coconut and to heighten the artificial flavor poured these in. To adorn the cake I found a pint can of Hershey's Dutch chocolate frosting. On the cooled and sliced banana bread I spread cream cheese and made a half-dozen sandwiches, wrapped them individually and ever so neatly in wax paper, and put them in the refrigerator against the moment I'd have to load the styrofoam hamper. In a pint plastic container I put radishes and celery, in another a pound of medium-old Cheddar cheese cut into delicately edible bits. Then with a flourish I frosted the chocolate marble coconut cake with the Dutch chocolate frosting, scraped out the can with a knife, licked the knife, and cut and wrapped four wedges of the cake. I located half a dozen apples, a bunch of grapes, and four cans of diet (a nice touch, that!) black raspberry soda.

Was this going to be enough? Better not take a chance, I thought. By then I was absolutely loony with industry. So anxious was I to make this gesture to the ghost of Wilson that I'd begun to resemble the proverbial mad chef preparing dishes for that joker Jackie Kennedy! I decided to make a couple of my famous tuna fish, chopped hard-boiled egg and onion sandwiches, the kind I'd made for Ms. Steinem. As tartly as a maiden aunt I then primly excised the crusts from some slices of white bread (which I hadn't dared do for Gloria, thinking it much too frivolous for The New Woman), and with the mixture made three of these sandwiches, wrapped and put them in the refrigerator. There was no room left in the refrigerator—it had begun to "swell."

I would have very much liked to make cucumber sandwiches but didn't know how. In English novels people were always sitting about sipping tea, nibbling at cucumber sandwiches, and saying marvelously subtle and witty things. But no English novelist had ever told me how to make such a sandwich—whether one simply sliced the cucumbers, chopped them up with mayonnaise and salt and pepper, or what. Then I started to chuckle. I was thinking how nice it would be if some brilliant Limey like Anthony Burgess or John Fowles annotated, with lengthy footnotes and for Americans only, an entire English classic, something of Dickens or Jane Austen, and straight-facedly detailed just such British cultural hang-ups as the proper preparation of a cucumber sandwich. In exhaustion and laughter I then lay down on the couch until it was time to go. When I started to pack the styrofoam container I discovered the Mason jars were cracked.

"Shee-it!" I spat the word into the back of my teeth and grudgingly settled for my single plastic bag of cubes.

My thinking was to take Mrs. Pcolar up behind the stone house to Flat Rock on the Sugar River where Wilson had himself picnicked for seventy years, to spread out a blanket, to settle all comfy down, perhaps in the yoga position, to nibble all afternoon on my lovingly prepared goodies, and to let Mrs. Pcolar talk while I scribbled on my yellow lined tablet. I don't know what I was after, certainly not an "article." I knew I wanted to take something of Wilson to carry with me, and I thought that in Mrs. Pcolar's laughter, her tears, some gesture, a tilt of the head, a coy shrug, some expression, grave, lightsome, even perhaps an imitation of Wilson—that in something meaningless to her I might abstract a piece of Wilson, however fleetingly minute, and in all the days ahead carry that abstract with me against my needs.

For the last dozen years of his Talcottville life, Mrs. Pcolar, a lovely Hungarian-American, acted as Wilson's amanuensis. She was his summer secretary. She was his drinking, dinner and movie companion, his occasional chef. Having helped him learn Hungarian, she was his teacher. She was forever his pupil, Wilson never abdicating his role as one-man faculty. She was his "niece" *Mariska*; to her he was *Kedves Ödön Basci*, Dear Uncle Edmund. To describe her in *Upstate* Wilson used the Hungarian *ezermester*, master of a thousand arts. Mrs. Pcolar was also Wilson's concern, his "problem," and in those pages he wrote, "I never leave Talcottville nowadays without an uncomfortable feeling of never being able to do justice to my relation to Mary Pcolar." Most of all Mrs. Pcolar was Wilson's friend. He sent her valentines, enclosing in one a handmade black paper butterfly which, on winding up a rubber band, was supposed to fly but didn't. In the center of a gilt-framed heart one read, "I declare by this EPISTLE," and overleaf, "That I'm yours should you but whistle." Beneath the verse a red plastic whistle was attached. That also didn't work. On her birthdays she received cards. "Happy Birthday to someone who's TOPS in my book!!" And on opening the card, and in obvious reference to *Memoirs of Hecate County*, "Of course my book has been banned in several states." As he did to all of his close friends, he sent her at Christmas the booklets of light verse and nonsense he composed and had specially printed for the season:

A dizzy old duchess named Sarah
Designed a delightful tiara.
It was made of live shrimps,
    Alternating with imps,
Who sometimes tormented the wearer.

On Mother's Day he took her and her family to dinner at the Fort Schuyler Club in Utica and to memorialize the occasion inscribed the menu with a suitable sentiment. He wrote her from Wellfleet, from Cambridge, from the offices of *The New Yorker*, from Lillian Hellman's New York apartment. He wrote from Israel, from Budapest, from Paris, and in the last winter of his life from Naples, Florida. On his last visit to Paris he petulantly complained that he was going to stay in his hotel room for the duration of his stay because Paris had changed so and the women no longer wore "pretty gowns." From Florida in that last winter he wrote that he couldn't abide being around old people. He was seventy-six. More amusing than anything, as though he were a just-published first novelist, he sent Mrs. Pcolar xeroxed copies of reviews of his books with arch notations to the effect that the reviewer may even have read the book.

As it got on toward ten, the sun was becoming increasingly merciless. My upper lip was coated and perspiration made its way in rivulets down the small of my back. Now certain I'd come on the wrong day, I was intently watching the front of the store when I detected something that stopped my heart. Across the façade at the top of the store was a yellow and red Coke sign bearing the name SANFORD DRUGS, and it struck me abruptly that I wasn't even at the right place! Nervously I stepped a few paces down the street to get a different perspective but, sure enough, coming out perpendicularly from the Coke sign and suspended above the walk was a white wooden sign on which in black letters was the legend KRAMER'S PHARMACY.

When at almost that very moment a profusely apologetic Mrs. Pcolar arrived, I asked her straightaway about the store's dual identity. She laughed and said it had been Mr. Wilson's doing. (Throughout the day Mrs. Pcolar was never to refer to him as anything but *Mr.* Wilson: "I never did in life. Why should I in death?") Cognizant of how little given to change we upstaters are, Kramer had retained the name of the previous owner, Sanford, when he acquired the store a dozen years before. Wilson, however, knew Kramer to be the new owner and in his finickiness that things be properly called had refused to bestow on the store anything but Kramer's Pharmacy, always using both words, as though down the street there existed the possibility of a conflict with KRAMER'S SALOON or KRAMER'S WHOREHOUSE. Mrs. Pcolar, who had gone to work there shortly after Kramer took over, told him of Wilson's stolid insistence; and in what one suspects was a larksome mood Kramer said if it was Kramer's Pharmacy to Mr. Wilson it had indeed to be KRAMER'S PHARMACY: hence the new sign appended to the old, a gesture whereby Kramer didn't alienate the old-timers by removing Sanford's name. I love these upstate* villages, and the unreasoning vestedness of their inhabitants, and on hearing this I laughed loudly.

In Alden Whitman's front-page obituary in the New York *Times* (and what other newspaper in the world would

---

* To a Manhattanite "upstate" means "the uthuh siduh Oddsley" ("the other side of Ardsley") but to true upstaters this notion verges on the laughably blasphemous. We do not even look on Albany, Schenectady, Utica, Rochester or Buffalo as upstate and feel that to be genuinely "northern" one has to know the Adirondack Mountains and the St. Lawrence Valley and towns like Old Forge and Hammond, Canton and Potsdam, Cape Vincent and Chaumont (never pronounced *Shummoo* as Wilson alleges in *Upstate*), Plattsburg, Gouverneur, Massena, Tupper Lake, Lake Placid—the list is as long as one cares to make it but does not include White Plains, which is "the uthuh siduh Oddsley."

have put it there?) he'd written that Wilson's marriage to Mary McCarthy had "tended to be troubled" and that in the McCarthy recollection everything that came under Wilson's hand was shaped into "an authorized version," not entirely excluding Miss McCarthy herself who had in a way become Wilson's version of her. She was to write: "Mr. Wilson said, 'I think you've got a talent for writing short stories.' So he put me off in one free room with a typewriter and shut the door," which seemed to me pretty much the way "Mr." Wilson had "shut the door" to any further dialogue as to what this rather nondescript drugstore on Boonville's Main Street should be called.

Unhappily, I very quickly came to understand that, like Kramer's Pharmacy or Mary McCarthy, Mary (I asked and was told it was okay to use her given name) had also become Wilson's authorized version of her. To escape the heat we went to Slim's café a few doors south on Main Street, slid into a booth facing one another, and ordered tea. Besides my pocketful of ball-point pens, I'd brought along a copy of *Upstate* with the pages on which Mary was mentioned turned over at the corners, and a copy of *A Fan's Notes* inscribed "For Mary Pcolar, 6/2/'72, Sincerely and with thanks, Frederick Exley." I'd had a difficult time obtaining a copy of the latter, and had finally got my lawyer's copy on the promise to get him another, and a first edition (very easy as there was only one edition). With a razor blade I'd excised the page on which I'd inscribed it to him, and on another page I'd written the one to Mary. At forty-three it was all I had to offer by way of portfolio. When I presented it to Mary I offhandedly said, "Here's a copy of my *last* book." I wasn't lying but I nevertheless delivered the line in such a way as to suggest that prior to this there'd been more volumes than I could at the moment recall, which in fairness might have been had I not been such an unregenerate drunk. I'd added the "and with thanks" in hopeful anticipation of the wonderful Wilson anecdotes Mary would pass on to me.

Mrs. Pcolar was a youthful-looking and strikingly handsome forty-four, not in the least reticent about her age. She had an erect sturdy bearing, and had she not been so oppressively feminine one might have thought her somewhat muscular. Save for the graying that would come with age, one was certain she'd look as good at sixty-four as she did now and not much different now from what she'd looked at twenty-four, the kind of woman—watching one's own aging by comparison—with whom it would be unnerving to grow old. Hence I was surprised to learn she'd once been fat.

"Yes," she emphasized, sensing my doubt as to whether *fat* was quite the word. "I was fat, ballooning up. I went to Dr. Smith"—the elderly Boonville doctor who'd ministered to Wilson and had been at his bedside when he died—"for some diet pills. He wouldn't give them to me, he brushed me off. He told me I was too good-looking and too intelligent to lay around the house all day, that my stuffing myself was just nerves, and I ought to go to work and the weight would take care of itself. So I did. I went to work at Kramer's. Then I met Mr. Wilson."

Mary wore her soft hair short, becomingly shorn just beneath the ears. It was light brown and wavy, attractively tinged with traces of blond coloring. By his own account in *Upstate* Wilson had once reprimanded her for making her hair too blond, which he thought unbecoming and cheap, and I smiled now to think that even from the beyond Wilson was holding dominion over her. There were the high striking Mongolian cheekbones Wilson had remarked, a facial structure inherited from her Hungarian ancestors. What Wilson had not got were her eyes. Although small, they were beautiful and of a pale blue so luminous they appeared flecked with a flashing silver quality, an incandescence so disarming that after a time I found I could not look steadily at her and rest easy. She wore a well-cut sleeveless orange dress, one of the new wrinkleless double-knits she'd bought for a trip to Budapest (on her way back through London, Mary was with a note from Wilson to visit Stephen Spender), a simple gold bracelet, a gold watch, and at the base of her strong columnar white throat a gold onyx brooch pinned to her dress.

The dress had been Wilson's favorite. "Mr. Wilson called it his orange sherbert dress." He had had his father's gold-rimmed spectacles fitted with his own prescription—"Mr. Wilson called them his Ben Franklin glasses"—and whenever she wore the dress he'd reach up with his right hand, with exaggerated drama lower the spectacles to the tip of his nose, look searchingly over their tops, issue a pleasurable *Ahhhh* and say, "You have on my orange sherbert dress." When she wore something else, Wilson would go through the same charade with his glasses but with mock exasperation at Mary's extravagance say, "Another new dress—*again?*" Her well-made legs were sheathed in flesh-colored pantyhose and on her feet she wore beige-colored shoes with squat blue heels and moccasin-style toes about which were decorative little gold chains. Even the shoes were Wilson's doing. Feeling audacious Mary had one day worn spiked heels and in a huff Wilson had remarked that *No, no they would not at all do.* Wilson had wanted her to wear "pumps." Mary had almost cried, "But these are pumps!" when it abruptly occurred to her that Wilson believed that pumps were necessarily low-heeled or walking shoes.

"And you never corrected him?" I asked, laughing.

"No one—at least not me—ever corrected Mr. Wilson." Mary sat pensively. "Besides, I guess now I'll always think of low-heeled shoes as pumps."

"I guess I will, too."

I'd asked Mary to begin at the beginning of the end, to tell me about the last days, and though I tried to take down most of what she said I found myself impatiently saying, "Yeah, yeah, but Wilson covered all that in *Upstate*." Then suddenly it occurred to me what was happening. It wasn't so much Mary's memory, her intelligence, or her imagination, which were all perfectly capable, as that she was so intimidated by Wilson she felt her recollection of their relationship must necessarily correspond with his, that under the distinguished Farrar, Straus & Giroux imprimatur *Upstate* had been set forth against posterity's judgment and she daren't contradict or elaborate for fear of toying with that judgment. Had I told her *Upstate* was one of Wilson's lesser efforts, one that probably wouldn't have seen print had it been offered over another's name, not only wouldn't Mary have believed me but it occurred to me that Mary herself as a person in the Wilsonian drama would have been eliminated along with *Upstate* and I couldn't say this without running the risk of hurting her.

I now asked Mary if we mightn't drive around and look at some of the places Wilson had been fond of, mentioning all the food I had in the back seat of the Pinto and how I prayed it wouldn't spoil. To this Mary suggested we immediately transfer the styrofoam container to her air-conditioned Impala and use her car.

I had to get out of Slim's. The village fuck, who because nobody said hello or paid her any mind must have been some other village's fuck, had come into Slim's and ordered a Coke. Her actions reminded me suddenly of someone else, and I found myself watching her intently out of the corner of my eye, hoping Mary wouldn't notice. I hadn't been fucked since the night of my farewell party on the island, nearly a month before, and that occasion had been one of the strangest encounters I'd ever had, as close to rape as I'd ever come.

We were having our rigatoni, marinara sauce and sausage feast at the big round corner table of the bar; the gang was shouting and laughing raucously; and then this woman I'd seen before came in, took a seat at the bar directly opposite our table, ordered an extra-dry martini, and turning her barstool halfway round to us got obliquely and mutely caught up in the spirit of the party, silently laughing on cue at the awful jokes, lifting her eyebrows in feigned but good-natured outrage at the furious obscenities, cooing with pleasurable surprise along with the others as I opened and read aloud my wacky cards and viewed my even wackier presents of farewell. She was about thirty, had short black hair, a marvelously compact little figure, and the fact that she was nicely groomed and always attired in dresses and heels—unusual in Florida—suggested to me she might be an interior decorator or one of the many real estate saleswomen in the area.

I'd seen her in the Islander Room two or three times late in the evening with one or another well-dressed, well-heeled-looking guy, and as nothing ever happened there until ten (at the moment we had the room almost to ourselves) when the first show began, I was surprised to see her that early and alone. So obviously did she seem to be enjoying our party from her short distance across the aisle, and so obviously did she seem to want to be a part of it, that I vigorously but with silent furtive stealth nodded my head two or three times for her to come over and take the empty chair next to mine, but to each summons she smiled jovially by way of declining, once wagging her finger fetchingly at me by way of saying I was obviously a nasty boy with nasty thoughts. Then she did something unmistakable. She asked the barmaid Diane for change for a dollar and directions to the pay phone and she did it so loudly that I had no doubt that whatever her motive—to prevent her calling another man?—she definitely wanted to be overheard.

Too excited to analyze motives, I said to myself, and I was sure I would, "I'm going to fuck her." Then I excused myself to the gang, saying that if we were going to go on all through the night I'd have to take a shower and would return momentarily. The pay phone in the hotel was located on the wall above a one-step landing leading up the front stairs, just off the lobby. I stood in the middle of the lobby watching her for some moments. She had her back to me, she was facing the phone, and in her uplifted left hand she tentatively held a dime, as though she were having trouble recalling a number. I thought, *That phony.* Moving quickly and noiselessly across the carpeting, I stepped up onto the landing, slid my hands around her waist, clasped them together at her tummy, and pulled her lovely little fanny back into my semi-erection. We hung suspended there, hotly riveted. She had the decency not to feign outrage or indignation.

Speaking quietly over her shoulder into her ear, I said, "Who are you calling?"

"A friend."

"Do you have to call him now?"

"Probably not."

Grabbing her still upraised hand with the dime in it, and squeezing with all the base fury of my excitation, I dragged her up to the landing of the second floor. There she yanked her hand free and in perfect control told me that that kind of thing was not in the least necessary. I then followed her—walking as cool as a Ziegfeld chorine up a ramp, she was—up to the third floor where I led her to my digs. Once there I was so distraught I couldn't wait for her to undress. Seating her on the bed, I took hold of her shoulders and pushed her back with her head against the pillow, then dropped my "foul fucking Bermudas" to the floor, lifted up her skirt, removed her panties, mounted and penetrated her wetness. Leaving her in the shower, where afterwards we'd gone together, I was back with the gang within a half-hour; and within another half-hour she—freshly showered and ready—had been joined at the bar by one of the suave joes I'd seen her with before. For the rest of the evening I watched her for some sign, but she never looked in my direction and all I could think of was Robertson Davies' Mary Dempster in *Fifth Business*. When she'd been found in the gravel pit by her minister husband and half the males of her village being passively mounted by a tramp, Parson Amasa Dempster had asked his heartfelt *why*, and Mary had said, "He was very civil, 'Masa. And he wanted it so badly."

And now this village fuck was doing the same thing that other had done, sipping on her Coke, turning round on her counter stool, and, trying her best to focus those hideous eyes, listing toward the various booths with people in them, including Mary and me, as though she desperately wanted to get invited into one of them and share the Sunday morning of less lonely souls. Too, I had no doubt that Mary's striking femininity was hardly abetting my abominable satyriasis—talk about prisoners of sex!—and I had to get some air in my lungs, to see the green lush of the early summer trees, to do something to help me get it together and keep my demeanor commensurate with the solemn nature of my pilgrimage.

9

On May 18, 1972, Wilson wrote Mary the last letter he would send to her. It was verification of an earlier telephone call from Wellfleet in which he'd designated his arrival time on the 31st and asked Mary to pick him up at the Utica airport. In the letter was a lengthy piece on Wilson from England with an accompanying caricature depicting him with prominent double chins. Wilson was pleased with the caricature, and shortly after his arrival he borrowed it back from Mary to show to someone else, promising to return it. Mary was never to see it again.

Recently direct flights from Boston to Utica had been

canceled by Allegheny Airlines and to his chagrin Wilson had had to fly to Syracuse. As it would do for twenty-two days of June, before and after both his death and Hurricane Agnes, the rain came in squalls the day of Wilson's arrival and his flight was put in a holding pattern over Syracuse for some time while Mary waited uneasily below in the terminal. At the announcement that his plane was at last landing, Mary ran to the parking lot and moved her Impala close to an exit to prevent Wilson's getting wet. When she returned to the disembarking ramp she found him waiting nervously in his wheelchair attended by a porter. As he invariably was, he was dressed in a brown pin-stripe suit, long-sleeved white shirt and dark patterned tie. On his lap he held a very British, scruffy and torn Mackintosh, and on his head he wore his wide-brimmed and floppy felt hat that might once have been beige but was now sweat and finger-stained to a dark unwholesome color. He had two pieces of old brown leather luggage, with straps and gilt-initialed EW, one stuffed with clothes, the other bulging with manuscripts and books. He was ready to do "a piece of work." He had his favorite walking stick made from the handle of one of his mother's umbrellas. Whereas years ago Scott Fitzgerald had remarked another stick of Wilson's as an affectation befitting a young *Vanity Fair* editor and dandy about Mahattan, time had done what it does—things, as Fitzgerald himself might have said, had now "come round" and after half a century Wilson had at last "grown up" to his walking stick. To Mary's surprise Wilson sported a McGovern button on his lapel. For years Wilson had seemed to despair increasingly of political solutions and when Mary playfully asked him what the McGovern button was all about, Wilson said, "But of course we must all vote for McGovern!" It was, Mary said, a trumpeting command issued from Wilson's Olympianly pedantic heights.

To Wilson's ironically apologetic smile at the porter—
it had the character of a bemused shrug at the fatuousness
of women—Mary focused her Instamatic, handed it to the
porter, and asked him to take a picture of Wilson and her.
She then sidled gingerly up to Wilson's chair and rested
her hand palm-down on his shoulder while he sat, a fallen,
embattled and tolerant eagle. Either because of the poor
light or the porter's incompetence the picture was never to
reproduce, and Mary was glad for the porter the camera
hadn't been a Polaroid so Wilson could have immediate
evidence that someone was screwing up. Had Mary ever
been cognizant of Wilson's much-remarked rudeness to
people (and on this score she insisted he was much ma-
ligned) it was with porters, waitresses, sales clerks—with
menials—and after she'd come to know him she viewed this
gruff impatience as little more than a comically Dickensian
eccentricity. She said he approached such people in a state
of heady exasperation, as if, before he even made his de-
mands known, he was certain the fates had set these people
to thwarting his simplest needs.

A dozen years before he had twice come into Kramer's
Pharmacy and without identifying himself had demanded
the New York newspapers he believed held in reserve for
him. When Mary explained she held no newspapers for him,
he had literally shuddered and left the store in a grandiose
huff, the magisterial frustration of the prince fully aware
that lackeys were conspiring to put him off his day. On the
third occasion Mary saw him coming and in literal fear fled
to the prescription section at the back of the store and
asked Kramer to wait on him. Afterwards Kramer explained
to Mary who he was (it meant nothing to Mary), that
Wilson was only in the area at certain times of the year and
that as he was a "big man" they best make sure he got his
newspapers.

Shortly thereafter Mary and Wilson became friendly.

She read his impressive biographical data in *Who's Who*, and he said he wanted her to do some part-time typing for him. Only recently he had learned that two of his plays had been translated into Hungarian, and he'd set himself the task of learning the language to check the translations. When he learned Mary knew Hungarian he was more insistent than ever.

Some days later Mary went to the stone house to discuss the job further, and when she knocked on the door a voice from on high demanded *Who-is-it?* in a tone that suggested Is-it-anyone-who-should-be-presuming-on-me? When Mary was at last told to enter, she did so and to her horror the first things she saw were white hairless bare legs descending the staircase. To her immense relief a bathrobe at last came into view, followed by the rest of Wilson, unshaven and holding in his hand a tumbler full of Scotch. It was ten-thirty in the morning and Mary's worst expectations were being borne out (what Mary didn't learn until later was that Wilson had worked all the preceding day and all night, which he often did in those days, and was only then unwinding and preparing himself for bed). When Wilson asked her if she had a typewriter, Mary said she did but wasn't all that sure she wanted to work for such a dangerous character.

"Dangerous?" Wilson said, whereupon Mary asked him what he had to say about his four marriages that were known to the gossips of Boonville. Wilson had this to say: "I don't recommend it." And Mary went to work for him.

By no means did Mary wish to suggest that Wilson was beyond inflicting hurt, but when he did so she came finally to understand it as Wilson's way of saying, But you are not living up to my expectations—you are not at all being the brilliant and stalwart person I know you to be. A few years before, in what one suspects was a Pygmalion gesture, Wilson had persuaded Mary to take night courses in English

‡   153

and literature courses at Utica College, and to her immense pride she had with some finagling persuaded Wilson to come and talk with her classmates in a journalism course. At that time Wilson was already "the dean of American critics," "the grand old man of American Letters"—substitute whatever cliché one wishes—and I doubt he'd condescended to have "a dialogue" with students for two decades or better. Mary, her classmates and her teacher Dick Costa were in a state of grand agitation at his arrival. Wilson's ground rules were simple. The student could ask anything he chose, and by the same token Wilson could if he elected choose not to answer. For most of the evening things could not have gone more swimmingly. Wilson was charming, witty, brilliant and direct, and he smilingly and tolerantly fended all questions, dumb and otherwise.

Because Mary saw Wilson practically every day, she felt it would be selfish and an act of extreme discourtesy to her classmates to take any of Wilson's time with her own queries, and she did not do so until late in the session when the questions from the floor appeared to be lagging. Now Mary could not even recall what question she'd put. What she did remember—what she would always remember—was that the words were no sooner out of her mouth than Wilson's eagle eyes beneath his massive hawklike brows narrowed furiously, and that his forehead bobbed angrily in and out at her, the predator signaling imminent attack.

"Mary! . . . You must never . . . *never* ask me a question like that again!"

Afterwards Dick Costa had a party at his house for Wilson and his students, but Mary had been so humiliated she abandoned Wilson and drove straight home, weeping. Wilson had to stay the night at Utica's Fort Schuyler Club and the next day get to Talcottville the best way he could. When some days later Wilson telephoned Mary he finessed the entire episode by ignoring it and instead inquired if the reason for her absence from his presence was illness. But he did apologize in the best way he knew how. Ordinarily it was his wont to summon by saying, "Come at four—I have some typing for you." On this day he asked if Mary might not do him the kindness of coming.

At her Impala at the Syracuse airport Mary became aware for the first time what a stroke of obstinate courage or of foolhardiness Wilson's trip had been. Scorning both her and the porter's help, Wilson rose from the wheelchair with the aid of his walking stick and with terribly protracted painfulness compounded by excessively labored breathing made his way into the front seat of the car. Mary recalled there was something indecent about his lingering performance. His movements owned the kind of duality that out of propriety forced one to look away at the same time they held one in thrall. When I asked Mary why Wilson's wife Elena had permitted him to make such a trip, Mary laughed and said that though she didn't know Mrs. Wilson well, she'd never seen anyone prevent Wilson's doing what he wanted to do.

"He was—"

"Spoiled?" I volunteered.

"Spoiled!" Mary cried.

Immediately after his death, obituaries and eulogies remarked Wilson's "stuttering" and "funny way of talking" but Mary chafed at these characterizations as wrong-headed. She never heard Wilson stutter in his life and his funny way of talking was simply that his voice had somewhat "a cooing pitch" and he seldom spoke save in grammatical sentences, structured paragraphs, and occasionally and off the top of his head in entire essays. If while having dinner Mary should ask him what constituted a good as opposed to a poor wine, there was apt to be an egregiously sustained pause before Wilson delivered, *in toto*, a history of vintage wine regions, the proper methods for tending the grape, and the mean temperatures and moisture amounts necessary to producing an exemplary bottle of wine. To be Wilson's friend one had of necessity to be his pupil.

Whenever Mary picked him up at the airport it was Wilson's custom to take her to dinner; and even after his near failure to negotiate the front seat of the Impala, Wilson insisted on abiding by custom and stopping at one of his favorite restaurants, The Savoy in Rome. Among upstate Italians The Savoy has the reputation of making the best sauce between the St. Lawrence and New York City, and though Wilson abhorred poorly lighted dining rooms, which The Savoy's is, he liked what he called the "garlic toast," the marinara sauce, and the owner Pat Destito who invariably greeted Wilson with "Dr. Livingstone, I presume."

Even at The Savoy, Wilson did not entirely relax. He could not of course abide the jukebox, and whenever someone got caught up in the restaurant's Italian atmosphere and played "Marie" Wilson literally cringed. For the life of him he could not fathom how the American Italian could turn the Italian *Oi* into the *Whay* of *Whhaaaaay Marie*, and though Mary couldn't remember all the details she remembered Wilson's once talking at interminable and pedantic length about the colloquial and exclamatory *Oi* being common to Venetian gondoliers—or something to that effect—Wilson's "setting the record straight." With what seemed to Mary a pathetic reluctance, Wilson on this night set his pride to rest and sought her help in getting himself seated at their table, then apologized for being too weak to talk. No longer were there two preprandial daiquiris, with Wilson then switching to double Johnnie Walker Red Scotches, followed by a bottle or two of Piesporter with the meal. As Mary had been expected to do for a number of years, she no longer had to caution Wilson about his alcoholic intake—to "ration"; he had tacitly taken this upon himself. They had a single daiquiri, Mary had scallops, and Wilson his "garlic toast" and scrambled eggs and marinara sauce.

During the meal Wilson perked up somewhat and there was a pretense of carrying on as usual, an implication that when he was rested from his exhausting trip he would as always take her to dinner and the movies. Wilson wanted to see *The Godfather*; Mary thought it was being held over in Rome and would check on it. By the time they reached the stone house at Talcottville, where Wilson's daughter Rosalind greeted them from the back porch, they were busy making plans for a night on the town. As Rosalind was helping her father from the car, she picked up on the conversation and offered her opinion that Mario Puzo and Wilson's dead friend Edwin O'Connor (*The Last Hurrah*) "wrote a lot alike." Wilson expressed surprise that Rosalind had read *The Godfather*. Rosalind hadn't but was certain the two authors wrote a lot alike in any event. With some exasperation Wilson said, *"But how can you know?"* And with that Rosalind ushered the great man into the stone house.

On Mary's telling me this, I smiled, not only because Rosalind had been right without reading Puzo (though not the Puzo of those wonderful early novels) but because I suddenly recalled that Edwin O'Connor had probably cost my meeting Wilson. In the mid-Sixties I'd twice written Wilson at Talcottville. At the time I was totally oblivious of the literary scene and knew nothing whatever of the notorious printed post cards with which Wilson put people so abruptly off. The cards read, "Edmund Wilson regrets that it is impossible for him to:" after which he listed about twenty items it was impossible for Edmund Wilson to, including such choice chores as *judge literary contests, take part in writers' congresses, autograph books for strangers*, and the item that most likely would have applied to me had

Wilson checked it off and to my horror mailed it to me: *receive unknown persons who have no apparent business with him.* According to Mary these cards were no mere conversation piece and did indeed get sent; and once when my editor, the late David I. Segal, was writing me I learned that he had received one of the cards. When I proudly told Dave that Wilson had twice answered me, in longhand, Dave made me fetch the letters and show them to him, after which he sat, shaking his head wondrously, and said, "Goddam, Exley, what did you say to him?"

I didn't remember then and don't now what I said in those letters. I'd just begun to work seriously on *A Fan's Notes*, and I of course admired Wilson immensely. I wrote him because he was nearby, because we were "neighbors," because we were the only two "writers" in the area. When to my exhilaration he answered me, he explained he was leaving Talcottville the next day to return to Wellfleet for the winter but said he was listed in the Boonville directory and I should telephone him the following summer and we could arrange to meet.

In that year I read Richard Gilman's "Edmund Wilson, Then and Now" in *The New Republic*. Gilman took Wilson to task for having recently "substituted the superficies of literature for *its* real life" and for fifteen years having failed to mention any recent American novelists save Baldwin, Salinger and Edwin O'Connor. When I wrote to Wilson to take him up on his invitation I had no idea that he and O'Connor were friends, a friendship which had extended to a light-hearted collaboration on an unfinished novel about a conjuror, with Wilson and O'Connor "feeding" each other alternate chapters. Least of all did I understand anything of Wilson's fierce loyalty to his friends, and with a kind of numbing naïveté I made the mistake in my letter not only of agreeing with Gilman's assessment on this point but of asking Wilson how he could ignore so many recent American novelists at the same time he could straight-facedly praise "that guy who writes fat novels for Spencer Tracy movies?" In a single line to the effect that he came to Talcottville to concentrate on "a piece of work" Wilson now put me off. After swilling a six-pack for courage, I telephoned him and reminded him of his invitation. Wilson said he did not recall. My tongue thick with booze, I then read him his letter. He refused to acknowledge it.

"Who are you?" And there was no doubt that he meant was I someone of such eminence that I should be pushing myself on him.

"Well, nobody," I said. "Look, I'm sorry, *really sorry.* I shan't bother you again."

Before ringing off, the great man, in his cooing pitch, spoke his last words to me:

"Stout fellow!"

Wilson's routine at Talcottville his last two weeks was not markedly different from that of previous stays. To be sure, he was dying; but he'd known that for ever so long and to delay that death he'd been offered a pacemaker for his heart but had scorned it as a foolish idea inconsistent with his acceptance of Darwin's theory that nature knows best. A trained nurse, Mrs. Elizabeth Stabb, came to attend him three hours in the morning and came back to stay over on those nights Wilson was feeling worse than even that to which he'd grown painfully accustomed. Mrs. Stabb and Wilson had an easy rapport and soon had worked out a ritualistic exchange. Mrs. Stabb would tell him that having to charge a trained nurse's fee to attend such an exemplary and lovable character as he made her feel a thief.

"Would you take half?" Wilson would ask.

Mrs. Stabb would reply, "Would you?"

There was also the ominous presence of the green oxygen bottles that did not go unused. An "emergency" telephone had been placed on the card table in the northeast downstairs front room in which Wilson worked at a window opening to the distant Adirondacks. His daughter Rosalind Baker Wilson was staying within easy access to him in a yellow clapboarded house a few doors south of and a few paces from him.

During that fall in Wellfleet and winter in Naples, Florida, Wilson had completed a definitive edition of his classic *To the Finland Station*, had collected his fourth book of essays called *The Devils and Canon Barham*, and had put together his assessments of Russian writers from Gogol to Solzhenitsyn, *A Window on Russia*, in which writing on Nabokov he would continue the "feuds" by being astonishingly simplistic. At Talcottville he now tried to work daily at his memoirs or diaries of the Twenties he was preparing for publication in *The New Yorker*. He had an occasional glass of white wine (one likes to think of him "keeping his hand in"); he played Ravel on the phonograph, and he spent his final days reading—no doubt through the sound of the bulldozers—a volume of Housman's *Last Poems* which as a boy he'd given his Aunt Laura. As I have noted above, sixteen years before Wilson had with some wonder remarked the sense of his continuum—that with so many of his admired contemporaries gone to alcohol, insanity and suicide he could sit yet in that stone house surrounded by memorabilia of his boyhood—and he must now have looked on that ancient volume of Housman with something approaching awe.

On at least two occasions he "did the town." As he promised he would he took (was taken by) Mary to dinner at The Savoy in Rome, thence to see *The Godfather*; and in the company of his dentist's wife, his "other girl," the attractive Anne Miller of Lowville, he went to dinner at the Fort Schuyler Club in Utica, thence to see *The French Connection* in that city. Immediately struck by the coincidence that these had been the last two movies I'd seen, the ones with which I'd had so much trouble, I wasn't surprised to learn the evenings weren't successful and that Wilson had difficulty discovering what was happening on the screen—nor was he averse to annoying his neighbors by asking his "dates" aloud—and I wished I'd had a chance to tell Wilson that his difficulty wasn't so much his hearing or the damnability of his aging as it was something a good deal more profound: the generations at their inevitable cross-purposes.

On the Saturday night before the Monday morning of his death, when Mary came to do his mail for him, Wilson asked her to abandon that for a moment and go to Boonville for his newspapers, some hamburger steak (never simply hamburger, always hamburger steak) and some Neapolitan ice cream—Mary had to settle for black raspberry —for his supper. Mary had once chided Wilson for the pretentiousness of calling good old upstate hamburger "hamburger steak." He had good-naturedly accepted her chiding without rectifying the habit, and when later I read his delightfully cranky attack on the Modern Language Association in *The Devils and Canon Barham* and came across his notion that we should have been well rid of our oppressive Ph.D. system if "at the end of the First World War, when we were renaming our hamburgers Salisbury Steak and our sauerkraut Liberty Cabbage, we had decided to scrap it as a German atrocity," I saw for the first time how much this upstate Hungarian-American woman, with her high school education, a major in typing, shorthand and commercial subjects, had indeed helped, in some small but significant way, to shape and moderate Wilson's pedantic way of thinking.

Wilson was feeling down. The day before, his publishers, Farrar, Straus & Giroux, had sent the photographer Nicholas Sapieha from the Rapho Giullumette studios to photograph him, and Wilson was not unaware that though he had books coming out warranting such picture-taking

Roger Straus, Jr., might be seeking some "last images" of him. He had also just learned that the son of his long-time housekeeper and friend Mabel Hutchins had had an accident with his logging truck outside Syracuse and the early prognosis indicated he might lose the use of his legs. A few years before, Mrs. Hutchins' husband Everett, also a trucker, had died of a cerebral hemorrhage shortly after the strain of a long and tiresome haul, and in his boundless sympathy for the "mechanics" of Lewis County, Wilson had used the occasion to damn to hell and back the capitalist system that demanded so much of its workers for so little recompense. He also heaped scorn on the much-despised Internal Revenue System bureaucracy which, according to Wilson, pettily demanded of these drivers receipts from those innumerable diners where they drank coffee to stay awake, and alive.

Surprising for one who could "talk" whole essays, Wilson did not trust himself to dictate. In his fine, not always legible hand he scribbled his manuscripts and letters on lined yellow legal-size pads and Mary typed from these. Ordinarily when she was doing this Wilson sat slightly behind and out of view away from her. When he would hear the typewriter pause, thinking Mary unable to decipher a word or phrase, he would impatiently say, "What is it?" On this day, however, the watching and listening were reversed. Wilson's breathing was the most excessively labored Mary had ever heard it, her fingers were constantly freezing in the air above the keys, and she found herself repeatedly saying, "Are you okay?" "Are you all right?" The last letter she typed for Wilson was a note to Auden at his home in Austria, a "Dear Wystan." Wilson congratulated Auden on the cottage he'd been given by Oxford University and told him how pleased he was that Auden could live out his life comfortably and free from financial anxieties.

Wilson's lightly sardonic view of awards and grants was consistent with his Auden letter, a view that must appear blasphemous to most writers with their scrambling and backbiting to get anywhere near A Prize: unless the compensation was commensurate with the amount of work expended Wilson considered awards little more than patronizing pats on the back, and even if the remuneration were substantial he was amused and touched by the "prize-longing" he saw among his peers and obviously viewed it as a facetious waste of energies that might better be put to another "piece of work." On being awarded President John F. Kennedy's Freedom Medal in 1963 he wrote this two-sentence missive (and one cannot conceive another writer in America answering in the same way, certainly not one in trouble with the IRS) to the President of the United States:

"I am of course extremely appreciative of the award of the Freedom Medal. I am sorry that I shall be in Europe in September so that I shall not be able to be present at the ceremony."

Wilson was apparently happily unaware that without him there could be no ceremony. As a result President Kennedy sent an envoy to Italy and presented Wilson the award at our embassy in Rome. In 1966 a committee of the National Book Awards gave him $5,000 and a National Medal for Literature for his "total contribution to American Literature," but he did not attend the ceremony (where some of his peers were undoubtedly calling "press conferences" to damn the other judges' choices) and the committee was forced to send the check and the medal to the Fort Schuyler Club in Utica where with food and wine he accepted them among his friends and relatives, including Mary Pcolar and his daughter Rosalind. Wilson received awards from both the American Academy of Arts and Letters and the National Institute of Arts and Letters but in *Upstate* he seemed vague as to what precisely these institutions were. In 1968 he received from the Aspen Institute of Humanistic Studies the $30,000 Aspen Award.

Because the altitude of Aspen was eight thousand feet and Wilson's doctor deemed the thin air risky for Wilson's heart, and because the $30,000 was tax-free (a fact which would not go unremarked in Wilson's acceptance speech), Wilson could not go to Aspen but did agree to a small dinner at the Waldorf Astoria in New York City where, by William A. Stevenson, President of the Aspen Institute for Humanistic Studies, the award was given to Wilson as a "man of profound erudition" who "has effectively demonstrated that for a humanist, literature is an art as well as a medium for the uplift of mankind."

Novelist-historian Paul Horgan was present at the ceremony and tells me that "attached to it were details of such hilarity and temperament, fumble and grumble" that he wishes he could tell me about it, but that he one day plans to put it down in his own inimitable way. Mr. Horgan spoke at the ceremony. Citing Wilson's "hatred of humbug," and quoting the "terrible Samuel Johnson" to the effect that the "reciprocal civility of authors is one of the most risible scenes in the farce of life," Mr. Horgan, happily, and save for remarking a lifelong addiction to Wilson's books, chose not to embarrass Wilson with maudlin or fatuous praise and instead related his personal relationship with Wilson. In the Sixties Mr. Horgan had left his beloved New Mexico and come East to be Director of the Center for Advanced Studies at Wesleyan University, Middletown, Connecticut, where one of his chores was luring the distinguished men and women who would come there as yearly Fellows. Mr. Horgan immediately, and with that trepidation inspired by the reputation "the world's great have for being personally formidable," set out to "ensnare" Wilson and was unsettled by the "almost dream-like ease" with which he managed it, the agreement being struck over drinks and dinner with Mr. and Mrs. Wilson one Sunday evening at the Ritz in Boston.

During Wilson's year in Middletown the other Fellows remarked his extreme professionalism (he was at his desk all day every day) and also his courtesy, warmth, humor and gaiety—Wilson occasionally entertaining his peers with his much-remarked abilities as a prestidigitator with playing cards. On completing his day at his desk, Wilson took to drinking in a "crummy spot" on Middletown's Main Street, where he sat at a "banquette" behind the cash register and where he often invited his colleagues to join him at what he had promptly dubbed "The Ritz Bar."

In President Stevenson's remarks I recognize possible sources of "fumble and grumble." I don't know the extent of Mr. Stevenson's intimacy with Wilson but he twice refers to him as "Bunny," a sobriquet I've read, and also have had verified by Mary Pcolar, Wilson brooked from nobody save long-time intimates and such long-ago friends as F. Scott Fitzgerald and John Peale Bishop, a nickname whose derivation is even uncertain, one story having it that it was given him by his mother because of his early interest in magic (pulling bunnies out of hats?), another that he picked it up at the Hill Prep School in his teens, and a third that it was acquired at Princeton; a fourth version, no doubt apocryphal, was that it made humorous and indecorous reference to his youthful sexual capacities. Too, unless the program contains a typographical error, Mr. Stevenson calls Wilson's *A Piece of My Mind*, to me the most confessional of all his works, and in which Wilson documents his father's pathological chronic depressiveness and even implies that had his father not had the stone house to which he could retreat, and to which later in his life Wilson would also "retreat," his father wouldn't have endured as long as he did—Mr. Stevenson calls this book *Piece of Mind*, which save for the spelling might have been something written by *Doctor* Norman Vincent Peale.

In his acceptance speech Wilson is wonderfully brief and apposite to what precisely this "humanist" has been "up to" with his life. He admits right off to being "no good at making speeches of any kind." Hardly pausing for breath, he says that he is "immensely gratified that not a penny of the money that this Institute is awarding me will have to be contributed to the eight billion nine hundred million which are going for this horrible war"—Vietnam, of course. Wilson then says, as he has said elsewhere, that, despite readers who insist Wilson's main influence was Sainte-Beuve, it was Taine's *History of English Literature*, which as a mere boy of "about fifteen" he read for the first time in H. van Laun's translation. "He [Taine] had created the creators themselves as characters in a larger drama of cultural and social history, and writing about literature, for me, has always meant narrative and drama as well as the discussion of comparative values." Certainly no sentence could more succinctly, forcibly or subtly sum up Wilson's two undisputed classics, *To the Finland Station* and *Patriotic Gore*.

Wilson never won a Pulitzer, he never won an NBA for any single volume, he never won the Nobel (an award given to Sinclair Lewis and Pearl Buck!), and though for the amounts of money accompanying the latter he surely would have made the trip to Stockholm, it is also certain he never fretted about not having received it. In *Upstate* he touchingly relates that the last time he saw his friend James Thurber at the Algonquin Hotel in New York City, Thurber had become "haunted" by the Nobel Prize; and with the exiled Russian novelist Aldanov, Wilson felt he could see the Nobel hovering before Aldanov's eyes "as if it were the Holy Grail." And Wilson leaves us no doubt as to his droll contempt for the fatuousness of this kind of yearning. Wilson took his philosophy of awards from the aging sculptor who in his seventies suddenly found himself acclaimed and being rewarded accordingly.

When asked to account for this abrupt acclaim the old sculptor said, "The thing is to outlive the sons of bitches."

On Monday Wilson was returning to Wellfleet. His daughter Rosalind was driving him first to Northampton, Massachusetts, and he was looking forward to spending a few hours with his friend Helen Muchnic, the distinguished critic of Russian literature. Mrs. Wilson was meeting him there, driving him on to the Cape, and he was returning to Talcottville later in the summer. Upon his return he planned to have Mary drive him to Potsdam to visit some academic friends who were to be at the State University College there. When Mary finished the Auden letter and assured herself she needn't prepare Wilson's "hamburger steak" (Rosalind was coming to fix it), Wilson and Mary made their last goodbyes. Wilson meant to tell Mary the date he'd return for his trip to Potsdam but the date eluded him. He hesitated for a long time before adding "until" to the only words that Mary would afterwards remember:

"I shan't see you again . . ."

Nothing of Edmund Wilson save his ashes ever got back to Cape Cod. He died in the stone house of his mother's forebears a few minutes past six-thirty on the morning he was slated to return. Sunday he'd spent a happy day with his Lyons Falls friend, Glyn Morris, an ordained Presbyterian minister who hadn't for years practiced his calling, having forsaken it for a federal job bringing culture to the hinterlands. They had gone on a long drive through the Lewis County countryside Wilson so loved; they had joked and they had laughed. The following morning Wilson had

‡ 167

wakened just before six and had just been asked by Mrs. Stabb whether he first wanted his bed bath or his breakfast when he began to convulse. By phone Mrs. Stabb summoned Rosalind from down the street. "Your father is having a bad spell, come over." When Rosalind arrived in her night clothes, Wilson was in his chair (ready to do "a piece of work"?) and Mrs. Stabb was administering him oxygen from one of the green bottles. Rosalind then called Dr. Smith in Boonville. Wilson was unconscious when Dr. Smith arrived just before six-thirty and he never regained consciousness.

At three Mrs. Wilson arrived from Cape Cod. As Wilson had specified in his will, a brief service was held at six that evening. Only a few Talcottville friends and neighbors were invited, his dentist Ned Miller and his wife Anne, his nurse Mrs. Stabb and her husband, his housekeeper Mable Hutchins and her daughter Beverly, Mary and George Pcolar, and a few others. The only "literary" figure present was the historical novelist and neighbor Walter D. Edmonds, accompanied by Mrs. Edmonds. A few minutes past six Rosalind Baker Wilson opened the doors to the "long room" and said to the mourners:

"I think this is all of us. We'll not wait for anyone else."

When Rosalind said this Mary Pcolar was struck by how much the phrasing and even the tone resembled Wilson's. In the long room Wilson was laid out in his white iron bed—"as though he were sleeping"—dressed in his blue pajamas and maroon bathrobe. On the nightstand next to the bed Rosalind had placed Wilson's watch and his final reading, Housman's *Last Poems*. The mourners had sent or brought flowers and to these Rosalind added a bouquet of lemon lilies and a bridal wreath she had picked the night before. Save for one man who broke down, and some touch-and-go moments for Rosalind, the ceremony was very brief and very controlled.

168   ‡

As Wilson had requested, his friend Glyn Morris read from the first lines* of Ecclesiastes ("I communed with mine own heart, saying, Lo, I am come to great estate, and have gotten more wisdom than all they that have been before me in Jerusalem; yea, my heart had great experience of wisdom and knowledge. And I gave my heart to know wisdom, and to know madness and folly: I perceived that this also is vexation of spirit. For in much wisdom is much grief: and he that increaseth knowledge increaseth sorrow") and the 90th Psalm ("The days of our years are threescore years and ten; and if by reason of strength they be fourscore years, yet is their strength, labor and sorrow, for it is soon cut off, and we fly away. . . . So teach us to number our days, that we may apply our hearts unto wisdom"). Mrs. Wilson blessed herself in the old Russian way. Wilson's body was taken to a crematorium at Little Falls, and Mrs. Wilson then returned his ashes to Wellfleet.

The ceremony on Cape Cod was attended by about thirty mourners and was made only somewhat more impressive by the half-dozen literary figures in attendance, Lillian Hellman, Arthur Schlesinger Jr., Harry Levin, Jason Epstein, Roger Straus, Jr., Morley Callaghan. Wilson's friend of fifty years and Wellfleet neighbor of thirty years, Charles "Charlie" Mumford Walker, a classical scholar, delivered the briefest of eulogies. On finishing, Mr. Walker bowed his head, stretched out his arms, and said, *Shalom*, dear Edmund." Wilson's daughters, Rosalind and Helen, his son Reuel by Mary McCarthy, and his wife's son Henry then consecrated the ceremony by taking turns committing a scoop of the Cape Cod sand to the grave. At Talcottville Rosalind had unearthed four of Wilson's much cherished Lady Showyslipper orchids and she now planted these at

* Rosalind Baker Wilson says that in his will her father had asked for the last lines of Ecclesiastes, but it was the first lines that were read.

the gravesite. Edmund Wilson was no more. In many of the eulogies and obituaries it would be noted that American Letters would never again see his like. American Letters had of course never seen his like before.

10

My picnic proved a disaster. After we'd transferred the
food to the back seat of Mary's Impala we drove first to
The Savoy in Rome, going down through The Gorge be-
tween Boonville and Rome through hamlets with wonderful
names like Ava, a drive Wilson had much loved, especially
in the autumn when the green pines embracing the road had
so vividly contrasted with the reds, oranges and yellows of
the hard maples. Mary had asked me if I minded the car
radio, which Wilson had deplored—"Turn that damn thing
off!" She also told me that Wilson had forbidden her to

drive over thirty-five miles an hour but that as soon as he became engrossed in the countryside, or in his long thoughts, which was very soon, she could drive as rapidly as she cared to and he wouldn't notice.

Here Mary laughed. If Wilson had ever accepted that her new Impala had air-conditioning, he never gave indication of it; and though Mary had reprimanded him for "cooling the countryside" he continued to leave his window on the passenger's side open. At The Savoy we parked the Impala behind the restaurant on a shaded elm and willow bluff overlooking the Mohawk River, high and surging and mustard-brown now from the awesome June rains. As we entered the back door I noticed a sign over it that read PLEEZA NO PARKA DA BIG CAR IN FRONTA DA DOOR, or something equally absurd and corny, and I smiled to myself imagining what Wilson had made of that request.

Inside Mary went so unwaveringly toward a table at the front of the dining room that I was sure it must be her and Wilson's table and I began to see that some stand-in role I couldn't possibly fulfill was going to be expected of me. Coming down through The Gorge, Mary had told me how mischievous Wilson could be while ordering drinks. Like an upcountry yokel he'd begin by asking Mary if she'd care for a DIKE-her-*rheeee*. Later, if a waiter or wine steward asked Wilson to sample the wine, which wasn't always the case in these rural eateries, he often took the most absurdly delicate sip, made the most exasperatedly sour face, feigned gagging the wine back into the glass. While Mary repressed joyous giggles, he went through an entire spectrum of hyperbolic disgust and dismay before allowing, with a curt affirmative nod of the head, that the wine was after all okay.

When Mary ordered a daiquiri I knew I was expected to do the same, but I ordered a bottle of Schaefer instead. I wanted to explain to Mary my "problem," that I might not stop with a single daiquiri, but I didn't feel I knew her well enough for that and said instead it was too early in the day for me to get into the hard stuff. Then I almost broke up at my own preciousness, imagining, as I was, the reaction to that of the gang on Singer Island, my cold island, where for weeks at a time I'd gone from literal sunup to sundown on double vodkas and grapefruit juice. I wanted to talk with the owner Pat Destito and study the man who'd got away with addressing Wilson as "Dr. Livingstone, I presume." Mary had told me that Destito had returned from Florence not long before, and the last time he and Wilson had got together the two men exchanged some amusing notes on Italy. But Destito wasn't there and as it was Sunday it was likely he might not be there at all.

It was one o'clock, but the dining room was already filling up, mostly with families. The beer was compounding my tiredness, the atmosphere and the heady aromas of sauces from the kitchen were diffusing me with nostalgia. In our neck of the woods Sunday is pasta day, families such as those around us would be coming and going all afternoon, and I was thinking of all the Sundays I'd spent in my extended exiles from Watertown in futile search of a decent dish of macaroni and sauce. In Palm Beach County I'd given up and had long ago decided the Florida Italian didn't really know what pasta was (though he argued, perhaps rightfully, that the tourist didn't know and wouldn't in any event order anything but the blandest dish of spaghetti and meatballs—or pizza!). On my infrequent visits to Watertown over the years I'd spent half my time trying to convince the Canale brothers of the fortune their food would make them in Palm Beach County. Most of the Watertown Italians of my generation (I'd got to know them in high school playing football, the great equalizer) were, like the rest of us, living on tasteless packaged steaks and packaged processed cheeses, but Sunday was still their day to return to the Sand Flats to visit Mamma and *really* eat, and those of us who were unfortunate enough to have no Italian Mamma went instead to the Sand Flats to Canale's or Morgia's. Nor was this custom or this longing unique to exiled Watertownians.

Whenever anyplace in America I ran into an Italian from the Northeast, we got round to food immediately and it was axiomatic to our exchange that Italian cuisine was unknown outside our part of the country. (One theatrical little trumpet player in Denver swore convincingly to me that there were more authentic Italian restaurants in the twenty square blocks comprising the Newark "Guinea section" than there were in all of the South, the Midwest and the Far West put together. "*Meenkyuh*," he said. "You can do better in Providence, Rhode Island, than you can in all of Los Angeles County.") On Singer Island we had taken to making our own, creating the one other occasion on which I could be persuaded to leave the island.

When we could stand our drought from lasagne no longer, we threw our odd singles into a martini shaker on the back bar until we had accumulated forty or fifty dollars. Then Diane the day barmaid and I crossed the causeway and went to the House of Meats, thence to one of the supermarkets on U.S. 1. Shopping, Diane and I had a game we played, she the domineering forceful shrew and I the servile Milquetoast spouse. Diane owned the kind of totally impressive looks and figure (once coming down at five to join the cocktail-hour regulars I noticed that of six guys sitting at the bar five of them were her boyfriends!) that made my dopey cringing toadyism utterly credulous—as though I were one of those unhappily damned souls hopelessly enslaved to whatever it was this stupendous creature was doing to me in bed. As she pranced up and down the grocery-lined, shockingly lighted aisles, the cheeks of her marvelous ass bouncing with mighty purposefulness, I sorrowfully and meekly wheeled my little wired grocery cart at her tight-stepping feet, saying Yes hon, yes dear, yes mam. Into the cart Diane piled the cans of plum tomatoes, purée and paste; the cheeses, ricotta, mozzarella and provolone; the boxes of pasta; the meats, pounds of hamburger and Italian sausage, sweet and hot, a shank of veal or pork to flavor the sauce; the bell peppers, the mushrooms, the garlic. And as she did so she issued abrupt commands.

"Put the cart right here, Frederick." Or, "You stay here, Frederick. I'll be right back and I don't intend to be looking all over hell's half-acre for you!"

We had husbands, more sure of their places in the marital universe, shaking their heads in heartfelt rue and sympathy with my plight. One day a pimply, aproned, white-shirted, black-bowtied stock clerk, totally unnerved by Diane's stunning looks that so clashed with her brutal stri-dence, toppled over a huge triangular tier of quart cans of prune juice (a big item among the retirees in Florida). I didn't think Diane and I were going to make it to the car. When at last we did so and had the bags of groceries in the trunk, we fell into each other's arms in the front seat and clung to one another in riotous exhausting hilarity. The real fun had only just begun. If one fancies himself a chef, one hasn't lived until he's been turned loose on a completely equipped hotel kitchen, with its pots and pans and kettles, its sharpened knives and racks of seasonings glimmering all in place; and because Big Daddy liked lasagne as well as the next guy, and was besides a prince of a man, he'd turn Diane and me loose. All day long we simmered our sauce in a four-gallon vat (it has to go *tapocketa tapocketa* like a volcanic crater). And while I sipped at my vodkas and grapefruit juice, and with a great wooden spoon occasionally stirred the sauce, the regulars, drawn as to a magnet, came round and round through the swinging waitresses' doors. They would sample a spoonful of the sauce, go *Ahhh*, blow a French

‡ 175

chef's kiss, and make their suggestions as to what little touch would lift it to the airy regions of perfection. McBride's little touch was invariably "Don't forget the motherfucking bay leaf!" The lasagne was reserved for the second night. In a great steel dish five inches deep we'd make up and bake about forty pounds of it, then put it in the walk-in cooler to "firm" before rebaking it the following evening. On the first night, as a kind of mouth-watering foretaste of the heavens to follow, we'd cook some rigatoni or linguini and use the remainder of the fresh sauce on that.

And now, sitting with Mary, between the beer and the ambrosial aroma of those sauces from this other kitchen I was dying of some sort of Sunday afternoon blues, longing terribly for a bowl of pasta, wondering if I were ever going to escape that accursed island, and thinking that in my search for something of Wilson I seemed destined to be interrupted by things of the flesh, sex or pasta, always something, and feeling downright shameful about my loony banana bread and cream cheese sandwiches. Mary, too, had been rendered nostalgic by her Wilson-less return to The Savoy and her daiquiris. Remembering the good times with Wilson, she had begun a discreetly quiet but steady weeping, petite tears coming steadily out of those small incandescent eyes and making their way over those lovely Hungarian cheekbones where she daintily stayed and absorbed them into her hanky.

The funny part, she was saying, was that though Wilson loved going out he cared nothing whatever about food, and though he owned the epicurean lines of *le grand gourmet* she never accounted for his figure save by thinking it derived from the sedentariness of his monklike existence or understood the relish with which he talked or wrote about food. So that Wilson's own order might not seem ludicrous or insulting to the chef by comparison, or that he and Mary might not appear a couple of "real losers," he'd force Mary to order one of the grandest things on the menu—lobster, Delmonico steak, scallops—and then his eyes would sheepishly avoid the waitress's as he asked if it might not be possible to get him a fried-egg sandwich. Wilson's teeth had been bad for years, but even after his Lowville dentist Ned Miller had put them right, Wilson seemed not to care about the choicer dishes or because of his teeth to have fallen into the habit of softer foods. Moreover, Mary insisted, if Wilson had ever been as interested in food as those outings to restaurants in *Upstate* had conveyed she'd never been cognizant of it. "Sometimes he didn't even finish his fried-egg sandwich!"

Because of the past days' furious rains and the possibility of a washout, Mary chose not to attempt the old road that led up behind Flat Rock, and we went instead to a little stream, a tributary of the Sugar River, that coursed rapidly among hillocks in a miniature valley behind a weathered upainted barn. After first going through a barbed-wire fence, I was handed the styrofoam container by Mary, and then I in turn parted the barbed strands so Mary could get through. I decided to be "heroic" and stake out our passage down to the stream, finessing the cowpies as I went. On my feet I wore a pair of rubber-soled suede ankle shoes—what we used to call "fruit boots"—and as I suavely took my first bold step the ground was so dismally wet that my foot kept going breathlessly down and didn't come to rest until mud as oozy as baby feces came over the top of my shoe and into my sock. The night before I'd been reading Iris Murdoch's *The Unicorn* and had just got to the part where the heroine is told of some pathetic creature who had sunk and "drowned" in the bog and how as he was oozing excruciatingly down his hideous screams could be heard all through the night but no one had been able to get to him. Now I started composing my obituary for the Watertown *Daily Times*:

"Frederick Exley, 43, reported to be on a pilgrimage to Talcottville in search of the ghost of Edmund Wilson, sank and drowned in the bog of Lewis County yesterday afternoon. His bloodcurdling, cravenly screams were heard for miles about but no one was able to reach him. His companion, Mrs. Mary Pcolar of West Leyden, related it had been a horrible death and that Mr. Exley had not died well."

By the time we got down to the stream, Mary had abandoned all hope of keeping her feet dry. She removed her blue-heeled beige "pumps" and was negotiating the stream by walking right through it, soaking her pantyhose up to her shins. Even the ground where the sun hit was impossible to sit on, and we settled atop a great round rubber tractor wheel, junked in the middle of the stream and as imposing as the legendary table of King Arthur. Putting the diet black raspberry soda into the stream to chill, I gave Mary a breast of my Shake 'n Bake chicken, one of each of my various kinds of absurdly genteel sandwiches, and some sweaty Cheddar cheese, some plump red radishes, some celery, and so forth; and though I tried to eat I wasn't in the least hungry and was by then totally exhausted and heavy with despondency that my picnic had turned out so farcically. I sat on that part of the tire closest to the bank so I could rest my feet on the grass, as on an ottoman. To do so I had to stretch my legs uncomfortably, and Mary was trying to coax me to be less uptight.

"Take off your shoes and relax," she said. And I could tell by the way she said it that she thought me too "proper," one of those fearful of deferring to the spirit of a predicament. She was also making mental comparisons, and I could have guessed that these words would follow: "Mr.

Wilson never cared a darn how he looked. In fact, he never cared about anything and least of all what other people thought about him."

I pondered that. "Was he not vain about his writing?"

"Surprisingly, no. I'd done a little work on the manuscript and galleys of *Patriotic Gore* and naturally wanted to read it. But Mr. Wilson wouldn't hear of it." Mary said Wilson thought the book too scholarly, too much for the professors, and he felt Mary wouldn't understand or like it. "I think he lived one life for his books, and another for his family and friends, and he didn't want those two lives to clash, to come into conflict. I think he didn't want me to read anything of his that set him apart from—or above me, so to say."

"That's admirable," I said, "and understandable. Though I know some academics take *Gore* to be his masterpiece, it's not one of my favorites and it gets somewhat heavy-handed."

Then for the first time I told Mary about my teaching assignment at Iowa and how much I wanted to pay Wilson homage by reading *Hecate County* but didn't think the young people would take kindly to it. "Even though the course specifies fiction, I suppose I could do *To the Finland Station* and get away with it, as it reads better than most novels. On the other hand I don't want to go to a new job arrogating to myself a change of curriculum before I even start!"

Mary laughed. "God! Don't worry about *Heck-it*! If there was any book Mr. Wilson was vain about it was that damn thing. That was the one book he gave me to read, and kept asking me if I'd finished it, but he certainly wouldn't have been upset about your feelings. I didn't like it and told him as much. I said, 'This effort at fiction is just a silly attempt to keep your finger in every pie.' "

"*You did?*" I cried. "And what did Wilson say?"

‡   179

"He just laughed," Mary assured me, and I thought how admirable to unearth a writer who hadn't made an "adoration" of his work a condition of his friendship.

When Mary was driving me back to my borrowed Pinto at Boonville I remarked how difficult it was to feel badly about Wilson. He'd done precisely what he'd set out to do as a young man—"to get to know something about all the main departments of human thought"—he'd lived to be seventy-seven, he'd died a lot less uncomfortably than he might have done, and at the end he had in tasteful ceremonies been put on his way by his friends, his relatives, his widow and his three children by three different women.

"Even the fact that he'd managed to hold on to all of his children indicates a kind of—well, stunning integrity."

"Yes," Mary agreed. "I guess everyone he really cared about was with him at the end." She paused and wet her lips. "Except his cousin Otis. Otis didn't come to the ceremony at the stone house."

"He didn't!" Of all the people who had populated the pages of *Upstate* I had admired the portraits of Otis and his wife Fern only second to Mary, and I now said, "But why didn't Otis come?"

"I don't really know. I know Otis hasn't been feeling well himself. But I know, too, that Otis was bitter about the references to himself and his wife Fern in *Upstate*. It was all spelled out in a letter Otis sent to the Boonville *Herald*. I'll send you a copy."

"I hope you do," I said. Then I said, "I'm really sorry about Otis. *Jesus, I'm really sorry about Otis.*"

Otis Munn's and Edmund Wilson's grandmothers were two of eight attractive Baker sisters. At the birth of their brother and the ninth and last of the children, a son born with a harelip and a cleft palate, their mother died and their father (Munn and Wilson's great-grandfather), Thomas

Baker, "something of an operator," thereafter married the spinster Sophronia Talcott and with his eight daughters and deformed son moved into the stone house which Wilson eventually inherited from his mother. One of the sisters, Wilson's "attractive" grandmother Baker, married the Reverend Walter T. Kimball, the pastor at Locust Grove, a hamlet (from what remains it could have barely been that) three miles north of Talcottville, and by this marriage there were three boys (two of whom became prominent New York City physicians for whom the Kimball Memorial Hospital was named) and three girls, one of the latter of whom, Helen, married Wilson's father, a brilliant but pathological ("a chronic depressive") crack trial lawyer from Red Bank, New Jersey. Wilson's father became Attorney General of New Jersey, and in that capacity so impressed Governor Woodrow Wilson that when the latter moved on to the Presidency Wilson's father undoubtedly would have ascended to the Supreme Court (though Wilson claims his father was bored by the law) had a vacancy occurred during President Wilson's tenure.

At the same time, Otis Munn's "attractive" grandmother Baker, Adeline "Addie" (Wilson's favorite great-aunt), married "the quite well-off financially" Thaddeus Munn whose father had once owned 55,000 acres of timberland in Hamilton County. Thaddeus was an 1861 graduate of Union College, he returned upstate, married, bore Otis's father, also called Thaddeus, and served six consecutive terms on the Lewis County Board of Supervisors. As was deemed proper for an affluent landowner's son, Otis's father Thaddeus was accorded privileges, at an early age sent away to the best of schools, and so forth, but he became a drunk and a wastrel and "within a few short years he was able to dissipate the entire [estate] . . . with the exception of an income to take care of his mother for the remainder of her life . . ." and the heavily mortgaged farm "which had been in the family since 1836." At his father's death Otis was only thirteen but the bank agreed to carry the mortgage if the farm was deeded to his mother. At thirteen, then (and Edmund Wilson has by now had the privileges of his Princeton education, has been twice to Europe [once as a thirteen-year-old on the "grand tour" and once with the military in World War I, and was even then becoming known as a reporter and literary critic]), Otis is forced to roll up his sleeves and save the family patrimony, at which he will succeed admirably, now owning one of the larger and more prosperous dairy farms of Lewis County.

When in 1950, two decades before his death, Wilson suddenly became anxious about the family house at Talcottville, he said nothing to his mother ("she did not like other people to meddle with her property"), to whom the house now belonged, and decided to go from Wellfleet on Cape Cod, where he'd been living for ten years, and determine the condition of the place. Wilson had not been there in seventeen years, since as a writer for *The New Republic* he had in 1933 covered a strike by Boonville dairy farmers trying to get a fair price for their milk. And his return now is not only touchingly and regally ominous, it seems to herald his eventual trouble with Otis. As neither Wilson nor any member of his family drove a car in 1950, he engaged a taxicab in Wellfleet and had himself, Rosalind and his son Reuel chauffeured from Cape Cod to Talcottville. On his arrival Wilson went to his cousin Otis and the first mention of Otis in *Upstate* is also prophetic: ". . . Otis and Fern Munn . . . kept the keys to the house and acted as caretakers." From the beginning Wilson seemed disposed to relegate Otis to the role of retainer.

The following year, on February 3, 1951, Wilson's mother died bequeathing him the stone house and he had a new well dug; in 1952 he removed the Franklin stoves from all the bedrooms ("one designed like a cathedral") and sold them to Mr. Parquet for the Parquet Hotel in Constableville; he began to have the place cleaned—"books caked with thick dry white mold or dotted with spiderwebs"—and had a new furnace installed; and in his mid-fifties he appeared at long last to have come "home." His friend and contemporary F. Scott Fitzgerald had been dead a decade; by the end of the decade to follow his contemporary Hemingway will have decided against enduring and getting his work done and with an inlaid shotgun will blow away everything of his head save for the lower cheeks and jaws; and at fifty-five, as a "child" of that "hard-used and damned" generation Wilson will yet go on to produce, among other things, *A Piece of My Mind, Apologies to the Iroquois, Wilson's Night Thoughts, Patriotic Gore, The Cold War and the Income Tax, O Canada, The Duke of Palermo and Other Plays, A Prelude*, a revision of *The Scrolls from the Dead Sea* called *The Dead Sea Scrolls: 1947–1969*, the final book published in his lifetime, *Upstate*, the posthumous definitive edition of *To the Finland Station*, and also the posthumous volumes *A Window on Russia, The Devils and Canon Barham*, and his diaries of the Twenties.

It was the publication in *The New Yorker*, in June 1971, of two segments of *Upstate*, under the title "Talcottville Diary," that caused the break that appeared to result in Otis's not attending Wilson's memorial service. The break is odd and sad and not a little funny and one that could only occur among relatives where the blood runs scaldingly deep and with it the capacity to hurt each other at the marrow where ultimate grief resides.

In Wilson's childhood the stone house had been the place of summer reunions for the children and grandchildren of the various Baker sisters, and Wilson was hardly settled in in the early Fifties when in a kind of sentimental effort to recreate that happier, less complicated past (and because his wife could not at that time abide the place) he persuaded his cousin Dorothy Furbish Sharp and her husband Malcolm, a University of Chicago law professor, to spend the summer months near him at Talcottville. Malcolm Sharp had taught with John Gaus during the Meiklejohn administration at Amherst, Gaus was now a professor of government at Harvard, an authority on upstate history and geography who passed his summers at nearby Prospect, and Sharp introduced Wilson to Gaus. Wilson, the Gauses, the Sharps, and occasionally the historical novelist Walter D. Edmonds and his wife, soon made up the nucleus of an intellectual buzzwuzzie that came together for drinks, conversations, and long drives or outings. Wilson's relationship with Gaus was to last until 1966 when at a dinner party at the Gauses' there was an uncomfortable scene—"We had an unfortunate dinner at the Gauses'," Wilson records—in which Gaus espoused a reactionary position vis-à-vis the government's position on the Vietnam War, nastily implying that by abhorring the war as an obscenity Wilson was following the Communist line. Afterwards, having walked Wilson to his car, Gaus would not offer Wilson his hand. Wilson had also persuaded his cousin, the writer Helen Augur, to come back to Talcottville summers and this proves his undoing with Otis.

Although Wilson goes to great pains to describe Helen Augur as "a true Baker woman" with "a passion for managing," "an intellectual but not quite enough of one," a person so different from Fern Munn (and how one wished Otis had taken from the text these compliments instead of what he did take!) in that Helen Augur "seems to have no real relations with anybody, and is always attempting . . . to substitute for [relations] by importuning people with *petits soins* . . . to make them pay attention to her." He implies that Helen Augur is catty, domineering, unfulfilled and unhappy, with a "lack of self-respect" due to "her failure as a woman." In the *Upstate* excerpts that appeared in *The New Yorker* as "Talcottville Diary," Wilson recorded that "Helen does not like the Munns' bad grammar, and they don't, or I think that she thinks that they don't, understand her kind of literary work. She said to Paolo Milano"—an Italian writer and Queens College lecturer—"that Otis's father had married a 'peasant' "—Otis's mother, of course!—" and that Otis had married 'another peasant' "—Otis's wife Fern! And though in the diary Wilson defends Otis, Otis's mother and his wife Fern, we have no way of knowing whether Wilson did so to Helen Augur's face. Wilson writes, "She [Helen Augur] has no respect for the fact that Otis and Fern between them rescued the family from a tragic decline," and that Otis, in reaction to his father, never touched alcohol.

But this is too feeble. For though the Munns come through more vividly than anyone else in *Upstate* save Mary Pcolar, with a kind of unbecoming crotchetiness Wilson himself is not above recording foibles that make Wilson appear a lesser man than he was. Wilson continually extolls the Munns' virtues of industry, cleanliness, decency and family loyalty, and then abruptly he stuns the reader by deriding them for "no exercise of taste"—one wonders when Wilson expected Otis to cultivate that taste, at thirteen having set himself the task of supporting his mother and saving the farm from the bankers— "hardly any pictures—two heads of deer in the dining room and the Doig portraits of trout caught by Thad, two small bookcases, piles of newspapers, and among them, when I first came in, Otis was asleep on a big red couch. . . . Otis asked me whether he was 'stunk up' from the cow barn— they got used to it and didn't notice it."

In June, 1959, Fern and Otis drove Wilson to the Mohawk Reservation at St. Regis for some research that would eventually be used in his *Apologies to the Iroquois* and Wilson records, with a good deal less sympathy than he gave to the mumbo-jumbo rituals of the Iroquois in his book, that on the way Otis stopped at a cheese factory and bought a paper bag of cheese curd which Otis and Fern ate like popcorn. "Fern said to Otis, 'It squeaks good,' and Otis said, 'It squeaks good.' They were talking about the sound you can feel it making when you bite it. This means that it is of the right consistency." Certainly Wilson is here affecting an ivory-tower syndrome and might be a novice anthropologist who has just discovered a tribe of aborigines whose locomotion takes the form of "walking" about on the fingers of their right hands. Having grown up in Watertown, the largest city in the upstate region that holds interest for Wilson, I have as a "city boy" always been aware of the splendid small cheese factories in the area, have always known that many truck drivers and traveling salesmen carry on their dashboards bags of the curd they eat like peanuts, and that the test of the curd's "body" is that "it squeaks good."

On the publication of "Talcottville Diary" in *The New Yorker* Otis, a proud man, and rightfully so, protested this treatment in a long letter (September 15, 1971) to the weekly Boonville *Herald* (and *Adirondack Tourist*). Apparently Otis had hoped *The New Yorker* would publish it. Near the end of the letter he wrote, "I hope the New Yorker magazine will accept and publish my article because I strongly feel that I should be entitled to tell my side of 'Talcottville Diary.' " But *The New Yorker* apparently declined —one prays they didn't do so with one of their nastily arrogant and aloofly anonymous rejection slips—and Otis was forced to settle for the weekly where his "side" would at least reach his neighbors.

Otis begins by admitting that he and Fern are mentioned frequently in his cousin Edmund's diary which appeared in two installments in *The New Yorker* and that they—realizing their limitations—are pleased to have a part in the life of a genius. Citing these "limitations," he ironically invokes his cousin Helen Augur to the effect that the Munns have lost their education and have bad grammar. He also says that of course both he and his father Thaddeus married "peasants."

The letter here takes one of those nasty "family" turns by implying that at some past time Helen Augur had coerced their Uncle Tom, the stone house's then owner, into leaving the property to Wilson's mother (had Otis hoped for it?). Otis indicates that when his Uncle Tom was enfeebled, Helen Augur had the foresight to ask him to spend the winter with her in Milwaukee. Uncle Tom died shortly thereafter and the house went to Wilson's mother. If this is the kind of advantage that accrues to the educated, Otis then rues not having gone on to school. For all Helen Augur's "intellectuality," Otis says, her gardening took the form of cutting down the currant and gooseberry bushes which had been thriving for twenty years and as a result Wilson had to go without his berries for a few years. He follows with an attempt at humor which, though funny, is awkwardly written and charged with the hurt Wilson's references to him and his family must have prompted.

In his diary, Otis says, Wilson spoke of Fern walking in her high heels about the farmyard and through the goose manure; but as the Munns raised only turkeys Otis has been meaning to write to Princeton—Wilson's alma mater, of course!—and inquire by what miraculous chemical process turkey manure is transformed into goose manure. For all Wilson's education, Otis points out that Wilson himself is helpless in many respects. Citing Wilson's attempt to learn to drive years before, Otis claims Wilson got into a car and drove for miles "trying to probe the intricacies involved" in bringing it to a stop. As to Wilson's much publicized battle with the IRS, Otis says Wilson didn't file a return for years because Wilson assumed it was being taken care of by an attorney who had been dead for some time and that, in compliance with their demand for a yearly return, the IRS had received no monies from the hereafter. Being "uneducated," Otis says he has to fall back on his own resources and make out his own returns, as well as those for sixty or seventy of his neighbors.

Otis's bitterness surfaces when he points out that superior education had not prevented his father from all but destroying the estate and with it the family. Attempting to establish his heritage in America as every bit as ancient as Wilson's, he places the first known Munn in America as a soldier in the 1637 Pequot Wars in Connecticut. Otis concludes by saying that he is proud of owning a dairy farm he can leave to his children and implies that his life seems of more durable stuff than it would have been had he written a few lines of prose and poetry which is read and soon forgotten.

To Wilson, this latter must have been the unkindest cut of all, characterized as it is by that unfairness that only members of a family are capable of hurling at one another, for there was hardly a reference to Otis and Fern in *Upstate* in which Wilson's affection and admiration for them didn't come through.

And yet, when I read Otis's letter in the newspaper Mary had sent to me, I was made terribly sad and found myself wishing that Wilson hadn't published *Upstate*, wished he'd taken his cue from his own 1928 essay I'd read for the first time while waiting for Mary that Sunday morning, and instead of indulging his passion for reminisence—what Cheever has so marvelously called the "lust of arteriosclerosis"—he'd passed his final days sitting in judgment of contemporary writers, a judgment they all but begged for. And now, and as I'd done that day in Mary's air-conditioned

Impala, I found myself saying, "Jesus, I'm really sorry about Otis."

From Rosalind Baker Wilson I later learned that there was no need whatever to feel badly about Otis and her father. Had there ever been a break between the two men (and even in the face of the letter's bitterness Rosalind Baker Wilson would deny that any hard feelings had ever existed; but then, I soon learned that Rosalind Baker Wilson has one of those likable and naïve capacities to see things as they ought to be) it had ceased to exist at the time of her father's death. On the Sunday night before Wilson died, Fern and Otis had in fact been Wilson's last callers at the stone house. When Rosalind Baker Wilson helped him up from his chair by the window to take him into the living room to greet the Munns, Wilson said:

"Oh, that I should have come to this!"

After asking Fern and Otis to stay with her father until Mrs. Stabb arrived, Rosalind Baker Wilson said: "Goodbye, Father."

11

Rosalind Baker Wilson, Wilson's daughter and his eldest child by his first wife Mary Blair, is fiftyish. She has never married. Like her father she is short and fleshy, somewhat pugnacious of eye, formidably and imposingly eagle-like of brow, impatient and crotchety, and seems bent on conveying to people she isn't much impressed by EW's eminence— proudly: "I've only ever read two of his books, *Night Thoughts* and *Upstate*." Too, she goes out of her way to make those people interested in her because of their interest in her father dislike her. From a man who knew her well I once heard, "It's very simple—she hates her father." As it happened this was patently untrue. Although she had me constantly dancing to her selections, although if I persisted in what she chose to believe was "prying" into areas where I shouldn't pry—and in her scrupulous ferocious eyes these included almost any areas at all!—she was rude to the point where on two occasions I had to restrain myself from telling her to stuff it, although she refused to acknowledge my interest in her father as an interest worthy of me, I outlasted her and came finally, in one awful grief-wrought moment, to see how much Rosalind Baker Wilson's life had been bound up with that of her father and saw with rueful clarity the reason she could not bring herself to talk about him.

At Wilson's death I had written and sent to her at Wellfleet a note of condolence in which I said that I had been commissioned by the *Atlantic* to do a piece about her father, especially as to Wilson's life and days at Talcottville. I also said that to make money from another's bereavement seemed to me the action of a scoundrel, but that if she'd consent to see me and I published anything as a result I'd give the monies to the Red Cross (fat fucking chance!) or any charity she chose. I had not even really been "commissioned" by the *Atlantic*. That magazine's editor Bob Manning had been kind enough to let me use his publication as a means of introduction to Wilson's friends and neighbors in the hope that I might put down some words he could use, but I was so vague about my conception I don't think Manning was much impressed or—perhaps knowing something of my reputation for procrastination—that he really believed he'd see any words.

Not that it mattered in Rosalind Baker Wilson's case: she never answered me. When I told Mary this during my day with her, she suggested it might be because the note had gone to Wellfleet and might not have been forwarded to where Rosalind had been living for the last two years—

three doors down the street from her father's house in Talcottville. A few mornings after my ill-starred picnic I therefore telephoned her and was immediately struck with her volatile impatience. When I tried to explain I'd written her and the contents of my letter, she cut me dead by saying she was sure the letter would have been forwarded from Wellfleet. In any case it hadn't made an impression and she couldn't at the moment recall it. She would look for it. She then rang me off posthaste as she was in the process of cooking up "a good old-fashioned country breakfast" for some "good old friends" who had come to pay their respects. Two days later I received a curt and avuncular note reminiscent of her father's chilling post cards, in which she told me that it would be her policy not to talk about her father with anyone. Following so close on her father's death, the thought of further intruding myself upon her bereavement seemed to me distasteful in the extreme, but even as I came to that conclusion I couldn't help thinking she'd never escape being Wilson's eldest child and couldn't help smiling wondering what her reaction would be when the academics and the "authorized" biographers, lustfully rubbing their hands, descended on her, the stone house, and the eighty-odd inhabitants of Talcottville. Then abruptly I got another letter from her.

Rosalind Baker Wilson was in a grandiose snit, one that would have become her father in his most polemical moods. She began by telling me that if I were going to do anything on her father not to give the money to the Red Cross, to get as much as I could and have a grand time with it. Then she got on to what was so distressing her. Rosalind said she hadn't read anything on her father but the Watertown *Times* obituary. Now a friend had sent her Jason Epstein's piece in *The New York Review of Books*; and though it would be the last thing she answered, she had to write Epstein. For my perusal she had enclosed a copy of a letter she'd sent to Jason Epstein in care of the *New York Review*. Of all the obituaries and tributes I'd read I'd liked Epstein's best. I'd never heard of him—I heard later that he'd been (perhaps still was) a Random House editor—but there could have been little doubt from reading his eulogy that he and Wilson had been on easy terms. On reading Rosalind's letter to him I had to go back to the *New York Review* to find the part that had so aroused her ire. Of the ceremony at Wellfleet Epstein had written:

> There were moments of humor I had not anticipated: the young Orleans curate, like a scrubbed Beatle, shyly adjusting his lacy canonicals beside his blue Volkswagen in the Wilson driveway, as if he were hanging curtains; Edmund's daughters, Rosalind and Helen, his son, Reuel, and Elena's son, Henry, smiling as they took turns shoveling sand back into the grave where Edmund's ashes had been placed, like children playing at the beach. . . .

—an "indiscretion" which had prompted Rosalind Baker Wilson to tell Epstein that she personally found the way he lounged over the grave repugnant; that he'd tried to play head mourner while Wilson's insensitive children were caught up in gaiety. Again I read Epstein's words, but for the life of me I could not see in them any conscious effort to inflict hurt or, for that matter, any effort to suggest that the ceremony had somehow been less grand than it ought to have been. Again I telephoned Rosalind Baker Wilson. That she had even written and included me in what was obviously one of those family-friends' contretemps common to almost everyone's death seemed some reaching out to me, some unexpressed hope that if I were going to do anything on her father I might at least get things "right."

"I'm flexible as hell, Miss Wilson. I don't really know what I want but whatever I do probably won't be any more accurate if no one agrees to talk to me." I then pointed out that if nothing else came from our talking she could tell any future pilgrims that she'd already talked with one "writer, Mr. Frederick Exley"—I liked that!—and intended to talk with no more.

With what seemed to me a somewhat hostile guardedness Rosalind Baker Wilson at last agreed that I might come on a certain early evening for drinks and a hamburger—not "hamburger steak." If the weather were sunny—and the rains were continuing—Rosalind Baker Wilson suggested that I could take her to a "nice" restaurant on Bob Manning and the *Atlantic*. As I had no such expenses agreement with Manning, and as for months my wallet hadn't been used for anything but a frayed and forlorn container for expired driver's and current fishing licenses, I prayed the foul weather would hold. Fortunately it did.

I liked Rosalind Baker Wilson immediately. She wore a Mexican-style black cotton skirt, a white cotton blouse, she was barefooted and her sturdy legs were badly scratched as if she spent a lot of time going barelegged about the yards and fields of Talcottville or as if she were one of those odd blustering people who can't avoid the piercing edges of kitchen cabinets. She shook my hand with warmth and firmness, and laughed with a kind of shakingly bouncy and unaffected joviality that suggested she was genuinely pleased to see me. She began by apologizing for the sparsity of the furniture, which she said she was in the process of rectifying by having on order "some things." Almost instantly she ordered me to a typewriter at a card table in the front room and set me to copying for my "records" the brief eulogy Charles Mumford Walker had delivered at the gravesite at Wellfleet. Mr. Walker had been kind enough to send her a copy, and though it wasn't at all the kind of thing I wanted, I dutifully copied it off, trying to act as solemnly earnest as a cub reporter "getting the facts."

When I'd finished she gave me the rye and water I'd

requested on her asking me what I'd have, I took a sip, made a face, and doing a Jackie Gleason said, "*Boy, that's goooood!*" Rosalind Baker Wilson was not impressed by my fraudulent attempt at gentility, my trying to suggest the drink was a trifle strong for me. Because she, too, had never heard of me prior to my letter, she'd set herself to finding who and what I was—in her father's lexicon what finally I was "up to"—and she'd been told by Dan Wakefield, a mutual acquaintance, that though I spilt more than most people drank I was "apparently" still functioning. She read Dan's letter to me. I had no doubt Dan's words had prompted Rosalind Baker Wilson to open her portals to me, and on that score was immensely grateful, but I didn't much like the letter. My own "recommendations" are as simple as *he's okay*, or *he's a prick*, and Dan's letter seemed to me somewhat patronizing in tone, self-protective (in case I got drunk and puked in Rosalind Baker Wilson's lap she'd have been amply forewarned), and I made a mental note to thank Dan for the letter before I gave him a spanking.

When we were seating ourselves in more comfortable chairs, I brought the subject back to the Epstein piece.

"I didn't even know we were supposed to fill in the grave till the last minute. If Jason saw anything humorous about it, what he took for us playing a bunch of prancing idiots was probably bewilderment on our part. Besides, who wants to bury their father with some joker hovering about taking notes." She paused, those hawklike eyes narrowed ominously, she was preparing to strike. "*Jason!* You know what he is?"

"What?"

"*A con man.* You can quote me on that!"

She looked steadily at me, with no little defiance inviting me to write it down. Up to this point I hadn't written anything down. With Mary Pcolar I'd filled up an entire legal-size pad, had spent two weeks studying the notes, and had determined that none of them had really contributed to catching the flavor of the afternoon, least of all the quotes. With Rosalind Baker Wilson I'd hoped to chat and afterwards put down only what I could remember as having stood out, if I put down anything at all. Now she was giving me the eagle eye, and as I'd seen the results of Jason Epstein's incurring her wrath, I removed my ball-point pen from my shirt pocket and with timid, rather quaking dutifulness and feeling downright cretinous wrote *Jason Epstein— Con Man!* Giving me an abrupt, affirmative so-there nod of the head, one of those I've-said-it-and-I'm-glad gestures, Rosalind Baker Wilson then digressed to substantiate her "charge," looking pointedly at me to make sure I was getting it all down. And though I made my cute little ball-point go furiously on the page nothing but frantic curlicues was recorded. She said that when she was an editor with Houghton Mifflin Jason Epstein had tried to get her to release for a pittance—perhaps nothing—a bunch of her out-of-print titles for a Random House paperback line.

"I told Jason Epstein what he could do!"

"Certainly your father and Epstein were on amiable terms?"

"Huh! Who knows? To me Jason was just another courtier. Maybe father only used him. When there were any difficulties with his contracts, I know he used to kid Roger Straus, Jr., that he could always take his manuscripts to Epstein at Random House." Suddenly Rosalind Baker Wilson's eyes again narrowed furiously. "Jason! I don't want to talk about Jason Epstein!"

We sat in charged silence for a moment. Then she asked, "What have you done so far?"

"Not much. I've read all the obituaries and eulogies I could find. I've talked with a few people."

When she asked if I'd read anything I liked I said I'd liked the Wilfred Sheed piece in the *Times*, not daring to tell her I'd also liked the Epstein piece. She was skeptical that the Sheed piece could be any good and challenged me to illustrate what was any good about it.

"It was nice," I said, trying to get the conversation on a jollier plane. "Sheed began by saying that only a knave would profess to an intimacy with a dead man he hadn't had in life, he wanted it understood he had no preferred place among your father's acquaintances; then he went on to say your father had once invited him to Wellfleet for Christmas, how once invited he'd be damned if he'd let your father back out of the invitation, how he and his wife had got snowed in at Wellfleet, and the pleasant week they'd spent with your father, drinking and talking books on snowbound Cape Cod."

Rosalind Baker Wilson said, "You're darned right Sheed wasn't going to let Father back out of his invitation!"

I did not know what to say. Was she going to tell me that Sheed and his wife had forced themselves on Wilson during a family holiday? Certainly everything that was known about Wilson made this impossible, and I sensed some need on her part to preclude anyone's having had any significant place in her father's life. To point out subtly the implausibility of what she was suggesting—Wilson's opening his doors to anyone he didn't want to open his doors to—I told her I might once have met her father had it not been for my unfortunate mention of Edwin O'Connor. She really laughed at this, bringing her knuckles to her cheeks to steady her face, and slapping her bare feet on the floor.

"Don't worry about that!" she assured me. "Ed was a helluva nice guy but no writer!" Once she'd told a friend that if O'Connor had never written a word the loss to American Letters would be negligible, and as she'd then done for the friend, Rosalind Baker Wilson now lifted her glass ceilingward and in a gay toast said, "Sorry about that, Ed, wherever you are up there!"

After a few more ryes we had our hamburgers, and I had mine with the works—mustard, mayonnaise, ketchup, and a slice of raw. Rosalind Baker Wilson defied me to convince her I really believed she'd give me hamburger.

"Why wouldn't I believe you? It's delicious."

"I thought you'd really expect something fancy. When I say hamburger, you get hamburger!"

I told her I'd talked with Mary Pcolar and to my immense relief she nodded her head approvingly and said, "That's okay. Mary's okay. You can trust her." Feeling emboldened, I then mentioned another couple with whom I'd spoken. Rosalind Baker Wilson came boltingly off her chair. I literally shrank back in my own, my mouth went slack.

"God, that's a laugh. I'll make us another drink. You'll need one to hear this. *Take this down.*"

When Rosalind Baker Wilson came charging back from the kitchen and handed me another "good" one, she told me the couple with whom I'd talked were health-food quacks. A few days before Wilson's death they'd come to the stone house bearing bottles and bottles of vitamins—B_{12}, C, E, the gamut—and for a long time the man had sternly lectured Wilson on his health, giving Wilson directions for the taking of the pills, the numbers and times of day and so forth. Having at seventy-seven reached an age "off the charts" for a writer, having been told he hadn't much time left without the insertion of a pacemaker and having scorned the extra time under such clinically aloof conditions, living constantly within the foreboding arm's length of bottled oxygen, Wilson had apparently viewed the offer of yellow and orange capsules as the kind of unconscionable black humor that can only issue from people totally oblivious of their hang-ups. Aware of the generosity of their offer and out of politeness Wilson had heard the man to the near-interminable end of his lecture on robustness, and then Wilson had looked quizzically and ruefully at the man and with an ironical and theatrical longing had asked, "What about griddle cakes?"

I smiled, I choked on my drink, I roared.

"But that's not even it!" Rosalind Baker Wilson cried. "The ceremony at the stone house was no sooner over and the guy wanted his vitamins back! The body was still warm!"

"Aw, Rosalind," I said. "Now take it easy on me— take it easy."

"I *swear*, Fred. And he kept after me. I finally sent him a check for fifteen dollars and told him not to bug me anymore."

I said, "But surely people don't do those things."

"But surely people do," Rosalind said.

After that we relaxed with several more ryes, and Rosalind set me "straight" as to her father's relationship with her Uncle Otis. I then read Rosalind a few pages about her father I had in first draft, and to my unabashed pleasure she laughed heartily and asked if I thought Manning would publish it.

"I doubt it."

"I doubt it too. It's not the kind of stuff the *Atlantic* publishes. And even if they do they won't give you any money."

"I know nothing about their rates."

"Forget about it," Rosalind assured me.

From that point on she refused to say anything more about her father, anything at all, leading me to believe that if ever we met again the subject of Edmund Wilson would be taboo, and by way of thanking her for her kindness I asked her if she might not come one day to Alexandria Bay and let me take her for a ride through the Thousand Islands in my brother-in-law's speedboat. "Then I'll feed you some spaghetti or something." Rosalind had again become Rosalind Baker Wilson and would have to think about it.

Going out the door, I said, "I know it sounds corny but your father meant a great deal to me. More than writing about him, which will be done by the scholars and academics qualified to do so, I was hoping to have something of him to carry with me. Would it be awful of me to ask for one of his walking sticks?"

For the first time Rosalind Baker Wilson became angry with me. She did not think it would be in the least possible. Someone had already walked off with Wilson's favorite stick, and what if everyone who had admired him sauntered off with one or another of his possessions? More than that, I could see that I had disappointed her. Before even going to her I'd surmised that all her life people had undoubtedly tried to use her to gain access to her father and I could see now that with that one unfortunate request she'd relegated me to that damnable category. I smiled apologetically. "I thought I'd ask. I'm sorry." We said goodbye a final time. I did not think I'd see Rosalind Baker Wilson again. Afterwards, thinking what I'd asked for, I didn't much blame her.

To my great surprise I heard from her twice within the next ten days. In her first letter she told me she probably shouldn't have read Wakefield's letter to me but she thought it so complimentary she did. Rosalind Baker Wilson again straightened me out on her father's relationship with her Uncle Otis and now reiterated that if the two men had ever broken over the contents of *Upstate* it must have been a trivial business. On Wilson's death, Fern Munn had been the first to arrive at the stone house, and the Munns' flowers had been the first to come. Because of Otis's bad heart and the fact that the service was at milking time she had telephoned Fern Munn and specifically requested they not attend as she didn't want Otis put under the strain.

Rosalind Baker Wilson then implied that her disparagement of the health-food addicts hadn't been prompted by grief, any distraught condition brought on by her father's death, or the amounts of rye we were consuming that evening. She assured me that the wife had been even more boorish than the husband, the wife worrying about a paperback she'd left with Wilson. Rosalind Baker Wilson said she was surprised the couple hadn't asked for the "inlays" in her father's teeth. Her last line informed me she was looking forward to a boat ride if I was still game. I telephoned her immediately and we made a date for a week from the upcoming Friday.

In the week Rosalind Baker Wilson was scheduled to come I had another letter from her, a carbon copy of a letter she'd sent to Bob Manning at the *Atlantic*. Apparently she hadn't been as offended with me as I'd thought and had now decided to "champion" me. In her letter Rosalind Baker Wilson told Manning—and I smiled sadly thinking it'd be the first and last time Manning got tied up with a loony like me!—that I was uncertain he'd publish what I wrote, that she was very spoiled where editors were concerned, used to letters of introduction, and so forth. She then told him she'd heard nothing but good about my first book, that I had been considerate, and that she could tell from the pages I read her I was a talented writer. She said she hoped Manning published me and that he paid me a lot of money, which he probably wouldn't—that is, pay me a lot of money! Oh, Lordy, I thought, had Manning ever intended to publish me, he must be having serious second thoughts by now. On my copy she had added a postscript in ink in which she said that she hoped her letter helped me. That, of course, was a matter of opinion. But I promised myself that, grit my teeth if I must, I wouldn't bring the matter up when Rosalind Baker Wilson came for her boat ride.

In the early afternoon Rosalind Baker Wilson arrived in rain squalls. She was wearing a blue cotton dress with a flare skirt, ocher ruffles at the cleavage and at the sleeves more ruffles and little ocher bows. She'd brought from the cheese factory at Lowville a five-pound wheel of Cheddar for my brother-in-law, as it was his boat we'd be using. For me she had a tin of fifty Turkish cigarettes, which I opened and started wolfing then and there, not having tasted such a robust smoke in the twenty years since I'd worked with a guy whose father had sent him cartons of Picayunes from New Orleans. Almost immediately Rosalind Baker Wilson seated herself in the big easy chair in the front room and asked if it was okay (it was) to remove her tennis sneakers. I had some Frank Sinatra albums on the stereo, had fixed some rye and waters for her and my mother and was telling her that if the weather didn't clear we'd never that day see the islands. In her letter Rosalind Baker Wilson had told me that the longest boat ride she'd ever had hereabouts was a half-hour tourist ride and her disappointment now was profoundly obvious. I quickly proclaimed, "Think positively!" Then I turned to my mother and for emphasis said, "*Everybody think positively!*"

Attempting to leaven my faux pas of having asked for Edmund Wilson's walking stick, I then chidingly gave Rosalind Baker Wilson hell for not bringing me one of them, sure that she would detect in my kidding tone that it hadn't really meant that much to me. But she was without subtlety when it came to impositions regarding her father, and to my red-faced uneasiness she took my chiding seriously and again became upset and huffy. "But, Rosalind Baker Wilson," I protested, "I'm only kidding, for Christ's sake, *only kidding*."

That was one of the occasions I almost told Rosalind Baker Wilson to stuff it. Thereupon my mother, who lacks subtlety on most scores, jumped into the breach and said that if I really wanted to appear a dandy and buffoon and carry a walking stick about Iowa City I could have the silver-handled, hand-tooled one that had been owned by my Great-grandfather Champ. When she went off to the storeroom to fetch it I took her drink to the kitchen, poured most of it out, and diluted the rest of it with water.

My mother cannot drink, has never been a drinker, she does not know how to drink, and yet she had this nutty compulsion to the social amenities which makes her feel she ought to do what everyone else in the room is doing. An irreverent friend of mine once characterized it by saying, "Old Charlotte's got a lot of heart. She really tries to hang in there with the big folks." Charlotte's trouble is that she understands none of the niceties of highball sipping, and she pops off a drink as if it were a glass of ice water and she'd just come from weeding her flower beds on a sunny, oppressively humid day. After three drinks she brings her elbows up on her knees to steady herself, and without saying anything lets her eyes drift from speaker to speaker, as if she were politely listening to native chieftains converse in Swahili. Sooner or later she finds her way to her bed. On this day, however, I had not only to entertain an already disappointed and huffy Rosalind Baker Wilson but I was counting on "Old Charlotte" for a chicken and dumpling supper and wanted her sober and out of bed. Outside it continued to pour, and the three of us drank and listened to Frank Sinatra and examined Great-grandfather Champ's silver-handled, hand-tooled walking stick. I made sure I mixed the drinks so I could prevent Charlotte's going dodo-eyed and coming on like Dopey Dildocks.

At four, when I felt a little dodo-eyed myself and there was still no sign of the rain's letting up, we drove to the camp on Dingman Point and I persuaded my nephew Ed, who knew the river better than I, to take Rosalind Baker Wilson, his mother (my sister) and me on a ride through the islands. Ed was an all-league high school halfback, and at seventeen he owned the swaggeringly intrepid way of that breed. I was sure the rains and the poor visibility held no wariness for him, and as he'd just come in off the river with a couple hoodlum footballer buddies he couldn't very well claim he wouldn't be caught dead out there on a day like this. Still, I could see that he thought we were all tetched and that the Point might better be named Dingbat. When I looked at Rosalind Baker Wilson to see if she'd caught Ed's attitude, I could see that she hadn't and wouldn't have been dissuaded if she had, so much was her heart set on this ride. The speedboat, a *Classic* (that, it isn't!), was a small inboard but the front half was securely battened down with canvas. Rosalind Baker Wilson had scorned a football parka I'd offered to keep her dry, and I assumed she was going to perch under the canvas in the cockpit and look out the plastic windows. I donned one of those hotshot royal blue parkas, with INDIAN RIVER CENTRAL lettered in white on the breast over the heart, and grabbed a six-pack. The four of us boarded, Ed started the engines and, shaking his head in sympathy with our dementia, roared off on the oddest boat ride I've ever had.

Rosalind Baker Wilson not only refused the canvas shelter of the cockpit but stood exposed aft in the boat, rocking uneasily back and forth on her sturdy scratched legs while the rains beat relentlessly against her, soaking her blue and ocher dress and gray-tinged hair so that both cloth and hair lay against her like seaweed. For the life of me I don't know what Rosalind Baker Wilson was up to. Perhaps it was her way of telling us that she knew it had been terrible of her to insist on a ride on such a day as this but wanted us to see that she was by way of enjoying herself immensely. Perhaps she was telling us that when all was said weather was no more than a condition of the heart, and that if we *really* looked as we sat huddled cravenly in the cockpit, throbbing to the roar of the engines, we'd be able to see that back aft where Rosalind Baker Wilson stood the sun was shining.

Compounding everything, Ed was expecting one of his cheerleader-type girl friends (oh, my satyriasis!) at the camp and to get the adult lunacy of this "tour" over as quickly as possible was traveling at speeds that gave the already frightful rains a near-hurricane impact so that they appeared to pound on Rosalind Baker Wilson's face, now thrust defiantly out in this forbiddingly stubborn and admirable attempt to enjoy herself. I think I never liked a person as at that moment I liked Rosalind Baker Wilson. At a severe nudging of my arm from my sister, indicating I should join my "guest" aft, I reluctantly snapped up my windbreaker, uncapped another can of Budweiser, sighed, took a deep breath, stepped out of the cockpit and was almost immediately drenched. Adapting myself to Rosalind Baker Wilson's Viking posture, I thereupon thrust out my jaws and began pointing out the various islands and land-marks, hardly visible through the rains pounding our faces a fierce pink. We stood together rocking precariously back and forth, back and forth, while to my barely seen sightings Rosalind Baker Wilson exlaimed "marvelous" and "great" and "lovely" and apparently everything was as wonderful, wonderful, wonderful as it could be.

Before supper there were daiquiris and more rye and chilled cans of beer and then we enthusiastically engaged our chicken and dumplings, tossed salad, bean salad, asparagus, green corn, olives and celery, and homemade strawberry cheesecake. By then I was very tipsy and do not know who was there when it happened; in any case I'd thought I'd told everyone that Rosalind Baker Wilson did not like to talk about her father. Not knowing who was present at the table had nothing to do with my being slightly inebriated. Ours is a family whose various doors are by tacit agreement left open to one another, and because it was Friday, the lead-in to a weekend of yet another waning season, nephews and nieces, brothers and sisters, boyfriends and girl friends, aunts and uncles, all having heard the magic words *chicken and dumplings*, descended on my mother's house, some eating and moving on, whereupon their places would be immediately usurped by someone else, others lingering at the table to smoke, drink, talk and laugh. Abruptly someone told me to explain to Rosalind Baker Wilson what I'd done on the publication of *A Fan's Notes*.

"What do you mean—*done?*"

Someone said I should tell her how I'd gone up to Wellfleet to await publication, thinking my proximity to Wilson would bring me luck.

"No, no, no!" I protested, the blood already rising to my cheeks. "Rosalind doesn't want to talk about her father."

"This isn't about her father. This is about *you.*"

To my furious discomfort someone then started telling the story, and telling it all wrong, and I found myself with no choice whatever but to interrupt and try to tell it "rightly" and in such a way as to cause myself as little shame as possible. Eyes cast downward at my drink, my cheeks inflamed, my voice hesitant, my tongue swollen, I did not tell anything like what follows because Rosalind Baker Wilson, sensing immediately what I was driving at, prevented my detailing the story.

Shortly before publication of *A Fan's Notes*, my wife left me. Barely able to abide my male chauvinism under normal conditions, as publication neared my anxiety increased tenfold and my disease of piggery took the form of staying away from home for days at a time, drinking heavily with the boys, and fucking waitresses, of reverting to nothing so much as once again being the perfectly "ineligible" bachelor. Thereupon my wife took off. Bewildered, hurt, alone, outraged (oh, I was beautiful in indignation!), I suddenly hit on the idea of climbing into my beautiful Chevrolet Nova, driving to Wellfleet, renting a weathered shingled Cape Cod cottage, trying to put down the early pages of *Pages from a Cold Island*, and waiting for the reviewers to notice me, in some odd way honestly believing that within the narrow orbit of which Wilson was the nucleus nothing really bad could come to me.

Which is what I did. It was early fall but already the Atlantic winds were cold, the waves wolf-gray and breaking frigid white, the beaches too soft to walk on. Instead I walked every afternoon—on those days I couldn't work on *Pages from a Cold Island* walked all day—on a high road overlooking the sea between the lookout pavilions at South Wellfleet and Wellfleet, day to day watching the sea transform itself from wolf-gray to slate-gray, the foliage of the shrubbery and stunted trees and vines of the Cape go through their autumnal change of colors. At night I had roaring fires in my stone fireplace, ate beans out of the can, and with the windows flung open to the incredibly stirring briskness of New England autumn fell asleep to dreams of a fame that never came. Mustering my courage, I drove into the village one day and inquired for the whereabouts of Edmund Wilson's domicile. At both the post office and the stationery–dry goods store people refused to admit they knew where it was. From their attitude they were obviously under orders not to disclose Wilson's homesite. By telling a gas station attendant I only wanted to look at the place I was finally told how to get there. I didn't go. The attendant had added, "If you see him, for Christ's sake don't tell him I told you how to get there"; and I thought that if Wilson so jealously guarded his privacy as to inspire trepidation in a grease monkey I'd best respect that privacy. And I continued to take my long walks, to look into my roaring fires and think long thoughts, and to wait for the fame that never came.

I don't know how much of this I told to Rosalind Baker Wilson—not much, I think. It seemed I'd just got into the story, head down, hesitant, groping, when my entire being was shattered by this wail—absolutely Biblical, it was!—and I looked terrifiedly up to see Rosalind Baker Wilson exploding in tears, coming apart. Straight up from her ladderback chair she came, knocking the chair into the china cabinet as she did so, and tearfully, wildly, blindly she made her way round the end of the table and fled into the living room, where for many moments afterwards, while we sat frozen at the table and stared astonishedly at one another in stony distress, we could hear, as though piercing our very beings, her heartbreaking, convulsive sobs and I found myself thinking how much different my "elegy" would be from Jason Epstein's larksome affair. When Rosalind Baker Wilson at last rejoined the table, and there would be no more talk of Edmund Wilson—indeed, from me there would never again be any mention of Edmund Wilson to his daughter—she said, "Excuse me, I'm sorry," and still looking downward in shame, I wanted to say that I was sorry, too, but I could not at that moment trust myself to say anything at all.

12

Tom Quinn is a friend of Norman Mailer, an ethereal condition doubtless demanding no little stamina. He is a successful young stockbroker, but doesn't much look it. When he was in the Marines he was the East Coast heavyweight boxing champion of the Corps. In Mailer's serious and campy, farcical and refreshing, intelligent and paranoid bid for New York City's mayoralty, he tried unsuccessfully to con his campaign manager, Joe Flaherty, into adding Quinn to the Mailer–Jimmy Breslin ticket. With his financial background, Quinn was to have been city controller. Flaherty's attitude was "Are you shitting me?"

Despite his fibrous neck, his thick and heavy shoulders, and the timidity his overall massiveness inspires in one, he has an Irish moon face out of which there issue continually, like sluice from a tropical sky, too many smiles, too many laughs, too many songs to convince one he owns the barbarousness needed to pound men into oblivion. Had he another thirty pounds one might picture him donning a 50-series green-and-white jersey, removing his partial plates, and on autumn Sunday afternoons pulling out of scrimmage to lead Emerson Boozer round the right side, erasing with effortless ado the opponent's left linebacker. Yet finally there is an easy joviality about Quinn which belies even this. If one were what he seems, then Quinn is a blustering, cock-a-hoop saloonkeeper in the Throggs Neck section of the Bronx; or a recently ordained, sanguine and rock-ribbed Jesuit striving mightily to erect another Boys Town in the ghettos of South Chicago. It was through Quinn that I got my first glimpse of the New York literati at their ease—or what I bird-wittedly believed would be their ease—and though I have elsewhere indicated that it was innocuous literary chitchat that set my stuttering Nova in its creaky motion back to Singer Island, nothing is ever that simple and it was actually a scene I had with this smiling Irishman—he wasn't smiling then—that set in motion the forces that prompted me to bid the New York literati a relieved adieu and to head back to where I belonged.

I had already seen the literati in quite another light. That spring I had received from John Cheever, in his capacity as chairman of the grants committee, a letter stating that I'd won the National Institute of Arts and Letters' Richard and Hinda Rosenthal Award for "that work which, though not a commercial success, is a considerable literary achievement." (With ironical sweetness Cheever's letter arrived within moments after I'd learned I didn't win the National Book Award—one had hoped, one had hoped.) In truth, until I got Cheever's letter I'd never heard of the National Institute of Arts and Letters, not to mention the Richard and Hinda Rosenthal Award; the world inhabited by writers stood as far removed from my consciousness as those inhabited by bird watchers or transvestites; I didn't know how one attired himself at such a function (the annual awards presentations); or whether I was expected to issue a few mellifluously enunciated words in acceptance. I found my nostrils dilating ominously at the prospect of a woefully uptight afternoon. I did not in brief want to go.

But the award carried with it some badly needed dough and I wasn't sure how long it would take me to get—or if indeed I would get—the money without attending. So it was that some days later I donned a newly purchased Paul Stuart summer suit of a rigidly cut and demure gray and went and got my first peek at the literati, if not ill at ease, at their austerely proper best, with legs crossed formally at the knees, hands crossed primly at the groins.

A luncheon was held prior to the ceremony for award winners, members of the grants committee, and officers of the Academy and the Institute, but certain that wine would flow in profusion and unable to trust myself to remain temperate in such patrician company, I eschewed it, arriving only moments before the presentations. To the relieved sighs of an anxious, tight-stepping little secretary—"We'd given up on you," she said severely—I was escorted into an impressive sitting room and left alone smoking cigarettes on a huge fawn-colored leather divan. Presently by twos and threes the room began filling up with luncheon guests—I spotted Robert Penn Warren, Lillian Hellman, Styron, Eudora Welty, Tennessee Williams, Ralph Ellison, DeVries —and, growing uncomfortable, I rose and narrowed in on George P. Elliott, who was there to receive one of the many grants being given that afternoon and was the only writer in the room I knew. Elliott disliked me intensely (he'd once made that very clear to me), but we had the same editor, and Elliott is a gentleman (the reason he dislikes me, I expect). I'm sure he sensed my alienation from the group and he kindly and not too self-consciously exchanged pleasantries with me.

In time we were interrupted by novelist and *The New Yorker* fiction editor William Maxwell. He introduced himself, said he was glad I'd finally made it, and explained that when my name was called it wouldn't be necessary to say anything, that I should just step downstage center to the lectern, get my hand shaken, and get out of the way as quickly as possible. As Maxwell talked, I found myself repressing a terrible urge to giggle. Because even in dress and manner Maxwell seemed so to represent *The New Yorker*, the very apex of literary probity, all I could think of was what his reaction would be if I asked him, seeing I couldn't say anything, whether it would be okay if I measured off a chunk of my arm and made a *fungoo* sign at the audience for all the copies they hadn't bought.

Now abruptly, as though we were nastily refractory sixth-graders on an outing our schoolmarm had already decided was an execrable boner, we were roughly herded onto a stage which had been set up in five or six wooden tiers, somewhat like the rickety stands at a hicky high school so undermanned they play soccer or six-man football. We located the seats to which we'd been assigned and found ourselves staring out at a lovely, dignified little candy box of an auditorium, with a gallery that appeared to sweep up and away into a chandeliered ceiling and ornate red and gold boxes overhanging the orchestra, the entire house jammed now with eight hundred of the radiant folk or whoever it is that finds their way to these fetes. For comfort I found myself searching for the faces of my editor, my agent, a childhood chum, and my brother Bill, a (is one ready for this?) full colonel, perhaps even a brigadier by now, in the

U.S. Army Intelligence, these people having been given the four tickets I was allocated. I was unable to isolate a single one of them.

I must here add that with but a few moments left in the ceremonies I saw my agent sneak into the back of the auditorium. She was impossible to miss: she wore a simply cut, sleeveless linen dress of canary yellow, with canary yellow pumps; her lovely black hair was flopping fetchingly around at shoulder length. I watched her creep in, crawl over a half-dozen people in the back row, aggravating them in the process, and slip with something very like stealth into what must have been the only vacant seat left. At the party afterwards I said, "How'd you like my acceptance speech?"

She pondered that a moment, her eyes narrowing, the blood already beginning to rise, then tried, "Well, like everything you do, it was different."

"Did you like the part about yourself?" I was really out to do it to her.

After a protractedly painful pause, during which the blood became a furious constant in her face, she said, "Hey, give me that part again—it was so hard to hear from where I was sitting."

"*You don't remember?*" I feigned a grimace of irritation. "I thanked my mom and pop; Miss Brainard, my fifth-grade teacher, who introduced me to the works of Lewis Carroll; my editor; and then finally, and most of all, my agent, Miss Lynn Nesbit, who stuck by me through more rejections than it makes me comfortable to recall but whose faith has instilled in me an adoration for her quite beyond my feeble powers to convey."

"Oh, Ex," she cried. "You didn't!"

"You're fuckin' *A* I didn't. I didn't say shit, and you weren't even there to hear the shit I didn't say. Where the hell were yuh? On the long-distance reassuring Charlie Portis what a genius he is 'cause you got him three-quarters of a mil so Big Duke Wayne can play the lead in his folksy *True Grit?*"

Nesbit gave me a sucker shot to the relaxed humerus muscles of my right arm, one of those female knuckle jobs done with the clenched index and middle fingers, and I carried the black and blue mark—turning purple, then that hideous purple-yellow, then yellow—for days.

Since I couldn't locate any of the people I'd invited, I zeroed in on a lovely blond woman in the third row, dressed in an elegantly tailored pants suit of an off-white shantung, and suspended from a gold chain about her regal throat a pendulous gold medallion the size of a one-egg cheese omelet. It was she who was a recurring cliché in that genius Groucho Marx's movies, the tawdry climber or, as they are known to belletrists, the camp follower. On first getting seated I'd noticed her directly, not only for her disarmingly well-groomed good looks but because her head, bearing her wide-set incredibly glistening violet eyes (contacts? I wondered), was sweeping so frenziedly back and forth she appeared desirous of taking in everyone on the stage simultaneously, her movements a parody of the aficionado at a tennis match. When at last her pulse simmered and the heavy medallion at her breast settled into the sea calm of her cleavage, she consulting her program, and literally began pointing out various people to her escort, vulgarly jamming the air with an exquisitely manicured index member, while at the same time her full pouty mouth formed itself into what can only be described as erotically suggestive orifices out of which there issued with each pointing a repressed but distinctly distinguishable little orgasmic yelp—yelp, yelp, yelp—which prompted me to smile inwardly and wonder if her bikini frillies weren't growing damp.

I'd focused particularly on her for two reasons. My

paranoia has never permitted me to be an eyeball-to-eyeball man; I view my eyes as an open window through which one too facilely discerns my transgressions; to the unavoidable discomfort of my colloquist my eyes evade and I shyly isolate a chin, a forehead, an ear; and unable to confront a person singly I was hardly up to taking on an entire audience. Hence, in the highly unlikely event that anyone was looking at me, and rather than stare distantly off at the façade of one of those red and gold boxes and risk being taken for aloofly indifferent, I chose her as a coordinate as inanimate as a cowpie for, despite the shrill exuberance of her movements, I knew that my name would mean nothing to her, that no manicured digit would be hurled in my direction.

Ironically, and not in the least untypically, her escort was a strikingly handsome man, a country mile more prepossessing than any of us on the stage, "artists" never having been remarked for their matinee-idol physiognomies; and indeed if those around me were anything like myself—and I suspected as much (it has something to do with being locked up too much with one's silent self, with becoming so oppressively inward that the least tummy rumble triggers horrendous premonitions of colonic cancer)— they were, whether scrubbed and benecktied for the afternoon's occasion or not, a grubby, scurvy, obsessively self-examining bunch, much given to toenail picking, ass and crotch scratching, farting, armpit whiffing, nose picking, penciled probings of the ear followed by minute examinations of the excavated wax, and even whacking off, it being known of no less than the great Flaubert that he used to pull his pollywogger right at his desk, with insouciant aplomb wipe the viscous semen on his velveteen smoking jacket, and go blithely and resolutely on with his masterpiece about the sappily romantic Emma.

"No, my princess," I thought, "you wouldn't be interested in any of the weirdos up here—you just think you would!"

Rather more than anything I was thinking how nice it would be if—in retaliation for the unforgivable assault on his manhood her shameless behavior must be causing him—her escort took it upon himself to repress one of those yelps on his own, if, for example, he rolled his own program into a phallic pipe the size of a penis in a state of inflammatory erection, waited for the initial signal of the manically extended finger, and precisely at that moment her attractively petulant mouth was forming its moistly hot oval poised to emit its goose-pimple-inducing little moan-yelp, he jammed it home! The other reason I selected her as an unresponsive —at least to me—coordinate was that prior to going onstage I'd promised myself, on pain of a later self-excoriation, not to rubberneck about and stare hot-eyed at any of my idols, especially Nabokov, whom I hadn't yet seen but who according to the program was that afternoon to receive the Award of Merit Medal for the Novel.

The State Department's George F. Kennan, the president of the Academy on the basis of his memoirs, I guess, made the opening presentations and remarks, assuring the uninitiated in the audience that the laurels about to be bestowed represented the highest a nation could pay its artists, and I don't know how those about me reacted but I crossed my legs, sheathed now in their demure gray Acrilan, folded my arms at my chest in what I supposed a sage posture, sighed, and let my eyes fall shyly to the floor, trying at once to appear both becomingly humble and fittingly meritorious. Then, as president of the Institute, Maxwell took over. He announced and explained the purpose of each award or grant, named the recipient, the latter stepped downstage center to the lectern, Maxwell read a line or two biographical sketch of him, followed by another two- or three-line citation on the nature of his work, and handed him a snowy envelope lovingly enclosing a check in the amount of his grant or award. The winner accepted his handshake and the well-bred, almost recherché applause and attempted—for the most part admirably—to file suavely back to his seat. Standing over Maxwell's left shoulder, I winced when he had me born in Watertown a mind-boggling fourteen years after my mother tells me I was born, wondering if even in one of Paul Stuart's laudably cut suits anyone in the audience could take me for twenty-four instead of thirty-nine, then fought down an outright groan when he said my work reflected a "maniacal and extended preoccupation with football and other games."

The biggest hand of the pre-intermission ceremony, during which, as it were, we minions were dispensed with, was reserved for Allen Ginsberg. He was seated two seats to my right on the middle aisle of the third tier, and his consistency was of arrestingly durable stuff: there was the magnificent black beard, striated now with gray; the small eyes behind the thick spectacles, looking watery and somewhat out of focus; the love beads about the neck; and what appeared to be a spanking new unfaded wrangler's suit of a starchy dark blue denim (had he bought it especially for the occasion? I wondered). Obliquely watching him nervously tap his walking stick on the floor between his legs, tut, tut, tut, I was not only surprised that the Institute had made him a grant and rather astonished that he had deigned to show up, but flat out mesmerized and oddly touched by the solemnity with which he appeared to be taking the occasion. Was he actually proud?

Then Maxwell called his name, then the house came down. Nothing whatever like the perfunctory applause which had preceded it, there was something rowdy and wild and even hooligan about it, the entire audience bursting forth from the shackles of its politesse. And though

Ginsberg's poetry had never been my poetry, I found myself clapping as loudly as anyone, which was thunderously, and literally gasping for breath, an absolute repression of the tears welling up within me. What was this ribald acclaim? A genuine respect for his work? Some concession the establishment was making to the singular, deviatingly fugitive road he had taken? Whatever, along with the Award for Distinguished Service to the Arts given to the eighty-seven-year-old Stokowski, talc-white in both face and hair but looking very chipper all the same, telling the audience to work and to work and to work, and finally to love one another, that that was all there was, it was far and away the most gratifying moment of the day.

Following a fifteen-minute smoking respite, the celebrated English poet and novelist Richard Hughes—a ghost from out of the past—delivered the Evangeline Wilbour Blashfield Foundation address, "The Novel as Truth." Older even than I'd imagined (and his *A High Wind in Jamaica* had been required reading in my own college days two decades before), he wore an inexpensive and poorly pressed suit of a mangy-looking rabbit-colored gray. While he read he kept slapping lightly and scratching abstractedly at the back of his bald, tanned and freckled pate, as though he were being stung. I'd read that for years Hughes had lived at Laugharne on the Welsh coast, a fishing village he'd once shared—somewhat reluctantly, I suspected— with the boisterous and doomed Dylan Thomas, and he looked to me now a minor dignitary in one of those Welsh mining villages poor enough to bring tears to the eyes. Throughout his delivery I found myself continually calling back the image of Frost trying to read his poetry on the glacially wind-swept day of Kennedy's inaugural, even to anticipating an abrupt an odiously arbitrary wind suddenly materializing in that chichi hall and sweeping his pages from the lectern. Because of his pronounced English accent

—which seemed to have become more Welsh than English —and the natural infirmities of age, it was nearly impossible to hear from where I sat. I'm sure the paper was a good deal subtler than the snatches I caught—this was, after all, Richard Hughes!—but it reminded me of nothing so much as those stilted, coma-inducing term papers students are made to read to one another in graduate seminars, and I couldn't help thinking how much nicer it would have been had Hughes read from the second volume of his *The Human Predicament* trilogy, a volume that even then he'd been working on for seven years.

Finally the *ne plus ultra* of the day arrived, the presentation of the gold medals for a body of work—for, in Faulkner's now fabled phrase, "a lifetime spent in the agony and sweat of the human spirit." Vladimir Nabokov became the sixth (only the sixth!) American, succeeding Dreiser, Sinclair Lewis, Faulkner, Hemingway and Huxley (the latter surprised me until I recalled that, like Nabokov, he too had become naturalized) in history to win the Award of Merit Medal for the Novel. He was the only recipient of the day not to appear. I remember thinking with a pang that if I hadn't come it would have been Nabokov and me (certainly the only way, however loonily tenuous, my name would ever be linked with his), but in acceptance he sent a charming, very funny, very self-parodying cable from Montreux, Switzerland.

An artist whose work I didn't know was the next recipient. He made a long, painfully esoteric acceptance speech in which he attempted to explain in terms of his work what his life had been all about. Words were not his vehicle, and knowing something of the enormous gaps in my education it was he above all I wanted to commune with me that afternoon. I was grieved that he hadn't—or apparently hadn't—permitted someone who knew words to help him say his thing, and all I could think

‡ 219

was that whereas what he said might have been just dandy sitting with Picasso, Matisse and Chagall in Gertrude Stein's Parisian salon of the preterite but still hungered-after Twenties, in this hall, on this waning afternoon, it was precisely the kind of turnoff that lends real poignancy to that mean cliché, "I don't know anything about art, but I know what I like."

Tennessee Williams was given the Gold Medal for Drama, the first recipient since Lillian Hellman, who presented the award, eight years before. Coming off the worst reviews of his career for *From the Bar of a Tokyo Hotel*, a play about creative stagnation (to a man, the asinine reviewers in what I'm sure they felt was wit incarnate pointed out that if anyone should know about artistic impotence it was the Williams of this play), Williams, apparently still stung, had insulated himself with booze or pot or pills or all three (he was to have a near-fatal heart attack within days after this), and as he rose and started down the floodlit area toward Miss Hellman—weaving, feinting, looking as if at any moment he might topple headlong into the orchestra—he cast a heart-stopping, utterly breath-intaking cast on the entire audience. With the literal body aid of Miss Hellman, and to the crowd's audible sighs of relief, he reached the lectern, grasped it frantically for support, and in an effeminate lisp grotesquely compounded by a ballooned tongue and the accents of his lingering deep South heritage, he said he had abandoned his speech (he couldn't have made it had it meant his salvation) and because he had always looked upon himself as a comic writer (like the guys who write for Red Skelton?), or something equally absurd, he was going to tell a story instead.

One day his actress friend Maureen Stapleton had telephoned him with the news that a lesbian of her acquaintance was being married to a homosexual by a defrocked priest, the only person they could get to marry them. And they had beseeched Maureen to get Williams to the wedding ceremony. "But my dear Maureen," Tennessee had said, "why in the world should they expect me to attend? I don't even know these people." To which Miss Stapleton had explained that whereas the other guests might view the proceedings as derisory, perhaps even emetic, they were confident that Williams would view the participants as "just plain folks."

The crowd roared its approval, more in relief, I think —I, for example, thought him constantly hovering on the abyss of some tasteless self-revelation—than at the story, though Williams told it surprisingly well; whereupon, still laughing, we went, eight hundred strong, into a huge courtyard and there under a brilliant candy-striped canopy set up against the infelicitous prospect of a rain which never arrived we sipped delicately at whiskey sours and daiquiris, nibbled at hors d'oeuvre, and as people do at such socially rigorous affairs kept within the orbit of our known groups, pining to drift off and talk with Warren, Styron or DeVries.

After that day I stayed in New York. I had had a second go at my marriage with a mightily chastened wife. It hadn't of course worked. Paraphrasing Warren's Jack Burden I'd said, "Goodbye, my lovely, and I forgive you for everything that I did to you," and in the Chelsea district I'd moved into the apartment of a young lady who had admired *A Fan's Notes* and had conveniently gone off to the Berkshires for the summer. For days I didn't do much of anything but stock up on whiskey, stake out the neighborhood for laundromat, dry cleaner, grocery store, and so forth, drink at the bar of the Chelsea Hotel, lie chain-smoking on the couch in the sunken living room of my rather swanky borrowed apartment (the girl was loaded), and wait for the phone to ring. Once I picked it up and it was my friend Ray Santini, who owned Chumley's in the Village and also Chumley's Steak House around the corner from Madison

Square Garden. He was calling from the uptown steak house.

"You wanna meet Mailer?"

"Mailer wanna meet me?"

Ray spoke with absolute menace. "Now, listen here, Little Muffin . . ."

Despite his Latin begetter (Ray is half Italian and once accused me, apropos of I forget what, of taking him for "one of these Greenwich Village wops"), Santini is fair-skinned with clear dark, slightly thyroid-looking eyes which glaze only with his infrequent drinking; a Nordic-shaped, handsome head; an abundance of black curly hair; and a broad-shouldered, commanding presence which makes him appear more Middle American than a Big Ten quarterback, a model they might attire in a space suit, sans globular glass helmet, and use in NASA advertisements to sustain an exasperated taxpayer's faith in our space program. I'd known him for better than fifteen years, since he was fresh out of Korea and I out of college. That he had never respected me I knew, but he owned affection as for a stray dog or a retardee. He had never called me by given or surname, believing that "real" names like Steve, George or Ray, Farquarson, Horsefield or Santini were tags one bestowed on maturity, on men, as it were, who had put it all together. And in his eyes I'd never done that, the Richard and Hinda Rosenthal Award notwithstanding. For as long as I'd known him he'd laid on me such sobriquets as Little Muffin, Nutsy Fagin, Baby Cakes, Goofy Gumdrops. It was an impetuous city personality dealing with an oafish rural one, the urbanite setting the tone of the relationship.

I own that peculiar cow-country mentality (Watertown is not in my marrow, it is my marrow) that causes me endless distress, as when, for example, I know someone is issuing a maxim, a hard-won wisdom nugget, know that my clear duty is a sophisticated crossing of the legs, a wise pursing of my lips, and an all-encompassing nodding of my noggin, yet against a thousand previous resolutions I find my lower jaw going as slack as a cretin's; I can almost feel my head rising into its pin shape; I find myself whinnying, "Whadda yuh mean by that?" In the early days of our friendship, when Ray was broke, unsettled, and anxious of the future, he often became so enraged with what he deemed my bumpkinry that with chilling earnestness he'd threaten to knock my teeth out. And though over the years, through the acquisition of the Village Chumley's, the uptown steak house, and a home in Westport, he'd mellowed somewhat, it was (as ineradicable as a birthmark) in his temperament that his Latinic quirks manifested themselves. Enraged once at the idiocy of a telephone operator, he stepped back from the wall phone in the galley of the downtown restaurant, doubled his fist, and did what every New Yorker has thirsted to do, threw it with all his might, leaving the blameless phone in uncountable black plastic pieces on the kitchen floor. Embarrassed, he told his bartender he had errands to run and expected the phone fixed on his return.

When hours later he called back, he talked about this and that, then said, "They fix the phone?"

Told that they had, Ray said, "What was the matter with it?"

It was impossible to stay angry with Ray. There'd be periods of two or three years we didn't see one another, but on arriving in the city I'd always go to him first. He'd circle me warily, stealthily, looking me up and down, over and around, as if he were scanning my clodhoppers for shit, as if he were having trouble placing me, as if he'd never seen anything quite like it. Then finally he'd smile and say, "How's it goin', Numb Nuts?" Ray'd take me to Chinatown for dinner, constantly reminding me throughout the meal that he was a frightfully busy man, that this was the only time he was going to give me during my visit, the implication being that even this was more time than I warranted. He'd let me drink on the house at Chumley's, with mock apologetics explaining to his bartender that "this fuckin' farmer can't handle these New York prices; where he comes from the shitkickers are still selling Genesee 12-Horse Ale for fifteen cents a bottle, ten cents less than they pay for it."

Santini was kind, and now he was going to do me the most delightful kindness of all—introduce me to Norman.

That evening there was a championship fight in the Garden. Apparently Mailer was at the bar of the steak house belting back a few in anticipation of the bout, and if I hurried I was led to understand I'd get a chance to swap badinage with him. Perhaps, I thought, Mailer'd even invite me to the fight. "Wonderful, Ray," I said, hanging quickly up. "Wonderful," I repeated dumbly to myself. This, I thought, was going to be nothing like the remotely formal world of the Institute. No, sireee, this was going to be just a couple writers, one famous, one unknown, bantering with each other, consigning this guy to hackdom, that one to "a nice little commercial novelist." Frantically selecting a blue button-down shirt with a maroon and gold regimental tie, a pair of gray flannel slacks, my black wingtip Florsheims and a beige corduroy jacket, an outfit I thought Norman would approve, I dressed, fled out of the apartment and hailed a cab.

13

"Where's Mailer?" I said to Ray.

"He's not here yet."

"Oh?" I was disappointed. "How do yuh know he's comin'?"

"Because a friend of mine made reservations for a party of people, including Mailer.

"He *specified* that Mailer was in the party?"

"Yes."

"Why?"

"What do you mean 'why'?"

"I mean, is Mailer a vegetarian or health-food addict? You have to order some special food for him, sauerkraut juice or something?"

"Now, listen here, Little Muffin—"

"Well, for Christ's sake, Ray, I thought I'd get a chance to pass some time with the guy. How'm I gonna talk with him if he's surrounded by a cadre of flunkies?"

"I never said you could pass any time with him. I said, 'C'mon up and I'll introduce yuh.'"

"You got me into a necktie to shake his hand? Should I kiss the hem of his jacket or anything?"

"Now listen, let's get this straight, Peckerhead. I've only met Mailer two or three times myself. If you're going to pull any of that Watertown cider-squeezer's crap on me, I won't even bother. Sit down."

I did, pulling myself up on the barstool Ray usually occupied near the reservations telephone at the dining room end of the bar. To his bartender Ray said, "Give Nutsy here some vodka," then to me, "Look, I'm busy as hell. If you want to meet Mailer, fine. If you don't, go fuck yourself." Already the bar was jammed with fight fans, and the tables, topped with their red and white checkered cloths, lining the walls of either side of the dining room were completely occupied, some people eating steaks, others placing orders. Then I detected that the tables in the middle of the room, which ordinarily were spread out singly to feed four at a sitting, had been juxtaposed to create one long table not at all unlike the table depicted by painters in their conceptions of The Last Supper. Like me, the china place settings sparkled in mute anticipation. I groaned, then chuckled, thinking that all the scene lacked was Christ and his apostles. And I had no doubt who Christ would be.

Well, I thought, what had I expected? Fifteen years before in *Advertisements for Myself* Mailer had told us that, like Bernard Shaw and Capote, whose publicity he had envied, he was embarked on a journey of self-aggrandizement and, if necessary, was going to pound the fact of his imagined superiority into our feeble domes. But he had also revealed—a bluff one had believed—that he was into a ten-year project out of which he'd come bearing an orange crate of manuscript containing something like a Proustian evocation of the entire sexual spectrum. He hadn't of course delivered, and despite the occasional flashes of brilliance in his "new journalism," which was neither new nor journalism, I was with my upcountry, whadda-yuh-mean-by-that? mentality perfectly prepared to demand of him what had happened, readily poised to point out that he hadn't made good on a promise he'd made me and a million other acolytes who, if not actually writing, were even then nursing our drinks, thinking of putting down words, and being dreadfully intimidated by the grandioseness of Mailer's stated designs, an intimidation I can understand now was utterly calculated for just such a purpose.

Moreover, in a touching attempt to keep the plane of his own ground airily lofty he had patronized or with wanton and spiteful arbitrariness shot down every writer who represented the least threat to his imagined eminence as King of the Heap—Bellow, Styron, Updike, Capote, Baldwin, Vidal: well, whom hadn't he patronized?—and even after he'd succeeded in his aims and with his swagger and bluster reduced the establishmentary committees of Mr. Pulitzer and the National Book Awards to their knees, when he'd been paid the homage of his peers, when he should have come to a little peace and got on to whatever it was he believed himself capable of, he would instead become "a media writer" popping up on TV every second week spewing his peculiarly sad venom, a pitiable performance that could only have been motivated by some awful disappointments within himself, something that rises up out of that terrifying place where ultimate grief resides, and probably something as obvious as that all those men he'd patronized had gone on to write their novels.

As I find myself saying this, I smile wryly, thinking that if the literary world were as clubby as generally imagined—as clubby, for example, as the United States Senate—Mailer would have long ago, like Senator Joseph McCarthy, been censured, but that the literary scene has yet to produce a writer of stature with the courage of a Margaret Chase Smith, a man to stand up to Mailer and say, "You are wanton, you are irresponsible, you are without the impulse to fairness or decency, and you are finally to be pitied." In time of course someone would step forward, and a woman at that, Kate Millett, but being vindictive and imperceptive she was the wrong woman. Instead of laughing and shrugging it off, Mailer in his melancholy game of one-upmanship took the time to devote an entire volume—*The Prisoner of Sex*, which was supposed to be about Women's Liberation—to nothing more or less than an attack on Millett, as though we were all too thick-skulled to grasp the unfairness of Millett's game.

And now, of course, Mailer is embarked on a campaign to garner himself the Nobel Prize. He wants us to believe that he possesses the generosity of spirit, the largeness of vision, the striking courage of a Faulkner, Mann or Solzhenitsyn, or for that matter the relentless dedication of an Edmund Wilson or the sheer genius of a Nabokov who never won the prize. Mailer opened his *Prisoner of Sex* waiting for a call from the wire services with the probable announcement that the prize was his; he modestly assured his gentle reader that he was sure the wire services had made an egregious error (indeed they had, indeed they had!), but he was unable to convince his new secretary who appears to have been transmogrified into a walking, talking mass of awe-stricken, admiring and gushy mush that Norman could take the whole business so cavalierly; and sadly, oh very sadly, we are left with the impression that Norman would not have been all that surprised had the wire-service man been right.

Even recognizing that he was nursing this kind of oppressive vanity, I could not guess he'd come to write about the lost and pathetic Marilyn Monroe, or that in the process he would make the great Arthur Miller, whose *Death of a Salesman* will be lighting up the world's theaters when Norman's books are being recycled to print Miller's words, an arch villain, or that he would seek to enlist our sympathy for his choice of subject matter by telling us—for Jesus Almighty's sake!—that he needs two hundred thousand dollars a year to live on. But one might have guessed as much.

Around the corner the preliminary bouts were already under way, both the bar and the tables were beginning to empty, and I had about decided he wasn't going to make it after all when I sensed an imposing presence behind me and heard, spoken to Ray with funereal gravity:

"My party is ready."

I couldn't help it, I started to laugh. Turning, I saw that it was this Quinn, the heavyweight boxing champion of the Corps, whom I didn't then know but who appeared to have way too much Irish-guy niceness to take a steak repast with Mailer so solemnly. Fluttering nervously, perspiring and wiping his brow with a handkerchief, he was an outsized Irish cherubim announcing the Second Coming.

Then the procession began, and in its ritualistic majesty it made the National Institute of Arts and Letters ceremony look like a thing of scant consequence, as pale as the talc hue of the great Stokowski's head. All together there must have been a dozen or fifteen of them—even including a priest I assumed was going to bless Norman's cauliflower—and as they filed behind me I noticed there was something

‡   229

utterly pilgrimatic or apostolic in their demeanors, that try as they would to glide nonchalantly by they were quite over-come by a ludicrous earnestness, a stealthy determined sense of importance, a kind of wait-till-you-see-who's-behind-me thing. And finally, a full thirty seconds—and what a theatri-cal effect this delay had—after the final disciple, He came!

Accompanied by his then wife Beverly, who was lovelier than I'd been led to believe from the single photo I'd seen of her, with dark taffy-colored hair, a peaches com-plexion and an outfit to match, Mailer was a good deal smaller than I'd thought, and thinner than in his recent pictures, though not thin enough for the vested—it made him look roly-poly—lightweight suit he was sporting. But here was his graying, kinky, pseudo-Afro hairdo and unlike the others his petite candy kiss of a mouth was giving off a smile, he was enjoying himself, which made me want to shout at his table, "Hey, you guys, look at Norman! He's smiling, you can smile now!"

I don't know why I stayed, but I did; and against a hundred resolutions not to, I found myself looking at his table, not much liking what I saw and wondering if ever again there'd come a time for him when he and his wife could slip into some corduroy slacks, some old and com-fortable cashmeres, have a couple of beers and a ham and cheese sandwich at the bar of Chumley's, then walk round the corner and see a fight together. I doubted there would. Mailer had made himself a literary Frank Sinatra, and where one could understand an egomaniac from Hoboken summoning and discharging flunkies to and from his private table way out yonder there in that ultimately vulgar Ameri-can dreamland of Las Vegas, Mailer yet owned something of brilliance, places in his recent work had taken on a com-passion I hadn't heretofore suspected him capable of, and at that moment he obviously housed the inner resources not to have to live his life, as it were, *en entourage*. And I knew then that, despite my grudging respect for some of his work, I couldn't like the guy, and that he'd never deliver on the promise he'd made us "lesser" talents.

Yet I persisted. At his table they were still sipping cocktails, and I implored Ray, before the steaks arrived, to get him and bring him to the bar so I could buy him a drink. Ray pointed out the obvious—that Mailer had probably never heard of me—but I countered with the truth that I didn't expect to confront him as an equal. "Just give him my name —I'll play the lickspittle—tell 'im I'm a votary, and ask him if he couldn't spare the time it takes to quaff a single drink. Christ, Ray, you're in this business, you know how to handle this corny fucking New York scene."

"What do you want to talk with him about?"

I was becoming bored. "Oh, for Christ's sake, Ray, who knows? Maybe I'll ask him if he's got an anal hang-up. He's always got his heroes shoving it up some broad's fanny."

"That's what I mean," Ray snapped. "I ain't even goin' to introduce yuh!" And for good measure: "Peckerhead!"

But Ray did. On his way out Mailer pulled up behind me, shook hands with Ray, thanked him for a lovely meal. I'd swung round on my barstool so Ray couldn't avoid me, and at the last possible moment he asked Mailer if he'd met me. We shook hands, and Mailer introduced me to his wife. He was, as people had so often told me, very much the gentleman (though with equal sincerity I'd heard as many stories about what, if true, could only be deemed a strident cruelty), speaking in a very low-keyed voice weirdly compounded by the staccato word-biting of the born Brooklynite, as though his vocal cords, quite independently of anything he was willing, were attempting the impossible feat of staying attuned to his acutely febrile cerebrum.

"You did well with your book."

"So-so," I said.

"Your editor sent me a copy but I haven't had a chance." He shrugged. "I've been, you know, sort of busy lately." He had of course been running and resoundingly defeated in the city's mayoralty primaries.

"I'm sorry," I said, meaning that I was sorry both that he had taken the time from his work for yet another ego trip and that he hadn't had the time for me.

"How's the book moving?"

"Seven thousand copies," and here I doubled my fist, projected my thumb upward, then turned the fist over and shoved it toward the floor, Nero giving the word to plant the sword in the throat.

Mailer laughed heartily. "That's about four thousand more than most of them do." By one, two, three of his courtiers he was being impressed with the urgency of the hour. "You going to the fight?" he said.

"No."

We shook hands again, then he was gone, lost now, because of his pint-size, amidst his entourage.

Although I never saw Mailer again, I began to see a lot of Quinn. I had found my way to Christopher Street and The Lion's Head Ltd., a bar—as I have elsewhere noted—frequented by poets, novelists, columnists, reporters, editors, agents and camp followers, and though Quinn must be relegated to the latter category, and though I'd already witnessed him in what I deemed a woefully unbecoming role, I found on acquaintance I liked him very much and hence never mentioned the circumstances under which I'd first seen him. That summer Quinn spent a lot of time on the West Coast and in Italy, putting together one stock deal or another, but whenever he was in town he was at the bar of The Head, as it is familiarly known, and the half-dozen times I drank with him there I found him generous, out-

232   ‡

going and sincere, a sincerity that bordered on the touching when one day he told me that with any luck, with the closing of two or three deals then looming on the horizon, he could get out of the business entirely within a couple years and be free to do his own thing, an appeal to accept him as a man of more substance than a shuffler and reshuffler of embossed certificates.

Had I then been sensitive to any appeals whatever, I certainly would have reacted to Quinn's appeal, but I was on a two-bender-a-day program, the first beginning in the swanky borrowed apartment shortly after I awoke in the morning, the second in The Head after I'd taken a late afternoon–early evening snooze; and my discourse during the latter bender was about as stimulating as *yup*, *nope* and *I'll-be-fucked*, none of which was destined to get enshrined among the provocative graffiti etched into the men's room walls of The Head. I was in effect in a state of total and constant inebriation and thereby not only insulated utterly from every kind of subtle human appeal but even "the great events," like Buzz and his Jack Armstrong buddies strolling among the craters of the moon, reached me with no more appeal than if those jokers had been exploring the marshlands of New Jersey.

Even inebriated I found it impossible to tune out the harsh noises resounding from Chappaquiddick. If there was a name that inspired in some of The Head's regulars more perked ears, more throbbing pulses, more stiffening of the backs than the name of Norman, it was the name of Kennedy. Not only had many of the patrons taken the assassinations of John and Robert as personal betrayals, it was as if they had seen shockingly and bloodily aborted some embryo that had promised them a greener, more lovely America than had heretofore been known; and now Senator Edward M. Kennedy, Democrat of Massachusetts and the last of the Kennedys, had yanked the rug from under them completely, rendering the politically inclined patrons bitter, spiteful, bloodthirsty.

On the night the Senator went on television to explain what happened following the "cookout" (ah, what PR genius came up with that one? Sorensen? Galbraith?), the bar was packed with no few of the men who set the temper, the moods and the opinions of the Republic. The Senator was minus the neck brace he had sported at Miss Kopechne's funeral two days before—"Thank the decencies," one reporter remarked—and the reaction at the bar drifted among deranged disbelief (one reporter bit his tongue, looked cross-eyed and did a little St. Vitus jig), uproarious laughter and strident hissing when the Senator —implying his house was as doomed as the house of Atreus—threw that "spitball" about the "curse" that haunts the Kennedy family. When it was over, Don Schlenker, the bearded, pageboyed bartender known affectionately as Prince Valiant, and one of my favorite people in all the world, volunteered a mot that perfectly expresses the awful division in this country. "I'll bet my mommy cried."

And I had to laugh, sensing that mine probably had also.

We drifted off into various groups, I finding my way to my favorite spot in the room, what I called "the paranoic's alcove," by the wall phone where I enjoyed leaning against the paneled walls beneath a framed glossy print of a dungareed Susan Sontag under which the novelist David Markson had written the legend "Is this really Joel Oppenheimer in drag?" With me were Markson, who if possible was even more apolitical than I, and Paul, a captain in the maritime service who wrote lovely poetry which on fear of rejection he never submitted. Never had I seen Paul so upset. A Jew, he loathed the Kennedys. It had to do with what he imagined was patriarch Joseph's position on Hitler when in the pre-World War II months the elder Kennedy had been our ambassador to the Court of St. James. Paul was convinced that the tragedy of the Kennedys was the Biblical sins of the father, whom he called "a fascist prick," being visited on the sons. To my shocked incredulity that such a gentle man could become so upset, all during the Senator's telecast Paul, who had stood beside me, had kept repeating, "Look at that farina-faced glob of puke."

Trying to retemper an ugly mood unbecoming to men who had neither columns to write nor editorials to compose, I now told Paul and David a joke I'd heard from the New Left writer Jack Newfield, who was a qualified Kennedy man and was even then writing an excellent memoir sympathetic to Robert Kennedy's last days. It is an old joke now, but I'd heard it from Newfield the day after Chappaquiddick, so it probably is that a joke that swept the country was born at The Head. At the "cookout" Miss Kopechne tells Teddy she is pregnant, Teddy tells her not to worry about it, Miss Kopechne anxiously exclaims, "But what are we to do?" and Kennedy responds, "We'll cross that *bridge* when we get to it." After that the three of us exchanged a number of stories more appropriate to our easy cynicism, Paul dropped from out of his loftily indignant regions, and shortly thereafter I was at the bar for a refill when I felt a meaningful tapping on my shoulder and turned to find an angry Quinn.

"Why don't you guys knock that shit off?"

I was surprised and bewildered. "What shit?"

"All those ugly jokes. Why don't you give the guy a chance?"

There was no doubt in my mind that Quinn was very upset, or that he wanted to knock me down, and that he would have little trouble doing so. Frankly, I was afraid, and felt that no matter what I said would be taken wrong and only further arouse his ire. So I didn't say anything. I took my drink and retreated back to David and Paul.

‡   235

The odd thing was that though I had no doubt that this joke would often be told in a cheap, sleazy or disparaging way, that sort of demeaning shot had been the furthest thing from my mind, as I suspect it had from Newfield's. For in my own drunken, aimless and sardonic way I was, and always had been, an unqualified Kennedy man. There was no doubt the Senator from Massachusetts had screwed up badly and had ended the near-incredulous tragedies of the Kennedy Decade in a shockingly shameful way, and if I chose to laugh at the black humor of this joke that seems so much more silly and inappropriate in retrospect than it then did, I'd chosen to laugh to allay the pain. I don't know David and Paul's motives for retreating with me to the paranoic's alcove, but as much as for any other reason I'd gone there away from the bar because if a single newsman had started talking in the jargon of tomorrow's columns and thrown at me a banner like "An End to Camelot," I doubt if I'd have made it to the men's room to do my puking.

Moreover, from at least two reporters in that room I'd heard about the Kennedy brothers' "notorious womanizing" (we did not hear such tales in Watertown, or on my island), stories told in a stout-fellow admiration that was apparently allowable among the "in-group" as long as it was not brought to the attention of the great unwashed out there yonder in that Outback west of the Hudson River. Even assuming that when he missed his turn and headed for that isolated beach sex had been the furthest thing from the Senator's mind, which I am more than willing to assume —though any American male who claims the possibility did not cross his own mind is a shameless liar or a eunuch—I loathed that America which lived in cowering trepidation of a politician with a pair of balls and continued to see some elevated and enduring virtue in the wan celibacy suggested by an Eisenhower or a Nixon, but not nearly so much as I

236 ‡

loathed the hyprocisy of that in-group America around me who could admiringly sanction a politician's womanizing as long as he did not get caught.

And moreover still, this pathetic bastard Kennedy had lost his oldest brother in World War II, had lost his only remaining brothers with their heads all but blown off before his eyes, and if any man was owed the right to an error it was he. Ironically, even then, even through my dark and constant inebriation, I was being more optimistic than most and thinking that this Kennedy might yet turn out to be the best of the brothers. Having spent more of my adulthood than it makes me easy to recall in and out of asylums, I could not at one time have lived had I not believed in second chances, and believed further that if a man could survive, heal himself and rise above what Styron has with such stunning eloquence called the "madness, illusion, error, dream and strife" of life, then he—yes, this Kennedy, Senator Edward M.—might yet come to know more of what goes into making a man than his brothers, taken in their primes, had ever known. Had I been capable of articulating anything other than *yup, nope* and *I'll-be-fucked*, these are some of the things I might have said to Quinn. But I didn't. In fear I retreated, and held my own counsel, warily watching Quinn out of the corner of my eye.

In the company of my young nephews I often used to watch a seven P.M. Sunday television show geared to the kids and called *Land of the Giants*. I never knew what it was about, partly because I'd spent the afternoon drinking and watching the football games, partly because comprehension wasn't of course in the least necessary. An Earth spaceship crewed by a bunch of guys who looked as if they might be the starting basketball team of a Kansas City junior college, along with a couple mini-skirted, cute-bummed cheerleader types, had force-landed on a planet inhabited by humanoids about three hundred times their size; and in every episode, to the great empathy of my nephews and millions of other "little people" around the Republic, the crew fled frantically in and out of ratholes in the baseboards, with ropes scaled office desks the size of Mt. Everest, and held at bay snarling, ferocious chipmunks as big as dinosaurs.

In contrast to the majority of the crew, who looked for all the world as if they could hardly wait to get back to Kansas City, have a cheeseburger, a chocolate malt, and take one of those cute-bummed cheerleaders round the corner to the Bijou to see, well, perhaps Nixon's favorite, *Patton*, there was another member of the crew, played with disgraceful, near-shameless hamminess by Kurt Kaznar, who was both my nephews' and my favorite, and who was a compendium of the most reprehensible neuroses known to man, a cowering cringing slob who constantly betrayed his gleaming-toothed All-American buddies, who began a blubbering, excruciating whining faced with the most trifling impediment, a man who could make the biting into an apple a vision of such nightmarish gluttony as to make one want to deny his human heritage. How my nephews and I roared our laughing approval at Mr. Kaznar's appearance in each segment, and how little my nephews— at their age sure they could never be like him!—realized that my own laughter was terribly compounded by the pain of recognition that I had somewhere along the line become so much like Mr. Kaznar.

On one of my stays in asylums I had had a post card from my brother, the military man. In its corrosive abruptness it was the kind of thing that only a career officer would have been capable of sending. It said simply, "What the f. is the matter with you?" In those days time was nothing to me but something to be got through, and when finally I sent him my answer I must have sent forty pages, all very rhetorical and highfalutin, and though

I remember hardly anything of that letter I know that in substance I told him that what was the matter with me, as he so stringently put it, was that I was afraid, afraid of too much beauty and of too much ugliness, afraid of loving and of going unloved, afraid of living and afraid of dying, so afraid of the sun that I could not open my eyes to the morning, and so afraid of the darkness I could not close my eyes to sleep, *afraid*.

When at length he answered, on another post card and in the abrupt military way, he wrote, "When I was on leave in 1945 I saw you, as a 140-pound sophomore, back Watertown High School's line. I do not accept your fears." In his peculiar way of loving he then added what I supposed was even a military solution: "Get off the sauce!"

At the time, wallowing as I was in my fears, I'd found the card vastly amusing. But after that incident with Quinn, my brother's words flew back to haunt me and I began to wonder if I ever had been man enough to tell Quinn to blow it out his ass and mind his own business and, sadly, began to suspect that once I had been man enough. Oh, I do not flatter myself that the best day I ever lived I would have come out of a scene with the heavyweight boxing champion of the Corps with anything less than two blackened eyes, a broken nose, and missing teeth, but that was beside the point. All that mattered was that I might once have been man enough to take my chances, and whether it was as simple as getting off the sauce or not I found myself once again thinking of the island, that world as seen through gauze, and those alienated youth on the hot bright streets beneath me. And so one day shortly thereafter I shook hands with and said goodbye to Markson and some guys I'd come to know and love at The Head, started the fluttering six cylinders on my beautiful Chevrolet Nova, and headed back to the island, to where I belonged.

On the way I took a detour. I drove north to the river

first, bid adieu to the family, packed a big brown paper bag with sandwiches so I could make Palm Beach County in one haul, stopping only for gas and Cokes, then started south, for a brief time pulling the car over and parking across the street from Edmund Wilson's stone house. I doubted he was in residence. No car stood on the lawns. The grass grew long in the yards. The house looked battened down and bleak; but it was a beautiful day in early autumn, the colors were splendid, the morning's autumnal mists had lifted, the sky was high, an exhilarating, heady blue, and way off to the east one could see—as was not always the case—the finely defined purple outlines of the majestic Adirondacks.

As I sat there, wondering why I'd stopped, I suddenly remembered something else. One of the first, kindest and most intelligent letters I'd received about *A Fan's Notes* was from a psychiatrist, doubly kind in that I'd spent no few pages deriding the psychiatric racket. He'd begun by telling me that he'd spent a number of years practicing in a state mental hospital and that my description of life there was the only thing he'd read that tells it "like it is." He'd then unnerved me. He said that being an analyst he hoped I'd forgive him and indulge him if he ventured a few observations on my character. I had of course winced, thinking that at me he was going to throw all those portentous catchall words like *paranoia, schizophrenia, manic depressive*, ad infinitum. I almost hadn't read on and at last had thought what the hell, the guy might give me a few chuckles.

Alas, I had not laughed. Not only didn't the wise doctor throw the asinine words at me, he immediately sent me reeling with a truth about myself I had never before articulated when he told me he had never before encountered "a man so haunted by sense of place." In this regard he cited my love for my hometown of Watertown, for the neighboring St. Lawrence and its idyllic green islands, for my mother's lovely limestone farmhouse, for the room I had built for myself therein, a room, as it were, of my own, and for Edmund Wilson's Talcottville stone house which even in those pages I had mentioned in passing. He wrote, and I can only paraphrase:

"Most advertising executives have their recurring dream of an antique shop in a red-painted barn in Litchfield, but with you this dream has been exalted to the grotesque proportions of a search for the Grail. You know of course that it is a dream. We live in a society mobile beyond our grandparents' brutalest dreams, one in which even the fucking corporations"—and how my heart leapt at finding a psychiatrist who also chose to tell it "like it is"—"transfer their personnel every other year denying them any sense of place, home, heritage, allegiance to community, this done by corporate psychologists in one of the most insidious and repellent uses of our damnable profession to keep the employee off balance and unaware of any possible loyalties other than those to the corporation. No, in a world where the kind of permanence you seek is increasingly unknown, unsought, and undesired by the money people, you will never find your haven. Which is not to say you shouldn't be looking."

And so remembering the good man's words, I once again started the engines, pulled out into the "high road" of Alternate Route 12D and headed south to Utica and the New York State Thruway where one again comes together with what I've always chosen to call "the rest of the world."

14

The temperature today, Christmas, on Singer Island is an unseasonable and stunning 90 degrees, the humidity an uncomfortable 86 percent. Having canceled my final week of seminars at Iowa, I arrived "home" two weeks ago, a week earlier than I otherwise would have done. Although it has been only seven months since I left here for the St. Lawrence, everything—to my displeasure—has changed (as always it does in transient areas like Florida), and I now wish I'd accepted Jack Leggett's invitation to remain and teach at The Workshop the spring semester.

Toni was of course gone even before I departed for

the river, and everyone else seems to be gone or leaving. To begin with, Big Daddy is selling the Seaview to a man intent on refurbishing it into ostentatious, expensive units, and those two or three of us who remain will for financial reasons be forced to move. In order to "get in on the Disneyworld dough" Big Daddy is opening a restaurant and night club on property he owns in Orlando; and though he tells me I am welcome to go with him—Big Daddy says I can stand at the bar as "local color"—and though I know that he takes my "sex life" with him in the persons of the strippers, Orlando is "over there" inland among the weirdos who punch clocks, make payments and accumulate things, and without the bright beaches and the blue seas and the alienated kids on the hot shimmering streets beneath my window, Florida has never made any more sense to me than the rest of America.

Speaking of kids, Gabrielle has married a young attorney and is living across the inlet in Palm Beach. She has three times asked me over for dinner and I have made one excuse and another, usually: "You know how I feel about leaving the fucking island!" Upon graduating from Harvard Law School, her young man needed a few months to prepare for the Florida bar. As nearly as I get the story from the kids around here, he slipped into a pair of shorn faded Levis, grew a beard, and studied the Florida law while lying on the beach where he met Gabby. When at length he was admitted to the bar, he and Gabby flew to the ranch in New Mexico or Arizona or wherever, and before God and Gabrielle's astonished (it was the first boy they'd ever seen her with!) parents they were joined in marriage. They returned to Palm Beach where he took a job with a small but snooty law firm and he and Gabby now move among the "beautiful people" over on Worth Avenue.

Although he still lives on the island and I see him and his girl frequently, Jack McBride has left the Beer Barrel and is working as a machinist on the mainland. Bob Schneider, who owns the Barrel, has a bad ticker and is not expected to live. Unable to run the place himself, he appointed a manager with whom Jack was unable to get along. The manager thought Jack "too casual." Ha! My Christmas dinner with the McBrides today will be my last meal with them. Alex has taken his pension from Pratt & Whitney; in order to be near Peggie's elderly mother they are moving to California on January 1; and I don't know whether Jack and his girl or I will miss the meals more. Although Jack tries to act nonchalant and philosophical about it, I keep saying, "Wait'll you start living on those fucking Big Mac hamburgers!"

It is yet a couple hours until drinks and turkey, and I have time to walk two laps on the beach between the inlet and Nigger Head Rock (McBride, a liberal, wanted to change the name to Black Head Rock but we decided this sounded more repugnant), which is about all I've been doing since my return. Between the rock and the inlet it is exactly a mile and a half; every lap is therefore three miles; and I walk stolidly, the sweat like vaseline in my eyebrows, head down or with my eyes eastward toward the blue-green sea and the Gulf Stream which, when the visibility is right, appears to ride choppily white at the horizon about a yard above the sea. Never do I look inland. In the short time I've been gone two new high-rise condominiums have gone or are going up. Looking inland at them reminds me of the doctor's words to the effect that money will not be stayed and that my days on this cold island are numbered. And as I walk I find myself thinking anxiously of the future, of other havens. I think, too, of these past three months in Iowa City.

On Labor Day at 10:40 A.M. I flew by American Airlines from Syracuse's Hancock International Airport to

244 ‡

Chicago's O'Hare Field, thence connected with an Ozark (wow!) flight which, thank the fates, put me safely down in the corn country of Cedar Rapids at 1:02 P.M. Novelist Vance Bourjaily is senior member of The Workshop's fiction staff, having been there fifteen years, and the day before I left I telephoned him at his home outside Iowa City, Red Bird Farm, to ask him to pick me up at the airport. A recording in the voice of his wife Tina answered the telephone. The recording, for which I was of course billed, told me that nobody was home, that I might take a chance and try another number in Iowa City, that I might call back later as the Bourjailys might be out walking somewhere on the grounds of the farm (a bucolic vision that! Squire Bourjaily, Tina and the dogs strolling about Red Bird Farm on a sunny September Sunday morning!), or that when the recording made a beep-beep noise I might talk back to it and make my wishes known. Unable to think of anything but "Fuck you, Vance," I demurred and resolved that my first order of business at Iowa City was to get my ninety cents from Vance, a fine, fine writer, a good and gentle man, at which time I'd give him a few verbal pops on the sconce for that pastoral recording.

I then telephoned Tracy Kidder, a twenty-nine-year-old Harvard man, Workshop student and English instructor who on my spring visit had been sent to Cedar Rapids to fetch me. I was told by his beautiful Vassar wife Fran that he was in California working on a book for Doubleday (everyone in Iowa City is working on a book) about Juan Corona, who is alleged to have sexually hacked up twenty-odd migrant farm laborers and then buried their mutilated remains among orchard trees in the idyllic Feather River Valley. Fran said, however, that she would see that someone picked me up, probably Jon Jackson, a likable Montana intellectual who comes on like a lumberjack in his Levis, hard-used work shoes and faded red hunting shirts. A

Workshop student, he is also an editor of *Iowa Review*, the university's concession to the verbal arts. From my memory of Jackson, my guess was that we'd hit every bar between the airport and Iowa House, where I was to stay, and that what should have been a thirty-minute drive through the tall green stalks would end by taking four to five hours.

And that is what happened, save that it took twelve hours. With him Jackson had brought a dozen or so *Daily Iowan* tear sheets of an article detailing my arrival to teach at The Workshop, and as the night and the drunkenness progressed Jon and I took a ball-point and with great scrupulosity wrote on the clippings, "Mr. Exley is 43, unmarried, heterosexual, lonely, and living at Iowa House." Then we tacked them to the walls of the various campus bistros. To my knowledge I had only one response to this drunken and optimistic bit of foolishness. But that one response proved more than enough.

When I had flown there months before to read from *Pages from a Cold Island*, I had been pre-registered at Iowa House, and while being driven there by Kidder had envisioned a white-columned, gabled, white-clapboarded *fin de siècle* inn—of the kind William Inge calls to mind—with old-fashioned, spacious and felicitously lighted rooms in which, on chain-flushing the toilet, the plumbing would make zonking, ominously gurgling noises. Instead it turned out to be a four-storied modern red-brick affair—the pedestrian creation of an architect obsessed with American-factory syndrome—with blue carpeting, green bedspreads, beige walls, functional maple-stained furniture and a nineteen-inch, black-and-white, metallic portable television set bolted firmly to the dresser. So eerily reminiscent was it of any middle-class motel in America that, on awakening, one could draw comfort from the hope that he opened his eyes to any place in America he yearned to be, Binghamton, Montgomery, Little Rock, Kansas City, Pueblo, Stockton—

or in my case, Singer Island. To commend itself it offered a Coke and an ice machine on every floor, daily cleaning service, a twice-a-week change of sheets, a cafeteria on the ground floor in which the coffee was okay but the food didn't work, an "art" theater in which they showed foreign or camp films (judging from the nightly queues in the lobby the biggest attraction this fall was something called *Reefer Madness*), and its walking distance to everything on campus, including The Workshop.

One stepped out the front door of Iowa House, crossed the street, bore right and southwest on a sidewalk to the left of which was a huge well-cropped green and to the right of which, between sloping green banks, the Iowa River flowed, serpentine, sluggish, lovely; now one walked through a concrete pedestrian subway (defaced with moronic and "revolutionary" grafitti) beneath a Rock Island Lines spur which farther to the right spanned the river, then stepped abruptly out into daylight again and was immediately confronted by EPB (the English-Philosophy Building) where The Workshop was located on the fourth floor.

It was on that twice-weekly confrontation with EPB that I began to fidget, and by the time I stepped into the elevator that ascended to the fourth floor, that floor of dreamers, madmen, cranks and ne'er-do-wells, the lonely, the lofty and the mean, I had begun to perspire. The truth was, I had so little to give the student and really had no understanding of what either he or I was doing there. For a time I justified my existence in Iowa City by telling anyone who asked that I had come on a sexual lark, a "last fling with young flesh."

A few days before leaving for Iowa I had received a call at my mother's house from a top editor in a prestigious New York publishing house. He was vacationing in Alexandria Bay with his wife, and they invited me to join them at Cavallario's Steak House for a drink. I had known him for twenty years, since June of 1953 when he had just come down from Yale and I had just graduated from USC (in America one "comes down" from Ivy League schools and the rest of us merely "graduate"). That incredibly hot summer twenty years ago our paths had crossed in various New York City placement agencies when he was seeking a job in publishing as a "reader" and I one in public relations or advertising. Although in those days he was so oppressively Ivy League from the tip of his close-cropped head to the toe of his Scotch-grained loafers, from his snug-shouldered J. Press seersucker suit to his shell-rimmed glasses to his scrupulously cultivated accent, and I was therefore disposed to view him with ironic distaste, we took to meeting for coffee to kill the endless and wearying hours among our various interviews. One day, to my astonishment, I learned that, as mine had been, his father was a lineman for a public utilities power company, in his case in Pennsylvania, and that he—I'll call him Richard—had got to Yale on an extremely generous academic scholarship and had besides worked for his meals and room.

"Well, look, Richard: at least with me, cut the fuckin' accent, will yuh?"

Richard had laughed, and had honored my request.

Richard had got his job with Harper & Row (Harper Brothers in those days) before I'd got mine; I'd bumped into him only a half-dozen times over the years, and I'd calculated the flourishing of his career as, at these rare and unexpected meetings, he'd tell me of moving from publisher to publisher and lay on me his title of the moment: reader, assistant editor, associate editor, editor. The last time I'd seen him I gathered he'd reached that exalted level whereon he could, on his own say-so, place any book he wanted on his firm's trade list, that is fiction or nonfiction as opposed to textbooks. His only problem arose with known writers whose agents were beginning to demand astronomical advances, at which time he'd have "to kiss the asses of the money boys" in the firm. On completing *A Fan's Notes*, and because, like every writer of a first book, I'd have published for the advance of a sawbuck, I'd first sent the manuscript to Richard as the only man in publishing I knew. He'd rejected it with "great reluctance." Although he'd never expressed sorrow for doing so, when the reviews began appearing later, Richard started sending me xeroxed copies of them with ironic notes to the effect that "you must be blowing this reviewer" or that this one must have cost my publisher a fortune as it "read like a paid advertisement written by one of those depressingly jolly young virgins two weeks out of Smith."

On our second drink at Cavallario's Richard told me that their three relatively young children were with his parents in Pennsylvania ("With the lineman?" I almost injected, but decided against it). They had rented a motel room in the village, had stocked it with ice and whiskey and intended to have a few drinks, repair to the motel and make mad abandoned love, "do all sorts of nasty things." Richard's wife, whom I'd never before met, was tall, trim, elegantly and goldenly tanned, and startlingly handsome with long dark brown hair streaked with the most attractive streaks of gray. She said, "We love our kids, *of course*, but you can't imagine how heavenly it is to be rid of them for a few days. And it's so, you know, romantic and forbidden and all. Especially in a motel room!" Looking at her, I envied Richard greatly. I said that it all seemed deliciously romantic and almost added that neither of my wives had stayed with me long enough so that I'd seen either of my children (one by each wife) reach the "nuisance" or "coitus interruptus" age. But it seemed somehow a dreadful confession to make, and I held my peace. Richard then asked me the state of *Pages from a Cold Island*, about which I'd written him when he'd sent a copy of one of my reviews and asked what I was up to now. I lied and said the state was wonderful as could be and that if my agent so chose he'd be seeing a copy soon enough.

When it came out that I was going to The Workshop to teach, Richard said, "But whatever for?" And in truth, I had no ready answer, notwithstanding my dream of taking a sabbatical there in order that I might return to the manuscript refreshed and prepared to outflank it.

As some *fucks* and *sucks* and *pricks* had already been unself-consciously introduced into the conversation, as they invariably seem to be among "literary" people (from what I've read *the words* are said to be seeping into every segment of our society—including pre-teens!), and taking Jack McBride as my guru, I started talking off the top of my head. I said that at forty-three, with a full head of hair and all my teeth but one (perhaps still lying on the close-cropped lawns of the Sheraton British Colonial in Nassau!), my sojourn in the corn country was no doubt motivated by little other than having a final indulgence with young flesh. Like Walker Percy's moviegoing Binx, I said, girls caused me real physical pain, explaining that when I was there in the spring for my reading I wasn't actually sure I was going to survive two days of walking about the campus among all those "creamy-thighed hog farmers' daughters," as Tom Wolfe has so aptly called them. "In their faded Levis—so cramped one could see the breath-taking indentures of their hot little crotches!" I cried. "And those tank tops covering those braless chests—chests that don't need bras! It was excruciating!" With both arms I formed a rood at my chest, doubled over in mock pain, and swooned. "Painful!"

Richard and his wife laughed. Richard said, "With all the manuscripts floating around Iowa City"—and he'd know!—"I think a published writer would have to do little more than snap his fingers. Out there it'll be as though you're one of those swinish, greasy-haired rock stars giving a concert to unchaperoned girls at Hollywood High School."

"Oh, Richard," I said, "spare me those literary group-ies with all those guys they call *Nah*-buh-kov and Prowst. Like a buddy of mine in Florida, I want something essen-tially dim-witted. Say, the captain of the girls swim team from Ottumwa. Long legs, pulpous thighs, great hips and buttocks, marvelous shoulders—oh, simply acres and acres of her! Someone so dumb she'll let her mouth droop open in vacuous awe at my ability to use a typewriter. Someone to train and then find oneself too old to handle. I'll have to abdicate and turn her loose on her own generation! Can you imagine teaching something like that to suck? What my Florida chum calls the snake motion? Oh, my sweet Eros!" Here again I sheltered my heart, doubled tightly up and groaned in mock pain. "When I turn her loose she'll go through whole dormitories of boys! Whole fraternity houses. The entire fucking football team! I'll be responsible for cleaning up every male pimple in Iowa City!"

We walked, still chuckling, to their car. With great envy and warm wishes I put Richard and his wife on the way to their motel and their simulation of abandoned, forbidden love, then returned to the bar for a beer. At the bar there were only two college guys dressed in dirty white deck shoes, hip-hugging faded Levis and yellow tank tops. No sooner had I ordered a beer than a girl such as the one I'd just described to Richard and his wife entered, rocked with haughty impatience on her long fleshy legs, and then de-manded from the bartender Jimmy Tousant the where-abouts of a wealthy local man notorious as a roué. On hearing this request, and the college boys were obviously as cognizant of the man's reputation as I, the three of us turned eagerly round on our barstools and stared lustfully at the girl. Told by Jimmy that the man hadn't been seen for a week or more, the girl pivoted with furious purpose, threw her tanned and regal throat back into a crisp celery arc, and in her glove-fitting Levi shorts showed us her opulent behind moving irately away from us, a blond ponytail flopping angrily at the nape of her neck. Shaking our heads in great envy of that old womanizer, the three of us swung back to Jimmy where we sat for some time in charged and heavy silence. Finally one boy spoke to the other. His voice was compounded of self-assurance, melancholy, lust, envy.

"I'd eat her until I caved the top of her head in."

I spat a mouthful of Schaefer all over the bar, coughed violently, then roared, enlisting Jimmy and those others in my laughter. For the autumn I'd found my goal—to cave heads in; and if not that, to have coeds shudder and faint in my arms. Accepting that long-ago Dong as my mentor, I wanted nothing less than to be forced to summon physicians to get pulse readings on the ecstatic lasses.

For the first three weeks in Iowa City I began to suspect that my dream of "corrupting" coeds was little more than a middle-aged impotent's sexual fantasy, wishfully depraved thinking. Although I made no concerted effort to do so, made scarcely any effort at all, I began to feel like the proverbial wan soul who couldn't get fucked in a bawdyhouse with the Hope Diamond. And how excruciating it was! All the blond hog farmers' daughters had come to town sporting their splendid summer tans; the weather the first month was excessively hot and humid, forcing the girls to wears shorts and tank tops, exposing lavish amounts of young flesh; and I found myself swooning and clutching my heart, and felt as though I were the ultimate satyr consigned to his rightfully deserved damnation.

Then one late morning at my room, just as I was preparing to go up the hill for a drink, I had an unannounced caller, a petite little golden blonde with the most innocent-looking cowlike gray-green eyes and a heart-shaped mouth that even unpainted was as red and as appetizing as cherry juice. She looked about fourteen, a veritable Lolita, and she carried under her arm a hardback edition of *A Fan's Notes* she said she wanted inscribed. I'll call her April and say that though she wasn't from Ottumwa or Omaha or Oshkosh, or even an Okie from Muskogee, she might well have been. She was Miss Middle America to a heartbreaking fault. It was raining that day, I helped her out of her canvas knapsack in which the Iowa coed was carrying her books that fall, her brilliant yellow rain slicker, invited her to sit in a chair, inscribed her book in the manner she prescribed, and we talked.

As it happened, she wasn't fourteen but twenty-one, a senior and a French literature major. She had read *A Fan's Notes* two years before in a course at a junior college she'd attended prior to transferring to the university, and she said she'd admired it so much she'd ordered the hardback, which she invariably did with those books she particularly liked. Although I'd have felt jollier had she told me that *A Fan's Notes* was one of a half-dozen volumes she'd acquired in this way, April said she now had upwards of three hundred books she'd gathered since first reading them in paperback. I thanked her in any event. Because she made no move to leave, I asked her if she'd like some vodka.

"*Sure.*"

Before going to Iowa I'd promised myself never, *but never* to drink in my room; that no matter the circumstances I'd force myself, for every single drink I had, to walk to one of the campus saloons and pay for it over the bar. But I was so horny at the moment, breathing labored, a profound ache at the pit of my stomach, and so counting on the aphrodisiac properties of the alcohol, that I would of course have bartered my soul for a whiff of April.

A close friend had taken me to the plane in Syracuse. Knowing my trepidation of flying, he had given me a pint of red-label Smirnoff in a brown paper bag just before I had enplaned. He told me it was to nip on if the weather got tacky, and added, "I'm not even a boozer but I'd have to drink about a fucking quart before boarding anything with *Ozark* painted on its fuselage!" But the weather had been superb; the courtesy and the service a damned sight more amenable on Ozark than on the American Airlines lag between Syracuse and Chicago; I hadn't even thought of breaking the seal on the bottle; and that is how I happened to have the pint, still in its brown paper bag, in my closet.

In the hall I got two cans of Squirt from the Coke machine and a styrofoam bucket of ice from the ice machine. Unable to appreciate the small and fragile Iowa House's glasses wrapped in their antiseptic wax paper, I had at a campus novelty store bought two heavy outsized old-fashioned glasses imprinted with moronic maxims, *Happiness Is A Warm Pussy* in black script on one and HORSE PISS in bold red letters on the other. On the utterly true psychological dictum that the mind is the most erotic organ of the body, I mixed April's drink in *Happiness Is A Warm Pussy*. In the next three hours we finished the bottle, talked eagerly, and at length I decided to take the bull by the horns, pull a Portnoy, and ask April point-blank if she'd like to get eaten.

April smiled, tilted her head in the most coyly affected way imaginable, and said, "Why not?" Standing up from her chair, she said, "Okay if I take a shower first?"

As the water was roaring in the bathroom, and both my heart and my intestines were roaring in tempo, I stripped naked, got into bed, pulled the covers above me, and lay waiting, loony with desire.

When at length April came from the bathroom, her blond hair darkened from the water and clinging to her head, a white Iowa House towel clutched to the top of her breast and falling suggestively to a point just barely beneath her pelvis, she walked as bold as brass to a point between the twin beds. Instead of dropping the towel and climbing

254　‡

into the space I had so eagerly provided in mine, she seated herself on the opposite bed, asked me to light her a cigarette from the pack I had placed handily on the nightstand between the beds, lifted her right leg up and rested her foot on my bed, in the process allowing me a breathless glimpse of her pubic area, then said, "I'll make you a deal."

"A deal?"

"A bargain. I'll make *a bargain* with you."

"Okay," I said, and might have added, "*anything, anything*, ANYTHING!"

Rolling over on my side to face her, so she wouldn't be cognizant of the embarrassing rise beginning to lift the bedcovers into a miniature tent, I lighted us both cigarettes, lay my head back and in utter incredulity listened to this Lolita's, this innocent's, this Miss Middle America's, this angel of the plains's "deal." April shared an apartment with three other coeds, two of whom had boyfriends who by agreement among the four girls came over afternoons, and afternoons only, "to fuck," and April was weary unto death of trying to study in the outer room with the raucous moans and groans of sex emanating from the bedrooms; even wearier of waiting to get into the bathroom and, worse, on once getting there of finding dirty skivvies, both female and male, all over the bathroom floor, of vile rings in the bathtub, of great globs of toothpaste dried on the mirror of the medicine cabinet. Oh, there were days when April wanted to scream, or puke, or both! April paused pensively and wet her lips. Her gray-green eyes avoiding mine, she said, "I saw one of your cute signs—you know, those corny clippings of yours?—in a bar a few weeks ago and since then I've studied your habits."

"*You've what?*" I cried.

April said that daily she knew I went late mornings to Joe's Place at the top of the hill, drank there for a while, then walked round to Donnelly's on Dubuque, drank some more, went then to The Vine on Clinton Street, and finally ended up next-door to The Vine at The Deadwood, the hangout for The Workshop students, where I drank with the Epstein brothers, the owners of the bookstore, until four or four-thirty, at which time I repaired to Iowa House and wasn't seen again until late at night when I went back up the hill and made the same circle of bars until closing time.

"That's every day except Tuesday and Wednesday," April added. "On those days you go directly from The Deadwood to your four-thirty classes, and when they're over you come back to The Deadwood and drink with your students."

"Jesus, April, you've been following me! Do you know what that could do to a paranoic like me? Had I caught you I might have strangled you where you stood!"

April thrust the palm of her hand abruptly upwards, the traffic cop admonishing the eager motorist, and demanded my indulgence that she might finish. April wanted a key to my room. Mornings before starting out for classes she could pack her book bag with fresh panties, with her shampoo and her toothbrush, and while I was up the hill drinking she could come and make her toilet in my "cool bathroom" with its roaring shower, immaculate mirror, clean towels, and so forth, after which she'd study until I came down the hill at four-thirty at which time we could "fuck or whatever you want to do." On Tuesdays and Wednesdays, the days I held my seminars, she'd stay as long as she had to or until I called and told her I was tied up. We could work out a code so she'd know when to answer the telephone, say, I could ring twice, hang up, then immediately phone back. She promised she'd never be around the room nights in case I had other "guests." Friday through Sunday was out of the question because on Friday afternoons April hitchhiked over to the state university at Ames and spent the weekend abed with her "sort of fiancé, a really groovy dude" who was as impoverished as she but who at least had his own pad where "we can fuck in privacy."

April paused, pondered her words, then offered her hope that if she pleased me I could perhaps throw her "a couple bucks a day" so she could get something to eat in the downstairs cafeteria when she was leaving. April didn't need much, a couple cheeseburgers, a Coke and a scoop of chocolate ice cream—butter pecan if they had it. Everyone who picked her up hitchhiking to and from Ames tried to fuck her and with the money saved on the food she could buy round-trip bus tickets. Too, April wanted to use my telephone to call her "sort of fiancé" one afternoon a week, Thursdays, to give him her arrival time in Ames of Friday and she promised—she raised her right hand as one swearing allegiance—that she'd talk only the allotted three minutes.

"Look, I know I look about eleven and a fucking half. You'd feel foolish being seen in public with me and I'd be embarrassed to be seen with you. But this way nobody'd even have to know we knew each other. And let's level with each other: you have your—uh—*needs* and I have mine."

The abrupt delicacy with which April delivered *needs* made it sound a word she'd picked up in a high school course in sex education, as indeed she probably had. At this point I began to roar, wildly, helplessly, unrestrainedly at the unabashedly shameless and calculating mercenariness of this whory angel of the prairie, this Miss Middle-America trollop, this harlot of the hog farms, and between wild howls I breathlessly shouted, "It's a deal! It's a *fucking* deal!" Whereupon I reached over, yanked the towel from her, pulled her into bed, and for the next two hours fucked her as though I were a depraved playboy who'd just presented a fifty-thousand-dollar pearl necklace to the most beautiful and sluttish courtesan-starlet in Hollywood and were extracting payment in kind, none of which bothered or unnerved my darling April in the least, and all of which she seemed not only adept at but to relish immensely.

From that day on April honored her bargain, and I honored mine, though from that very night when I picked up another girl in The Deadwood on my late evening rounds a strange phenomenon began occurring. Whereas for three weeks it appeared I couldn't have bought a fuck with that fantasized pearl necklace, after April I found myself smack in the middle of what the dopey sociologists call "the new permissiveness" and greedily relishing every moment of it. Girls seemed to be coming out the woodwork and there were days when, leaving April her two dollars, I'd write her a note to the effect that she'd have to be out of the room by four as I was expecting another "guest"—all of which, I must say, April took in great good stride, at least for a time.

A week before returning to the island, I was drinking at The Deadwood with Glenn and Harry Epstein and their aide-de-camp in the bookstore, Danny Farber, and without mentioning April by name I told them of my early sexual drought and how after April I couldn't seem to handle what was there for the plucking. In that they read and knew the books on their shelves, as did Danny Farber, the Epsteins were among the most literate booksellers I'd ever met. To pay the rent they stocked Jacqueline Susann and Irving Wallace and Harold Robbins, but I could never, without giggling idiotically, hang around the store and watch them hawk such wares. For *The Love Machine* they'd accept their money with a straight enough face, but to the purchaser, and speaking around their cigars, they could never resist an observation.

"You've got yourself a helluva book there. Solid stuff, *solid*. You're in for a real *heavy* read. *Heavy, man, heavy.*"

Harry and Glenn and Dan were all on the short side.

They had wild mustaches and equally wild heads of hair. As the autumn progressed and the cold set in, and with it the heart-stopping winds sweeping across the Iowa plains, the three of them took to sporting outsized wool greatcoats that fell almost to their shoe tops; and I never drank with them in The Deadwood without an uncomfortable feeling of being in a clandestine cellar in turn-of-the-century Moscow making elaborate "revolutionary" schemes and belting back vodka with Marxist bomb throwers. The three of them listened with great interest and solemnity to my tale of April and the subsequent turn of sexual events in my life. When I finished, Harry, the top of whose head came to my shoulders, looked up, removed the cigar from his mouth, focused his great baby eyes on me, and said:

"Broads can smell it when you're getting in. Then they all want some of the action."

15

In October a letter from Rosalind Baker Wilson arrived at Iowa House, offering me one of EW's walking sticks. Alas, there was a rather formidable condition. Although I don't remember the note in detail, it seems that Rosalind Baker Wilson was planning on doing some traveling and if my mother agreed to take off her hands four tomcats, a stray mongrel and a bike-riding chimpanzee, or some such thing, Rosalind Baker Wilson would throw in six cases of dog biscuit, fifty-two hundred tins of cat food, six old T-bones, a bunch of bananas, or some such thing, and into the bargain would present me with one of her father's walking sticks. I never answered her. In the first place my mother's health didn't allow for her to take on that kind or responsibility, and as I was already yearning to return to the island, dragging stray felines (which I loathe in any event) was out of the question. For another thing, I had taken my great-grandfather Champ's silver-handled walking stick with me to Iowa City and for a time I had foisted it off as Wilson's, thinking that by using it as a memento of him I might try to convey to the kids what he had meant to me and what I thought they might learn by his example.

But I hadn't the heart or the guile to continue the deceit of the walking stick; it seemed so much an uppity denial of my great-grandfather Champ and my own undistinguished heritage. Aligning myself with Wilson at the expense of my own blood seemed so much not my kind of thing.

John Champ was born in 1832 in Wantage, England, a hamlet about midway between London and Bristol, on the Bristol Channel of the Irish Sea. On my map Wantage appears to be within a reasonable taxi fare a few miles south of Oxford. As a very young man John Champ entered the military, became a batman, little more than a glorified valet and horse groom, to a cavalry officer in the light brigade; and in England's war with Russia over the rightful site of the Holy Sepulchre ("Even for an eggshell . . . but greatly to find quarrel in a straw when honor's at stake," the Bard says) he was in the Crimea and from the heights above Balaklava watched the famous or infamous charge and saw the six hundred and how "bravely they rode and well." Later in life he would claim that what he saw in "Lord Raglan's War" so abhorred him that on the troops' return to England he deserted on the spot, on the docks of Liverpool, and boarded a steamer to Canada. As in his old age he drew modest pensions from both The Crown and from our own government, this part of his tale could hardly have been accurate.

In any event, he made his way to Kingston, Ontario, across the St. Lawrence from Cape Vincent, and after some difficulty (he did "time" in the prison in Kingston) he forded the river border to Watertown and the Thousand Islands area. Hardly had he been settled in his "new land" than our own Civil War began. He volunteered his services to the 10th Heavy Artillery, then being made up of upstate New York recruits, and was assigned to Company E, in I suspect a lowly or noncommissioned capacity. Although he saw "sharp" action in a number of battles against General Lee's armies, he would later say he saw nothing in our monstrously bloody and internecine war that could compare with the glory and the madness, the courage and the foolhardiness, the resoluteness and the stupidity, the heroism and the slaughter of the British troops at Balaklava.

On returning to Watertown from the Civil War, he married a widow, Mrs. Fanny Smith, and by her sired a son John and a daughter Nellie (with a fucking *i* and a fucking *e*, as with one's mare!), my mother's mother and my grandmother. The maiden name of John Champ's wife, Fanny Smith, was McGuire. To flee the potato famines she had emigrated from Blarney in County Cork, had made her way to Canada, thence across the river to America. Barely literate, I'd guess, she made her living as a domestic for a time, then as a cook at the various hotels which began sprouting up in the last third of the century, turning our part of America into a resort area. After her marriage to John Champ, she continued to work, for on his return from the Civil War he never held a job for more than a few months at a time (I know from whom I inherited my lackadaisical and ironical view of our "work ethic"). He became a kind of ne'er-do-well "country squire" with a silver-handled walking stick, an incredibly handsome man with a magnificent mane of snow-white hair and a great gray beard, and lived out his life with his memories of blood and thunder, carnage and cannon, and died in his sleep at his Massey Street home in Watertown in 1909, age 77, the same age at which Wilson had died.

So this, then, is my heritage on my mother's side (on my father's it is, if possible, somewhat meaner), and yet one of the dreams of my life has been to make a pilgrimage to Wantage, England, in search of the boy John Champ (one of my relatives went and discovered the family thought him long dead and buried in the Crimea; they were "shocked" on learning of their "American family"), thence to County Cork in search of that never-known, never-seen (I can uncover no picture of her) colleen, Miss Fanny McGuire. Can one imagine Exley, middle-aged and sporting his youth-seeking faded Levis, walking stick in hand, great vodka tears in his eyes, his voice aquiver, strolling into the Bureau of Records in Blarney (*and how about that?*), in the County of Cork, the Republic of Ireland, and demanding, pleading for information about that long-ago Fanny McGuire?

Be that as it may, I found I had no gift for continuing the charade of passing the walking stick off as Wilson's, of seeking to align myself with princes, even literary princes. Unlike Ms. Steinem, whose father, by her own admission, had been a kind of itinerant or gypsy antique-junk dealer, I hadn't the capacity to scorn one who "should have been a sports reporter for the *Daily News*," least of all scorning grant-grandparents. But even without the walking stick I had mementoes enough of Wilson. In my bosom, as hot and as pestilential as a rotting and stricken heart, I carried the tears of Mary Pcolar and the awesome grief of Rosalind Baker Wilson. Constantly recurring behind my eyelids, as a picture flashing intermittently on a film screen, I carried visions of Wilson's stone house and something of what I thought it had meant to him. I carried—but enough. Oh, I had, I thought, plenty to give my kids!

My Tuesday afternoon class caused me the most distress and anxiety. In this section one or two students typed onto mimeographed paper a twenty- or thirty-page short story or novel segment, had it run off in the mimeograph room, saw to it that the various members of the class got copies in advance, and we spent ninety minutes or so discussing the pages. I seldom said anything (what I did offer was invariably kind), setting myself up more as a moderator, a role I know some of my students took to mean I hadn't read them carefully. The truth was something quite else. Although in the entire fall I saw nothing I deemed publishable, I saw stuff that was damned close to being so; and even above that, I read not a single manuscript that I would have been capable of writing at the age of these kids and I therefore had no inclination to discourage. I held my peace, fearful of causing the slightest hurt.

My moderation or decency, I must say, did not in the least restrain the students from commenting on one another's work. At our very first session, I laid out my ground rules, saying I was going to go from student to student around the seminar table, let each offer his opinion and criticism, and then afterwards see if we couldn't reach some accord as to how the writer might make his pages more successful. As Jon Jackson, my lumberjack-intellectual drinking companion, was in this group, and I of course knew his name, I went to him first. Jon was rocking back and forth on the heels of the rear legs of his straight-backed chair. He held and was rather grimly poring over the mimeographed pages in his left hand. In his right hand he held and with no little gravity was sucking on his pipe. Now he let the front legs of his chair settle jarringly to the floor. He nonchalantly flung his copy of the manuscript onto the seminar table. With great and theatrical deliberation he removed his pipe from his mouth. He slowly raised the bridge of his horn-rims farther up on his nose. Now he looked at and addressed the student who had written the pages.

"This is a bunch of shit. They never should have let you in The Workshop."

Jesus H. *Keerist*! And I had an entire fucking autumn to go! Enraged at Jon, I angrily stuttered something to the effect that I'd brook no more of that kind of nonsense masking itself as criticism, that *never* for the remainder of the fall did I again expect to hear any comment like that. But I must say that my passing rage did paltry good, and as the autumn progressed there were days when I felt the students' capacity to hurt one another bordered on the shamelessly boundless, other days when I literally thought I was going to have to break up fistfights! Then one day I recalled myself as I had been at these kids' ages and remembered my own insecurities and with what rage and contempt I'd often read even published books hailed by reviewers as "masterpieces." As the fall continued, I found that at The Deadwood I had to belt back a half-dozen double vodkas before even going down the hill to confront this group.

My Wednesday section was a good deal pleasanter but not, in its own way, without a certain amount of uneasiness. For this we read and discussed each week one of my previously selected "modern" novels, and I did my best to see to it that the student talked about the novel the author had written. For example, I didn't give one good shit what Lionel Trilling had to say about *Lolita*, I wanted to know what the student had to say about it; and there was one day—with an American novel I hold particulary dear, Robert Penn Warren's *All the King's Men*—that I disallowed any discussion whatever and instead spent the entire session reading aloud from the book. I read first Jack Burden's poignant account of first love with Anne Stanton, then his sad and hilarious description of his marriage to the "Georgia peach" Lois; I read, as it were, The Dream of Love and The Reality of Love; and after these two parts I read the entire concluding section which, along with the conclusion of *The Great Gatsby*, I hold to be the best ending in American fiction.

When I finished, I solemnly closed the book, picked it up, looked at the students, rose from my chair, and with furious joy hurled the book against the wall, the way I'd always imagined Red Warren must have kicked up his heels on writing his last paragraph.

"I understand that book cost Warren seven fucking years of his life and I utterly refuse to let our pale words decimate it as though we were talking about the trick endings of a corn pone like O. Henry! In Warren's own introduction to the Modern Library edition he invokes the great Louis Armstrong. When somebody asked Satchmo what jazz was about, Warren quotes him something to the effect 'that there's some folks that if they don't already know, you can't tell 'em.' And that's how I feel about the novels we've been reading. Do you fucking guys know what I'm telling you?"

To a man, and very gravely, they nodded, by way of assuring me that they did.

Admittedly, for the rather handsome salary I was receiving for a few weeks' work, this didn't seem an awfully lot to give the student. But beyond all this I did try to tell him something of Edmund Wilson and his stone house, and how Wilson had been *sui generis* to the end. I agreed that the student's two years at Iowa City was better spent than selling snowmobiles, that he was reading, getting some healthy fucking, and drinking beer among people "into books" and hence was unable to avoid the vibrations and the emanations, that he was coming of age in an idyllically conducive milieu; but that he must understand that for everyone of him there were two, three, four hundred young guys somewhere out there in the Republic, locked up, apart, confused, putting down words, trying to bring order out of that confusion, the way books are born, getting on with it in other words; and that I didn't much trust the insecurity that had brought him to Iowa City in search of his peers' laudations. As provocation, I said, I'd much prefer the student's invoking the image of those four hundred guys already working out there than listening to me, or anyone else in the room, or of resting smugly with the knowledge of having been good enough academically, which to a writer doesn't mean doodly-squat, to have been admitted to The Workshop.

"Your real literary life," I offered as my one piece of tendentiousness, "will begin the day you accept the conditions, apartness, confusion, loneliness, work, and *work, and work*—the conditions so many of your peers have already accepted and that Edmund Wilson and his stone house so vividly and hauntingly evoke."

I asked the student to accept this from me as a man who understood these things too late, when alcohol, fatuous dreams and disappointed life had all too dearly sapped the youthful ambitions. Wilson's stone house, I said, was a condition of the heart, a willingly imposed isolation from the "literary scene" or anything resembling that scene. If, like Mailer, I said, the student wanted to spend his idle hours running for president or hurling cruelties and spite at his peers or talking about "writing" with little Sir Richard Cavett on the boob tube; or if, like Steinem, he were handsome and striking enough to be introduced on the talk shows as a "writer" without, to my knowledge, having ever written anything, then he wanted something quite else from what I, with all my being, hoped for him. Do what I say, I said, and not what I've done, and I promised my student that, like Edmund Wilson, he would in the end hold up to

America a mirrored triptych from which, no matter in which direction America turn, she would—to her dismay, horror, and hopefully even enlightenment—be helpless to free herself from the uncompromising plague of her own image.

On settling into Iowa House my first order of business had been to write Jack McBride and remind him of his promise to leaven what in my mind had already assumed the proportions of an endless autumn by visiting me. His reply assured me that he fully intended to do so. He told me to send him "The Hawkeyes' "—apparently the appellative hung on the university's athletic teams—Big Ten football schedule and he would come on a game weekend, bringing with him a roast loin of pork or fresh ham from Peggie, out of which I could make "inch-thick cold pork sandwiches on onion rolls, with crisp cold lettuce, thinly sliced Bermuda onion, mayonnaise, and a shitload of salt and pepper." For the "personals column" of the *Daily Iowan*, which didn't, I don't think, have one, he appended an "advertisement" that I was to run the week immediately heralding his arrival. It said that the friend of a campus "dabbler in words, well-known to five drunks and a pseudo-intellectual dwarf at The Lion's Head in the Village" would be in town for the weekend of "the fucking Fighting Irish game, or what the fuck ever," that Jack resembled "that incredibly handsome and gifted leading man of such tour-de-force flicks as *Shingle Mountain*," but unlike him was "no fucking fag," and that for the weekend Jack was seeking "a strenuous and not in the least academic female, preferably someone as rum-witted as an arts and crafts major" interested in that "pure companionship" which follows a few laughs, a few drinks, thence to that "nastily wholesome and animalistic carnal abandonment that comes with the immunizing knowledge that neither partner will see the other again. No whips."

Unhappily, Jack never came. Since I've come "home" I've been meaning to ask him why not, but I keep forgetting to do so, though I expect it's as simple as that he got fired from or quit his job at the Beer Barrel and had to start looking for his new job as a machinist. For all that, though, from the autumn day I got his letter I began finding myself the "hero" of a recurring dream, that of a fucking sky-jacker, and as the autumn progressed and the cold weather set in the dream began to take on an alarming vividness. I have no doubt that the dream's high coloring grew in direct proportion to the complexity of my relationship with April and my need to escape that relationship. I'll not burden the reader or strain his credulity by confessing that I came to love April, or she me. Suffice it to say that the human ani-mal, even in our desperate sexual musical-chairs society, does not continue fucking the same partner without some-thing happening, for one must desist from fucking and suck-ing, and come at length to lie exhausted with love in one another's arms, whispering into one another's ears. And that whispering involves language, the loftiest instrument of man, and that language reveals to one's partner something of one's childhood, one's hopes and dreams, one's fears and aspirations, so that try as one will this *thing*, this syrupy delectable fucking and sucking instrument lying in one's arms, assumes a history, begins to seem after all a creature of sacrifice or of selfishness, capable of being done great hurt or of inflicting great hurt, becomes, as it were, *human*. Yes, immunize ourselves with the hardest, most impene-trable shell of which we are capable, trouble eventually begins.

The trouble with April began this way. Having one day left her a note telling her I wanted her out of the room at four as I was expecting a "guest," I unlocked my door at the designated time, my "guest" at my side, and, *lo*, there was April as she usually was, freshly showered, naked ex-cept for her clean and iridescent bikini panties, seated at my desk studying from one of her texts. My guest beat an angrily embarrassed and hasty retreat. April was profusely apologetic, wept rather histrionically, swore she'd been neglecting to watch the clock, and we made it up in bed.

Within the next month April repeated the scene two more times. On the third occasion I grew furious, slapped her face, and tried to get my room key from her. April threatened that if I took it from her she'd never leave me alone. She said she'd call me every hour on the hour until my life was such hell I'd wish I'd never been born, until they ran my "old ass out of Iowa City on a rail!" April said I was fat. She said I waddled when I walked. She accused me of living in the shower and said my penchant for cleanliness bordered on the pathological, "utterly Freudian," and was obviously a result of the guilt and disgust I must feel at degrading young and innocent girls.

"Like you?" I cried, a great smile forming on my face. "You horny little cocksucker of the cornstalks!"

April spat a great glob of saliva into my face and hysterically shouted, "*You filthy, dirty, evil old man!*"

I slapped her again, she spat again, I threw her onto the bed, and we made it up once more.

Now there came the weekend April didn't go to Ames. She said her sort of fiancé's grandmother had died in San Francisco and he had had to go out there "to plant her." April could stay with me the whole weekend—oh, joy!—as her roommates, her "wombies," would believe her in Ames. Two weeks later her sort of fiancé was off someplace else, digging for gold in El Dorado no doubt, and by then April had decided that for "an old fart" I didn't look *all that old* (here she twisted up her nose with mock distaste) and that if I put Vitalis in my hair, which considerably darkened the gray, she wouldn't mind my taking her out to dinner. April said I took everybody else out. "I've seen you with cunts I know aren't any older than me." I said no, emphatically no, we had a bargain, *her* bargain, and we'd goddam well stick to it. One late afternoon in early December I awoke to find April weeping terribly in my arms.

When I said, *"What is it? What is it?"* April, between the most heartrending sobs, said, "Why do you have to be *so old?"*

And listen to this, dear reader: without thinking, and absolutely sincerely, I said, *"Yeah, why the fuck do I?"*

In the next two days I told my classes that an emergency had arisen at home and that I was canceling my final week of seminars to flee home and attend to it. From that moment on my dream became alarmingly vivid.

I am on this completely jammed airplane in midflight, with fat Eugene, voraciously munching Mars Bars and lapping his thick fingers, in the seat next to mine; and his mom, her mouth still going like a whippoorwill's ass and mouthing indignities I can't comprehend, seated at the window seat. In every respect but the Mars Bars it seems to be the same flight as that other one, save that it can't be as I'm about to skyjack this flight, order it "back to where I belong," and I am only biding my time until the stewardess haughtily informs me that seven A.M. is too early for a double vodka, as she invariably does in my dream but didn't do, though she certainly thought of it, in "reality." And I am nervous as can be, sweating profusely, and downright dizzy with anxiety.

Now with the stewardess, who on close inspection turns out incredibly to be my darling April, I place my order for two miniature red-label Smirnoffs, and the abruptly nasty April adamantly refuses, telling me I'm a dirty old drunk and a degenerate prick besides! This, kind reader, is *my fucking moment!* Trying to act as suave as a British cabinet minister caught in a bawdyhouse, I ever so dramatically unzip my yellow London Fog jacket, reach slowly into it, furiously whip out my pistol (it is Yogi's .22 Magnum!), shove it between the startle-eyed April's tits, and snarlingly demand to be taken to the flight deck, in the process suavely patting April on her cute little bum and sophisticatedly remarking that "were I an anal man I'd have me some of that." At the flight deck I direct the captain to reroute to Jacksonville to refuel and to get me a parachute.

"How much dough you want waitin'?" the captain asks, quaking.

I laugh insanely. "None at all, buster."

Whereas other skyjackers are all asweat with crackpot and wild-eyed revolutionary visions of utopian Cubas and Algerias, to the pilot's consternation I order him, on refueling, getting me into my parachute and taking off from Jacksonville, to follow the east Florida coastline southward, losing altitude as he goes. Oh, I am crazy all right, crazier than a shithouse rat, which does not go unremarked by the pilot, the navigator, the engineer, and especially by my sweet child April who keeps telling me that I can, after all, have my Smirnoff and asking me if I don't have "loved ones" who will be shamed by what I'm doing. All are huddled together on the flight deck, wringing their hands, fearfully wetting their lips, mad with alarm, and begging me to give them my "destination."

"Just say," I say at length, and steely-voiced, "I'm going home."

"*Where's home?*" April cries.

"Home," I say, "is inside *here.*" With great, grave and theatrical deliberation, I lift Yogi's .22 Magnum and with its blue barrel go TAP, TAP, TAP against my right temple.

At Singer Island I leap. For a long time I float in free fall, face down on an eiderdown of air, twisting slowly, now buffeted dreamily, abruptly whipped now, now back face down on this eiderdown, this pillow of air, now into the ecstasy of watching the known places define themselves, the Beer Barrel, the Surf Apartments, the Seaview! Now I am shouting, "I'm comin' home, gang! Set up a vodka and grapefruit juice, Jack! Hey, Diane, start collecting the singles—we're gonna make us some motherfuckin' lasagna!" It is invariably at this point that I awaken. I don't know if I pull the rip cord or not.

So I am come "home," back to my island, and it is Christmas, the temperature is 90 degrees, the humidity a distressing 86 percent, and yet to me this island has grown "colder" than ever. In the back of the hotel in the trunk of my beautiful Chevrolet Nova, rustier than ever, its lime-white gone almost snow-white from the relentless sun, there rests the again snugly wrapped manuscript of *Pages from a Cold Island*, at which I haven't bothered to look since my return. While at Iowa I managed to bank, "bank" in my pants pocket, two grand; and were Big Daddy staying at the hotel, and lover of words and prince among men that he is, that two grand could be stretched into the year I need to remake the book. But alas, he is going; the high-rises, at which I will refuse to look when presently I walk my laps between Nigger Head Rock and the inlet, are climbing steadily; the money cocksuckers will not be stayed; and as I walk I will find myself thinking of stone houses, of Elysian havens, of last islands, of places that never were.

But enough of that. Today is Christmas, and Jack and Alex and I are sworn by Peggie to have no drinks until forty-five minutes prior to dinner, at which time we will be allotted two frozen daiquiris, though after the meal we can, Peggie says, get as loaded as we damn well please. Peggie's (nee Elizabeth's) maiden name is Godwin; her grandmother came from Bath, not far from Wantage, and on her death left Peggie a magnificent set of Wedgwood, the real stuff, on which we are dining today; and the reason we are sworn to sobriety is that Peggie is rightfully fearful that drunk we might break a piece of this ancient and precious china, for which, Peggie swore, "necks will get wrung!"

When Peggie called this morning to order me to remain temperate, she told me we were having three kinds of meat, turkey, roast beef, and roast loin of pork; mashed potatoes, sweet potatoes, squash; tossed salad, asparagus, green beans; cranberries; apple, pecan or pumpkin pie and home-made ice cream; God only knows what all. So I'll worry about "last islands" tomorrow. What can I do on this, the Day of Our Lord, but wish everybody—all the relatives; all the good, good guys at The Head; Big Daddy and his wife; the Dianes, Rent-A-Car and -Barmaid; Toni and Gabrielle and her husband; my wop acquaintance in Panacea; my students, the Epsteins, April and other lasses in Iowa City; fat Eugene and his mom; Mary Pcolar and Rosalind Baker Wilson; and—well, just everybody, not excluding the utterly thrilling Ms. Steinem, Gloria Wonderful, or even that mouthy and canny old *poseur* Mr. Mailer—what can I do on this day but wish everyone an altogether lovely and peaceful Christmas and an equally joyous, productive and splendid New Year?

ABOUT THE AUTHOR

FREDERICK EXLEY was born in Watertown, New York, and educated at the public schools there, at the John Jay High School in Katonah, New York, and at the University of Southern California, from which he received an A.B. in English in June 1953. His first book, *A Fan's Notes*, was nominated for a National Book Award, won the William Faulkner Award for "the year's most notable first novel," was awarded the National Institute of Arts and Letters' Rosenthal Award for "that work which . . . is a considerable literary achievement," and received a Rockefeller Foundation grant.

Mr. Exley divides his time between Alexandria Bay, New York, in the Thousand Islands region where he grew up, and Singer Island, Riviera Beach, Florida. He is now working on *Last Notes from Home*, the final volume of his autobiographical trilogy.